SLAM DUNK

SLAM DUNK

DAVE BRANON

MOODY PRESS

CHICAGO

PHOTO CREDITS

Cover: David Robinson slam dunks on his way to 1994 NBA scoring
 title. Photo courtesy of Allsport.
Page 285: Pete Maravich stretches for basketball. Photo by Ron
 Kuntz. All Pete Maravich photos courtesy of John Lotz.
Pages 33, 39: Mark Eaton photos courtesy of Scott Breen and Don
 Grayston, respectively.

All other player photographs courtesy of the Atlanta Hawks, Charlotte Hornets, Cleveland Cavaliers, Detroit Pistons, Golden State Warriors, Indiana
Pacers, Philadelphia 76ers, Phoenix Suns, Portland Trailblazers, San Antonio Spurs, and Washington Bullets clubs of the National Basketball
Association.

ISBN: 0-8024-7894-8

3 5 7 9 10 8 6 4 2

Printed in the United States of America

To the home team:
Steven, Melissa, Julie, and Lisa,
along with their mom and my wife, Sue.
Thanks for encouraging me to persevere at
this project when you would have preferred that I
was going to your games, helping you with your
homework, or just eating supper with you.

To Coach Don Callan of Cedarville College,
who first taught me—
through word and example—
that basketball can be used as a ministry.

Contents

Foreword

The summer of 1978 was a critical time for the Philadelphia 76ers—and for me as general manager of the Sixers. We were under a great deal of pressure to improve our team.

We had assembled a team that was noted for its great glitter and amazing talent. We had Dr. J, the great Julius Erving. George McGinnis, Lloyd Free, Doug Collins, and Darrell Dawkins all dazzled. We were a traveling road show of high-marquee players.

Yet we had not won the big prize. We had come close the previous year, winning our division by a wide margin over the Celtics before losing in six games to the Portland Trail Blazers in the NBA championship series.

And in the spring of 1978, after winning the Atlantic Division by an even wider margin, we didn't even make it to the Finals. We lost to the eventual champions, the Washington Bullets, in the Eastern Conference Finals.

When the season ended, we told our disappointed fans, "We owe you one." We knew that their patience was wearing thin as they waited for this team of All-Stars to bring the championship to Philadelphia.

As we faced the player draft that summer, two things were evident. We needed a point guard who could run our fast break. And we had to break up the tandem of Julius Erving and George McGinnis. Together they were a strong force, but we felt that it was time to let George go elsewhere. Maybe then Dr. J could really take control. And maybe the offense could be spread more evenly throughout the team.

The night before the draft, I got a call from the front office of the Denver Nuggets. They wanted George McGinnis in exchange for Bobby Jones and Ralph Simpson (and a couple of draft picks). We thought about it and decided that this would give us a better rotation among our forwards. We made the deal, and it worked out perfectly.

Then, in the second round of the draft, we used our 36th pick to get an unheralded guard out of West Texas State, Maurice Cheeks. In one swoop, we solved our frontcourt and backcourt problems. We now had the makings of a team with the chemistry to win it all.

But the catalyst for our championship drive would be Bobby Jones. We had been aware of his good reputation, but we had no way of knowing what Bobby's arrival would do for our team— both on the court and off. Bobby is one of several All-Star players featured in this book.

Bobby came to me that fall and said he wanted to start a chapel program. Here was this shy, somewhat introverted person who had something at work in his heart that made him want to put together this program.

During February of his first year as a Sixer, Bobby realized his dream. Melvin Floyd, a black Philadelphia policeman, was the first speaker for that chapel, and he was primed and ready to go. An hour or so before a game with Milwaukee, Melvin stood before Bobby, Julius Erving, assistant coach Chuck Daly, and Milwaukee's Kent Benson, and preached. He didn't just talk to the guys; he really preached. In fact, he had just gotten wound up with his message when I stuck my head in the door and said, "Hey, fellows! We've got a game to play here!" I think Melvin would still be preaching if I hadn't stopped him.

That small gathering, put together by Bobby Jones, was the beginning of what has become a strong, vibrant chapel program in the NBA. Till then, there had been sporadic services over the years headed by players like Bob Pettit of the Hawks, but it never really caught on.

We brought Bobby Jones to Philadelphia to help us win the NBA championship, which, of course, we did in 1983. But we— and the entire NBA—got a bonus.

Bobby was the player God used to provide a spark to get NBA chapel started. Soon John Tolson, who was then a pastor in Houston, began working with Robert Reid and the Houston Rockets, and a network of chapels was begun. Tolson has since moved to Orlando, where he is still active in our chapel program as the chaplain for the Magic.

In large part because of Bobby's efforts in getting NBA chapels off the ground, every team in the league currently meets for Bible study. There is even a coordinator for the programs, former NBA player Claude Terry of Pro Basketball Fellowship. Basketball chapels have become as much a part of the game as the backboards. The NBA now includes a chapel service as a regular part of the gala All-Star weekend. In addition, the owners and other leaders can attend a chapel program at the annual September meetings of the National Basketball Association.

As a result of all this, the lives of many NBA players, coaches, and officers have been impacted for eternity. Once it would have been considered a real coup to find one NBA player who would stand up for the testimony of Jesus Christ. Now the league has many men of faith.

In *Slam Dunk*, Dave Branon captures the stories of a dozen players who know how important it is to have faith in something much greater than ability and fame. He also highlights the careers and faith of five retired players who have made their lives count for God, including Pete Maravich and one of my all-time favorites, Julius Erving.

In this book you'll read about such players as premier guards Mark Price, Kevin Johnson, and Avery Johnson. You'll get to know some big guys like Mark Eaton and David Robinson. You'll relive the past glories of David Thompson, and, of course, Bobby Jones.

In the summer of 1978 we got Bobby Jones because we wanted to build a championship team. We got our rings, but we also learned by his example that building lives is even more important. I hope the testimonies in this book will help you see how vital it is to build your life around Jesus Christ, the only One who can make you a champion for eternity.

PAT WILLIAMS
General Manager, Orlando Magic
Author of *Rekindled*

Acknowledgments

Collecting the interviews needed to write a book like this is about as easy as trying to stop a Shaquille O'Neal slam. You can't do it yourself, you need others to back you up, and the task looks impossible at the outset.

For their cooperation and help, I would like to thank the public relations folks of the National Basketball Association. Dave Senko of the Spurs, Patti Balli of the Jazz, Jason Brannon of the Hornets, Bob Zink of the Cavaliers, Sue Emerick of the Pistons, Julie Fie of the Suns, and Terry Trebelhorn of the Blazers were especially helpful.

Special thanks go to Mark Stephens for helping hook me up with his friend Brent Price. And to Bruce McDonald for his assistance with Hersey Hawkins. Also, the people at A. C. Green Foundation for Youth were most helpful in arranging a chat with A. C.

To Focus on the Family, thanks for the Pete Maravich tape recording. This marvelous testimony was first broadcast by Focus on the Family in 1988, based on Maravich's testimony before a large audience a few years earlier. Copies of the tape can be obtained by contacting Focus at 800-232-6459 and asking for broadcast tape CS378.

To Bobby Jones and David Thompson, I appreciate your giving time on your visits to Grand Rapids. To A. C., K. J., and David Wood, thanks for your time in Detroit.

To Tony Bennett, Mark Eaton, Craig Ehlo, Hersey Hawkins, Avery Johnson, Clark Kellogg, Brent Price, Mark Price, David Robinson, Buck Williams, thanks for your interviews.

Pat Williams of the Orlando Magic deserves a debt of gratitude for his cooperative spirit. He is a one-of-a-kind front office executive. For being accessible and for being such a great example of Christian virtue, thanks.

Besides all the people who helped, several media sources proved other valuable statistics and quotes about the winning players featured in this book. The gold mine of information includes *Sports Spectrum* and *Sports Illustrated* magazines, *The NBA News,* the staff at Sports Spectrum radio, and the following publications: *The Information Please Sports Almanac, The Sporting News NBA Register, The Sporting News NBA Guide, The Sports Encyclopedia Pro Basketball Edition*, *The NBA News*, and *The Sports Illustrated Sports Almanac.*

Introduction
Slammin' It Home

All of us have dreams. For fans of professional sports, it's to swing the bat like Paul Molitor or hit "nothing but net" like Mark Price. Even the incredible Michael Jordan, who dunked with ease and power as an NBA superstar, wanted to pursue his —and his father's—grand dream of playing Major League ball: at age thirty-one he willingly reported to the White Sox's Double A team in Alabama in hopes of working his way to the Majors. No matter what happens with Jordan, he reminds us that we all have dreams.

Basketball was my game. I worked long and hard to polish my skills. I had worked on my jumping ability, for I wanted to be able to dunk a basketball. And eventually, at six feet tall, I was able to slam the ball home. Though I loved baseball a little more than basketball during high school, I enrolled in college to study some and play basketball a great deal more.

Now I had my own grand dream: to play pro basketball. The American Basketball Association (ABA), a rival league to the NBA, was going strong in the early 1970s, giving basketball wanna-bes like me a large selection of teams to dream about. Surely the Dallas Chapparals and their seventy-nine fans could use a small college, 6-foot guard who could shoot a little, handle the ball well, play monster defense, and dunk with authority.

To be sure, there were never any hints from another source that hoops heaven could be on the horizon for me. No scouts ever came to see our team play. No one from our conference had ever hit the big time. In fact, to actually voice this dream at the time would have been met with widespread derision.

But dreams of playing pro basketball don't have to be broadcast. They can be private thoughts, nurtured by an All-Star selection here, a 20-point performance there. They are musings that surely drive thousands of young basketball players who push themselves toward an internal goal.

And remember, I could dunk. One hand. Two hands. You name it, I could do it.

Unfortunately, I played during that oddball era of college basketball when it was illegal to dunk during the games but OK to slam it during warmups. Therefore, with my team, which wasn't all that good, pregame warmups were better than the game. But hey, if I could just get my shot at the NBA, the ABA, the CBA, or any BA that wanted me, I could show them my slam dunk. Coming from a Bob Cousy-sized guy, that would surely impress the pros.

Of course, I never got the chance. Reality set in during a rec- reational league contest the first year after college. I had obviously not parlayed my 12 points-per-game college average into anything that even hinted of pro ball. So, as for thousands of us who had given it four years of effort and then had to look for a real job, recreational ball was the remaining hoops outlet.

So here were dozens of frustrated players, all muscling and sweating our way through spectator-less games, still lying to our- selves that but for a break here or a 45-point performance there we would have gotten a shot at the big time.

Until one particular game. I don't recall many details, but I remember what it did to the dream. We were scheduled to go up against another local team. But they had a guy who had been invited to the Cleveland Cavaliers' training camp. In fact, he had been the last guy cut, and supposedly he had played Austin Carr, the All-American from Notre Dame, to a draw in camp. It was awe-inspiring. I would be guarding a guy who had almost made an NBA team. Life was good.

Until the first time down the floor. Nonchalantly I brought the ball down court, looking for someone to hit with one of my usual pinpoint passes. Quicker than you can say, "Grab some bench," this guy had stripped the ball from my hand and was headed for an uncontested layup.

On and on we battled that entire game. Me trying to get the ball across halfcourt and him trying not to laugh. It may have not been that bad, but it felt like it.

By the end of the game, this almost-NBA player showed me with his quick hands and faster step what the difference is be- tween good college basketball players and the pros.

And I relegated my own slam dunk to showing off for my basketball team on the first day of my first coaching job. I knew that if I threw one down in their presence, I would have them in my pocket all year. It's been quite a few years since I calmly showed them how to dunk, and they still remember it.

We all have dreams. If you're an NBA fan, this book will remind you that there's another side to the dream world of pro basketball. The spectacular slam dunk, the winning three-point play, the stolen ball that leads to the winning score are all there, but so are the hours of practice and repetitive drills. There is the applause, but there's also the wearying travel schedule, the temptations and boredom on the road, and the working your way into the starting lineup. The more I watch of the NBA, the more my respect grows for the players who have reached that level of play with a humble perspective, a balance to their lives.

The players I most admire are those who can play the game at the highest level and also maintain a testimony for Jesus Christ while doing so. In a world that is increasingly ruled by secular thought and in a sport that puts players under the microscope of scrutiny more than any other, these men stand out.

That's why *Slam Dunk* is so important. The exploding popularity of the NBA shines added light on this select group of men. They could take their stardom and use it solely for their own glory; indeed, some NBA stars have done that. Or they can do as Mark Price, David Robinson, A. C. Green, Avery Johnson, Kevin Johnson, and so many others do. They are using their platform to reflect the shining spotlight back onto the person who gives real meaning to their lives—Jesus Christ. Their faith focuses their lives on helping their families, their teammates, and even those in need.

Long ago, I learned how good you have to be to play pro sports. But many years before that I learned something immensely more vital about being good. You can never be good enough to get into heaven. For someone with the talent and acclaim of these men to agree with that truth is encouraging. These guys know they are good, but they also recognize that in relationship to God they can do nothing good.

They know they need a Savior.

They could be monster dunkers like David Robinson, Julius Erving, or David Thompson. Or they could be guards who can't or don't dunk much, like Mark Price or Tony Bennett. But they all know that just as a slam dunk is a sure two points, knowing Jesus is the only sure way to get to heaven and to have happiness in this life.

This book is for all who enjoy knowing more about those who reach the upper echelons of sports. It gives us a glimpse inside the lives of men who love basketball and have made it a career, and who, more important, love the Lord Jesus Christ.

Tony Bennett
The Coach's Kid

VITAL STATISTICS

Born June 1, 1969 in Green Bay, Wisconsin
6 feet, 175 pounds
College: University of Wisconsin, Green Bay
Position: Guard
1993–94 Team: Charlotte Hornets

CAREER HIGHLIGHTS

- Holds NCAA record for highest three-point field goal percentage (49.7%)
- Selected Mid-Continent Conference Player of the Year (1992)
- Named to *The Sporting News* All-America second team (1992)

PREGAME WARMUP

In the back of my mind, I always knew I wanted to play for my father. Yeah, I wanted to go on some recruiting visits and stuff," Bennett says. Then, laughing, he continues, "But to this day I think he was holding all my recruiting mail and never let me see it."

But when things got serious, there was no doubt where Bennett would play. "I really did know that I wanted to play for my father because he knew my game the best. His greatest strength is that he can get the most out of players on the team. I knew that if I wanted the chance of doing what I dreamed about—playing in the NBA—I figured he was the man who could help get me there. He did a great job."

Tony Bennett

When Tony Bennett's new teammate, Hersey Hawkins, arrived in Charlotte before the 1993–94 season, Hawkins
knew his status as an NBA player would change at Charlotte. He knew he would no longer be looked to as the go-to guy,
as he was in Philadelphia. Now he had to share playing time with
guys known as Grandmama, Muggsy, and Zo. Johnny Newman,
Del Curry, and Eddie Johnson also were there.

Guys who have marquee value. Name recognition. Players
who have huge statistics.

So if Hersey Hawkins, who has a career-high of 43 points in
one game and who once led the nation in scoring in college, now
would be playing second fiddle, where would that leave Tony
Bennett, the six-footer from Green Bay-Wisconsin?

Unawed.

The name Tony Bennett may be big only in music, but this
Bennett has learned that there is no reason for him to take a back
seat to anybody on the basketball court.

It's a little something his dad taught him and that Bennett has
always believed.

"My dad said, 'Good basketball knows no divisions or limits.
It doesn't matter where you're from, what school you go to, what

reputation you have, once you're out on the court, if you can play, you can play, and nothing can take that away.'"

Tony Bennett showed he can play during his senior year of high school. He was named Mr. Basketball in Wisconsin for his stellar play for Green Bay's Preble High School.

The Preble High varsity was lightly regarded, even though it had a good record. "We weren't a real strong team," Tony explains. But "we had great chemistry, and we were just a bunch of short guys who could shoot the lights out. It was a blast. People never expected anything from us. People would look at us and start laughing in warmups, but we could play."

But did they think they were playing with a guy who would one day be battling Mark Price and Kevin Johnson in the NBA? "I think some of them believed it. I wasn't very sure myself at that time. I never looked too far ahead. It was a dream, but I don't know if it was quite reality."

It's a dream he has followed since the seventh grade. Although he also played golf and tennis until he was in high school, when he entered junior high, he says, "that's probably when I made my decision that I wanted to be a really good basketball player. I started devoting myself to workouts. I knew I could be pretty good."

As he headed into high school he also learned that in his personal life being good was not enough. He had learned at home about "right morals and values and believing in God." But he discovered during his ninth grade year that "there was something that was not quite there. I knew I wanted to go to heaven. That's one thing I knew for sure.

"I said, 'Hey, after I die I want to go to heaven.' But I wasn't quite sure how to get there."

One summer Tony went to a Christian sports camp. There "the gospel was presented to me in such a way that I understood that through God's grace He gave us His Son Jesus Christ, who went to the cross for us. I realized that if we accepted the free gift of salvation, I could be saved forever and have eternal life and have life abundantly on earth and that peace that passes all understanding. I was inspired at that camp and I was ready."

Bennett started his spiritual journey with that decision to trust Jesus Christ as a ninth-grader. But his family had begun their earthly journeys much sooner. "My father was a coach when I was born, so we moved a lot," Tony notes. "I've lived in London, Eau Claire, Stevens Point, and Green Bay." Each move was the result of a new head coaching job for his father.

Watching his dad coach and observing the game developed Tony's interest. But Dick Bennett wasn't the only family member who helped Tony along the path to basketball greatness. "My sister Kathy was a big reason I've made it this far," he says. "She was a great high school player, but she went through three major knee surgeries. She also played in college. She always took me to the gym with her and let me play a lot of ball. She's six years older than I am. When I was in the sixth and seventh grades, she was better than me, but not that much. I played a lot with her friends. So actually, I got initiated playing basketball against women. She used to whip me all over the court. Then about ninth grade I could catch her. Then she quit playing me.

"She was a determined person. I watched her go through injuries. Whenever I see someone go through a tough injury and then just fight to get back, that inspires me. I saw how committed she was to it."

Besides Dad and Sis, there was a kind of a big brother who led the way for Tony. Entering his teen years, Tony watched his dad coach a future NBA great at University of Wisconsin Stevens-Point. He watched and admired Milwaukee native Terry Porter. But not from a distance.

"Every year I had the opportunity to be around the gym and my father," says Bennett, who didn't reach his optimum height of 6 feet until he was in college. "When I was a sophomore, I got to play with the college guys at Green Bay. That was a benefit for me, going up against guys who were so much more physically mature."

Soaking it all in from his dad, his sister, Terry Porter, and the other big kids, Bennett kept improving. After being named Mr. Basketball, he set his mind on college ball. And his dad was right there, at nearby University of Wisconsin at Green Bay. Tony would be playing college ball for his dad.

"In the back of my mind, I always knew I wanted to play for my father. Yeah, I wanted to go on some recruiting visits and stuff," Bennett says. Then, laughing, he continues, "But to this day I think he was holding all my recruiting mail and never let me see it. The funny thing about it was that we did go on a visit. We went on an official visit with some other guys. My mom came along. It was kind of amusing."

But when things got serious, there was no doubt where Bennett would play. "I really did know that I wanted to play for my father because he knew my game the best. His greatest strength is that he can get the most out of players on the team. I knew that if I wanted the chance of doing what I dreamed about—playing in the NBA—I figured he was the man who could help get me there. He did a great job.

"I mean it wasn't easy. Any father-son situation in sports puts a strain on a relationship. You go through the highs and lows. But then you have the successes. You play in the NCAA tournament, and you do it with someone you love. You can't beat that."

Not only was there the strain of a dad and a son coexisting on the same basketball team, at first there was just the adjustment of Tony having to take his game to the next level. It was a fast adjustment, for he averaged 19 points a game during his freshman year.

During his college years Tony faced stiffer competition and greater pressure to excel. He soon found out that the players were bigger and stronger and the game moved more quickly. He knew he had to adjust, and his heavenly Father helped there, he says.

"I don't get overwhelmed too easily. I'm not cocky, but I think there's a quiet confidence inside. I give all the credit to the Lord for that. I just believe that I have a faith that's not going to be shaken and I seem to deal with it OK that way."

But how could this relatively short kid from a relatively small school make the big jump—the one to the NBA? "I owe so much of my basketball success to my father," the younger Bennett says. "I knew he could make me the best player I could be. He knew I wanted to play in the NBA. He pushed me to the limit and he got the most out of me.

"But I don't think I really realized until after my sophomore year in college that I might have a chance at the next level. I started getting the sense that I could compete. After my freshman year I played in the Olympic festival with Kenny Anderson and guys like that, and I thought, *This is reachable,* and I started gearing toward it."

If stats were the only gauge of a player's worth, Bennett's college years would leave no doubt as to his value. He became the all-time leading scorer and assist man in the Mid-Continent Conference with 2,285 points and 601 assists. He racked up the all-time best three-point field goal percentage in the NCAA with a 49.7% mark based on 290 of 584 shooting. At Green Bay, Bennett holds 22 offensive records, including all-time scoring leader and most assists and highest free-throw percentage in one game. He was the MCC Player of the Year and the postseason tournament MVP.

He also made time for college studies. With his 3.46 grade point average, Bennett was named to the GTE Academic All-America third team.

The U. W. Green Bay Phoenix went to the NCAA tournament for the first time during Tony's junior year. One game prior to the tournament remains Tony's college highlight.

"We were playing Northern Illinois on ESPN for the right to go to the NCAA tournament. Green Bay's a football town, as everyone knows. And my dad and I had always talked about just doing it the right way—being from a small school and putting our name on the basketball map. It was an opportunity for us as a team to get into the NCAA tournament. That's a big deal for everybody.

"The conference tournament was at our place and I remember we came out and we played real well, and we won the game. After the game the crowd poured on the court and my dad got the old Gatorade thing dumped on him. It was just pandemonium. Somehow we found each other and the crowd broke and we embraced at halfcourt and just held onto each other. That was the most awesome feeling.

"They captured it on ESPN, and they made a lot of comments about it. Just to embrace my father and to realize what we had attained was the highlight of my college career. And we knew we did it the right way."

The intangibles that Dick Bennett taught Tony would help him as he left college to take his game to a higher level; his father's words and example would sustain him during a unique opportunity during the 1991 Pan American games.

Duke Coach Mike Krzyzewski directed the United States squad that summer, and Bennett became a starting guard.

"We had guys like Christian Laettner, Jimmy Jackson, Walt Williams. We had a lottery team, and I was a starting point guard. I took what my dad said with me, 'good basketball knows no divisions or limits' meaning, 'it doesn't matter where you're from. You just step out on the floor and you know if you've done it the right way, you can get there.'"

Many players might have folded under that pressure, but Tony performed well, and he credits his father. "What my dad taught me really helped me when I played in the Pan American Games." Tony returned to the Green Bay Phoenix a stronger player, ready to take on greater leadership.

Still, his move from college to the pros two years later wasn't easy. Think of all the good players on all the good college teams in the country—all vying for about thirty rookie spots in the NBA. Think of the talented players who take their game to the Continental Basketball Association, hoping for a ten-day contract to show their stuff in the NBA.

Getting there is a huge, uphill battle. And the climb for Tony Bennett was tough, even with the great attitude and the big stats. U. W. Green Bay did not receive much exposure through national TV or by "playing the big-time teams or the so-called big-time names," Bennett says. As a result, he participated in the NBA predraft camp in Chicago so scouts could see him, and then he attended the Orlando NBA camp. He devoted himself to preparing for both those tryouts, knowing a player "can really make or break [himself] at those camps as far as getting drafted."

During those two camps, with all their pressures to do or die, Tony "got convicted," as he puts it. "I said to myself, *You've got guys here basically playing for their careers and possibly millions of dollars. You've got the general managers and all the coaches sitting around the court watching you, and there is so much to it.*

"It made me realize that all these things we are doing are temporary. Important, but temporary. You've got to enjoy it and go after it, but there is something more important. And that's the thing that lasts and that's permanent. And that's my faith in Christ. It's the relationship I have with my family.

"I could see the strain," Tony admits. "I was under the strain, I'm not going to lie. But it struck me that there had to be something more. You have to have a foundation."

Bennett had that foundation, and it allowed him to relax and work at making the adjustments necessary to get to the next level.

The Charlotte Hornets were impressed enough with Bennett's adjustments to nab him with its second pick and the 35th selection overall in the 1992 NBA draft. So, on June 24, a lifetime of listening to dad and learning to adjust to changing levels of play paid off as Bennett got his chance at pro basketball.

Joining Georgetown's Alonzo Mourning as 1992 picks, Bennett became part of a Charlotte team that was beginning to stockpile a good combination of big-name players and young talent. Larry

(Grandmama) Johnson. Muggsy Bogues. Dell Curry. And now Alonzo (Zo) Mourning, drafted in the first round just before Bennett.

Tony Bennett knew he wouldn't play an All-Star role on the team, but he found that he could contribute to an up-and-coming NBA team. "It's about making adjustments. You always have to make adjustments. Each year in the NBA you have to find ways to improve and get better. Just find the little things. The size of the people in the NBA is impressive. I look at guys like Mugsy Bogues and think how amazing he is because he is only 5-3." Not that it was always easy as the new kid on the block. "There is some taunting," he recalls. "Especially for a rookie. They're going to test you and tell you if they think they can do something to you. But that's part of the game, and I try not to get involved in it and I try not to let it affect me."

Not that Bennett didn't have fun during his rookie season. He remembers his Hornets defeating the Boston Celtics in the first round of the playoffs. "When Zo Mourning hit that game-winning shot to eliminate the Celtics, it was unbelievable! There were grown men rolling on the floor, piling on each other. It was definitely the highlight of my rookie season."

And, of course, there was the time his teammates introduced him to the NBA with a little practical joke. Before his first home game at Charlotte Coliseum, his teammates told him that when they ran out of the locker room, it was his job as rookie to lead them out. So when the team was ready, he took off, running full speed onto the court—leading the charge. Problem was, his teammates were still back in the tunnel.

Laughing. Hysterically. "All of a sudden I get to half court, turn around, and they're all standing in the tunnel, laughing at me," Tony recalls.

All of Tony Bennett's experiences—the exciting, the embarrassing, and all the others—have given him a platform from which to influence kids.

"I tell them that all the stuff I've experienced is great and I'm very blessed because I know the Lord has given me great opportunities. Being in the limelight, having my face on basketball cards, driving a nice car, making money, and playing in front of all these people is great, but I say: 'It's going to go away someday.

It is going to go away. It's not lasting. You also have to put your time and your effort into the thing that is permanent.' For me, that is my faith in Jesus Christ and my relationship to Him and my family and friends."

Tony believes a lot of the teens who listen to him respect his warning. "The high school kids say, 'This guy's in the NBA with all these guys.' Then when you [talk about your faith], they kind of go 'Wow!'"

"I try to tell them if my career ended today, I think I could handle it because of the Lord."

Tony Bennett will make the adjustments and move to a new level. And that's just what a coach's kid should do.

Q & A WITH TONY BENNETT

Q: *Who were your sports heroes as you were growing up?*
Tony: My first was Gail Goodrich of UCLA and the Lakers. I remember when I was in first grade watching Gail Goodrich. He came to a camp when my dad was coaching at Stevens Point, and he was a lefty and he wore number 25. I'm a lefty and wear number 25. I liked watching Terry Porter. I've enjoyed watching Mark Price because of his commitment and what he stands for. He's just a great player. I appreciate all the guys who stand up for what is right.

Q: *What do you do to keep your relationship with Jesus Christ fresh and strong during the NBA season?*
Tony: There is chapel before the game, and I really enjoy going to those meetings. I've been blessed to have developed some special friendships with people who have really nurtured my walk with the Lord. One is my pastor in Charlotte, David Chadwick. He used to play for North Carolina in the early seventies. I've developed a special relationship with him and his family. So through chapel, through fellowship with others, through reading the Word, and through quiet time I get help.

The quiet time is so important. Whenever I get going too busy and too fast and I get away from taking the quiet time, it just doesn't seem right. Something's not in balance. Doing those things really helps me.

Q: *What do you think of the trash talking that is becoming so prevalent in the NBA?*
Tony: I'm not one to trash talk. I think the media has blown it out of proportion. They key in on it if they see it. I don't notice it too much. There are a few guys who'll talk some stuff, but not everybody does it. I didn't see too much of it. It's a little intimidating, but I try not to worry about that stuff too much.

Q: *What is the tougher assignment? Guarding the other team's best player or being guarded by the other team's best defender?*
Tony: That depends if you've got to guard Michael Jordan or he has to guard you. Guys are such great offensive players, and because we have to play defenses where you can't help as much, it's probably tougher guarding their best player.

Q: *What is the player's role in maintaining self-control as a good example to young people? Do you consciously think of your testimony in the heat of competition?*
Tony: I just compete as hard as I can. I'm not a basketball player who's a Christian, but I'm a Christian basketball player. I just remember that the Lord comes first in everything. It doesn't mean you're going to be perfect, you're not going to get mad and mess up, but I guess I've always felt that I have a control about myself and I try not to lose it. I've been intense a few times, and maybe stepped over, but I feel like there's a safe harbor around me, and I feel that from the Lord.

Q: *What bothers you the most about being an NBA player? What do you wish you could do without and still have the career you have had?*
Tony: Nothing bothers me about it, but it is not as glamorous as everybody says. It is exciting and there are so many great things. But it is a long season, and it is physically and mentally draining. You really have to keep yourself up and steady. I think it's important to be consistent and not get on the highs and lows. I think

that's important in life, just to have an even keel. Look at how the Lord handled everything that came His way.

Q: *You studied literature in college. What do you like to read now?*
Tony: My favorite book is the Bible. Also, I like Frank Peretti's *This Present Darkness*. Other books I've read recently include *In His Steps*, the Joshua books, *The Firm*, and *Of Mice and Men*.

Q: *When your NBA career is over, what do you think you might want to do?*
Tony: My dad said something interesting to me. He said I might make a good guidance counselor—junior high or something. But I'd have to go to school some more. I guess I just want to help people. Just to serve. That's what the Lord did. Just have a servant's mentality. Just to help people in a good and pure way. From all the experiences I've had, I think I could help some people and give people a good perspective on things. That appeals to me.

Q: *What is your favorite advice to kids about basketball?*
Tony: Obviously, you have to enjoy the game. You have to have a belief in yourself. A quiet confidence, whatever it is. I've noticed that every guy in the NBA is there for a reason. They all believe in themselves. There's a confidence that they can achieve and do it. They don't back down in tough circumstances. They have the ability to plow ahead and not look to the left or the right.

Also, it's important to have a focus yet always enjoy basketball and keep it in perspective. When you start to get out of that, if you start looking at basketball as everything, that's when trouble starts.

THE NBA ROAD

1992: Selected by Charlotte in second round

THE BENNETT FILE

Collegiate Record

Year	School	G	Pts.	Avg.	FGM	FGA	FG%	FT%	Asst.
88/89	UW-GB	27	516	19.1	179	343	52.2	84.7	138
90/91	UW-GB	30	499	16.6	179	355	50.4	85.9	155
91/92	UW-GB	31	665	21.5	229	419	54.7	83.6	154
92/93	UW-GB	30	605	20.2	205	384	53.4	82.6	154
NCAA Totals		**118**	**22851**	**19.4**	**792**	**1501**	**52.8**	**84.0**	**601**

Three-point field goals: 1988–89: 47 for 107 (43.9%)
1989–90: 68 for 141 (48.2%)
1990–91: 80 for 150 (53.3%)
1991–92: 95 for 186 (51.1%)

NBA Record (Regular Season)

Year	Team	G	Pts.	Avg.	FGM	FGA	FG%	FT%	Asst.
92/93	Hornets	75	276	3.7	110	260	42.3	73.2	136
93/94	Hornets	74	248	3.4	105	263	39.9	73.3	163
NBA Totals		**149**	**524**	**3.5**	**215**	**523**	**41.1**	**73.2**	**299**

Mark Eaton
From Engine Blocks to Blocked Shots

VITAL STATISTICS

Born January 24, 1957 in Westminster, California
7 feet 4, 290 pounds
College: UCLA
Position: Center
1993–94 Team: Utah Jazz

CAREER HIGHLIGHTS

- Named to NBA All-defensive first team three times
- Selected NBA Defensive Player of the Year in 1984
- Led NBA in blocked shots-per-game in 1984 (4.28), 1985 (5.56), 1987 (4.06), and 1988 (3.71)
- Holds single-season NBA record for highest blocked shots-per-game: 5.56 (1985)
- Holds NBA record for highest blocked shots-per-game average in a career (minimum 400 games): 3.68

PREGAME WARMUP

When I came into the league," recalls center Mark Eaton, "the Jazz were looked upon as the doormat of the NBA. Yet we became a very good team within a very few years, and people began to wonder, 'Why are they a good team?'

"It's a combination of things. We got some good players, but we also got some good defense."

To anyone who follows the game, the names of those good players are well-known, especially Karl Malone and John Stockton. They get the headlines and the cover stories. But they are just part of the tale of success in Utah. Another reason is Mark Eaton and his 3,000-plus blocked shots. He and Kareem Abdul-Jabbar are the only two players who have passed the 3,000 mark. That's why he gets a special feeling when those people who are trying to figure out what makes the Jazz tick say, "And you know, they've got Mark Eaton."

Mark Eaton

Picture this: Mark Eaton, all 7 feet 4 inches and 290 pounds of him, in the swimming pool—standing squarely in the way of any swimmer who would dare try to sneak a water polo ball past him and into the goal.

If you have trouble getting that image in your mind, try this: Mark Eaton, all 7 feet 4 inches and 290 pounds of him, squeezed underneath a small Yugo sedan, wrestling with a faulty ball-joint.

Do those images seem unlikely?

Of course they do. But that's only because we've grown so accustomed to another image: Mark Eaton, all 7 feet 4 and 290 pounds lurking near the basket, just waiting for some foolhardy guard to come sweeping down the lane for an attempted finger-roll. In that scene, Eaton waits hungrily for the opponent to release the ball so he can swat it out to teammate John Stockton, who will start a fastbreak to the other end. There, more often than not, Stockton will then give the ball up to a swooping Mailman by the name of Karl Malone. Malone, of course, will deliver the goods, thanks to the strong defense played by the big man in the middle, Mark Eaton. For a man who has led the NBA in blocked shots four different years, it seems like an accurate picture.

Images. Pictures. They can be so deceiving.

The image we now have of Mark Eaton differs radically from the images he had for himself as a kid. It was Mark himself who envisioned his role in water polo. It was Mark himself who saw the possibilities in auto repair.

In fact, Eaton today considers it a mistake that he gave up on water polo. In high school he played goalie as a junior and he reveals with some satisfaction that there was recruiting "interest from some different schools."

Besides, he enjoyed water polo more than he did basketball. "I grew up around the beach and enjoyed the water. I was a lot more successful at water polo than I was at basketball. And I had better camaraderie with the guys on the water polo team."

But when it came time to decide between the two—something that he was forced to do—he succumbed to the pressure of the expected. Coaches and other students alike were convinced that Mark, who had started high school at 6 feet 3 and was now edging toward 7 feet, should play basketball.

And so Mark went from treading water to dealing out shot blocks. But lest you see an image of high school player Eaton immediately swatting away a half-dozen basketballs a game, look again.

The future NBA defensive ace started slowly, and not primarily because of a lack of skills. What Mark lacked most was playing time. Thus he calls his decision during his last year at Westminster to leave the swimming pool for the basketball court "a mistake. I did not play at all on the team. I sat on the bench. I had coaches who did not know what to do with me. I'd play in the last five seconds of the game."

Now a new image emerges. One of a frustrated young man who has tried the sport everyone thinks he should play, and he fails miserably. It is the kind of frustration that defeats young people every day. It is a combination of failed expectations and questionable decisions. It is the feeling that can drive a young person into a shell or into trouble.

For Mark Eaton, it did neither. And he knows why. First, he had been taught to handle the coming onslaught that people who do not fit in the category "average" have to deal with.

"I was fortunate that my parents were very tall," Eaton says. "And they always told me to be proud of my height, walk with my head up, and keep my shoulders back. It has to come from parents to reinforce their kids' attitudes and tell them they're OK." Even if a son doesn't excel immediately at basketball.

Eaton still calls his father the most influential person in his life as he was growing up. "We were pretty close," he recalls. "He spent a lot of time with me. We did the Boy Scouts thing."

So no matter what the image other people had of Mark Eaton happened to be, he was not concerned. He had been taught by a caring father that there was no reason to let those who imagined him to be a failure at basketball ruin his life. "At the end of high school, I had no athletic inclinations whatsoever, so I decided to go on with life."

Mark Eaton was realistic. Basketball, he was sure, would not get him a scholarship, so he knew he had to prepare for the real world, including a regular job. And there was another reason Mark Eaton could look forward to a future that despite his height did not appear to include basketball. During his high school years, he made a teenage commitment that gave him direction.

Although Mark grew up in a church-going family, he felt that there was still a "missing link" in his relationship with God. "I guess the realization for me came when I was about sixteen," he explains. "I was at a retreat with our youth group, and there was another group from another church staying there as well. One of the members of the other youth group expressed to me the need to have a close relationship with the Lord. Growing up in my church I assumed that if you are baptized you are a Christian. This kid explained to me that this was not the case. That you needed a further commitment. It was kind of like a lightbulb went off there.

"*Wow*, I thought to myself. *This is the missing link.* So I made a commitment to Jesus Christ. I really started branching out at that point and attending different churches." Eventually he found a church that taught the Bible and settled in. It was Calvary Chapel of Costa Mesa, California, now a church of more than 6,000 but at that time meeting in a big tent. "From that point forward," Eaton explains, "I've been trying to develop a little closer walk with the Lord."

Secure in himself, Eaton said good-bye to Southern California and moved to Phoenix. There a trade school transformed him into an auto mechanic in one year. So, armed with a government loan, he spent the next year preparing for life as an ace mechanic. He returned to the Los Angeles area for work.

"My specialty was brakes and front-end work," he says of his job in a tire and auto shop. For the next year-and-a-half, he was content with life as it came. His future plans included management because, as he says now, "My back was in pretty bad shape already, after a couple of years of working on cars."

But that image thing kept intruding. A basketball coach at nearby Cypress Junior College noticed Mark and asked him to give basketball another try. "Forget it," Mark responded. "I was happy with what I was doing, and I figured that not everyone is cut out to be an athlete. But he persisted. One day he talked me into coming to the gym and working out with him for a couple of hours—just to get him off my back."

As they played, the coach, Tom Lubin, did something that Eaton says his high school coaches never did. Lubin showed him some big man moves that were "fairly simple and could be fairly easy to learn."

This time it was not prodding or making assumptions about what was expected of him that convinced Mark to give basketball another shot. "I was intrigued," he explains.

It was the spring of 1978 and Mark Eaton was a basketball player again. He and Tom Lubin were on a mission. The entire summer Mark met with Tom daily after work.

"I worked for about twelve hours a day as a mechanic, then I would go get something to eat and would work out with this coach until 10 or 11 at night. Over the course of the summer I became confident enough in what I was doing that I decided to return to school. I kept my job as a mechanic."

In the fall, Eaton enrolled at Cypress Junior College. Not as a big star on scholarship, but as an auto mechanic going to night school. It was a grueling schedule. "I worked from 7 in the morning until noon and then went to practice. At night I went to school. It was straight commission work at the shop, so I didn't get paid if I didn't get something done."

For the first time, Eaton found success between the lines of a basketball court. During his freshman season the team had a 34-2 record and reached the state semifinals. At that point Mark began to attract interest from several big-time colleges. In fact, the Phoenix Suns drafted him in the fifth round "on a kind of 'Let's see what happens in the next year' sort of situation," Mark recalls.

Basketball had cost him a spot on the water polo team in high school. It had caused him to drop out of the high school band. It had, as he describes it, "affected my whole senior year." And not for the better. Yet now he was willing to let it jeopardize the career he had trained for.

"It was at that point that I decided to get serious and just concentrate on basketball from now on. I wanted to play this thing out and see where it would take me. I quit my job and I got a job selling cars. That I could do at night, and I started going to school during the day like a normal person."

It couldn't have gone better in 1979-80 if he had planned it. "The next year we went 31-5 and won the state championship for California. And the night job worked out."

It was still not clear that Mark Eaton's day job would ever be basketball. Yet he was starting to attract some attention. More than 150 colleges and universities contacted Eaton and expressed interest in his coming to their school. Now it was his turn to do some imagining. Here was a kid who grew up in the shadows of UCLA. He had seen the success of John Wooden and his ten national championships. He had watched the Bill Waltons and Lew Alcindors come to Westwood as prospects and leave as wealthy pros. What other decision could he make but to enroll at UCLA?

"I was recruited for two years by UCLA," Eaton explains. "One year I was recruited by Gary Cunningham and Jim Harrick before Harrick went to Pepperdine. During my sophomore year, I was recruited by Larry Brown. I just felt that growing up in the L.A. area, I couldn't see myself turning down an opportunity to play for UCLA."

In addition to a new opportunity at the major college level, Eaton also took another step with huge future implications. Before heading to UCLA, he and his longtime girlfriend Marci were married. They had met five years earlier when Eaton went to an auto parts store to visit a friend. Marci was working there, and a relationship soon developed. So while he was fixing brakes, selling cars, and learning how to play basketball at Cypress, she went to nursing school for her training. After they were married and Mark was at UCLA, Marci went to work to pay the bills. "She was able to pay for the apartment and everything," Eaton recalls of those days when she brought home the bread.

Once on the UCLA basketball court, however, Eaton must have thought he was experiencing déjà vu. After all those years of training and working at his profession, he gave it up to play basketball, just as he had given up water polo as a teenager. Now, as then, it was coaches who had talked him into doing so. And now, as then, it was coaches who seemed to be making life tough again.

"I spent two years at UCLA, and things didn't go extremely well there. My junior year I played for Larry Brown, and he had a pretty small, quick team. He was nice to me and everything, but I didn't fit into his game plan. I sat the whole year.

"The following summer, Larry Farmer got the job. I initially had high hopes because I knew the kind of player he had been [Farmer played for UCLA in 1971, '72, and '73] and the type of style he was looking to utilize was much more low-post oriented. In any case, I actually went to him and received a list of things to work on over the course of the summer. All I did was work on those things off that list."

Coach Farmer congratulated Eaton on his progress, and seemed impressed, according to Eaton. But during actual games, Farmer chose a freshman, Stuart Gray.

Gray "was a 7-footer, and played in the NBA for a few years," Mark recalls. "Farmer had somewhere along the line decided that he was not going to utilize me, so I floundered on the bench to the degree that on the last road trip of my senior year, they left me home.

"So, again, not one of my better decisions. It was not a fun experience. One of the reasons I went to UCLA was for the notoriety that you receive for going to a big school like that. By not playing, I did not receive any help at all."

Another thing that didn't help were his statistics at UCLA. For instance, he logged only 191 minutes of playing time in two years at UCLA. He got into only 30 games, so he averaged only 6 minutes a game when he played. That actually exceeded his scoring average of 1.8 points per game.

He left UCLA "initially pretty bitter about the whole thing." It was easy to have second thoughts: *Perhaps I should have taken the Suns up on their earlier offer. Perhaps I should have gone somewhere—anywhere—besides UCLA.* And perhaps his dream of basketball stardom, prompted by faithful coaches, was dead.

But even if it was, Eaton would not have been left rudderless. "I always knew that whatever happened, I was going to be OK," he says in retrospect. "Even though I didn't always know where I was going, at least my life had direction. I knew that God would direct me to whatever my goal might be. Most important, my faith made me at peace with myself."

Surprisingly, the direction he was to go was still toward basketball. The experience at UCLA had not killed Eaton's chances at a pro career. The junior colleges who had watched him play cared

—and acted. The strong relationships he had established with the different coaches during his J. C. days was still there, and they helped him as he pursued basketball on the next level. The coaches started calling up NBA teams. "We tried to find out about All-Star games that you could pay your own way to, things like that. And I basically promoted myself over the next couple of months. I got myself to a couple of tryouts."

Then came perhaps the most important phone call Mark Eaton ever made. "I actually called up the Jazz on the telephone because they were last in the league in rebounding and blocked shots. They had never heard of me."

Keep in mind that he had already been drafted by the Suns a couple of years earlier and that he played for UCLA, one of the most visible college basketball programs in the country. And keep in mind that NBA scouts are paid to know who the prospects are.

Despite all that, they did listen when Eaton told them he was 7-feet-4 inches tall. They knew about images and the fact that tall guys must be basketball players. But they weren't ready to make any commitments. The Jazz asked for highlight tapes.

Highlights of Cypress Junior College would have been nice. Seven losses in two years, 14 points a game, almost 600 rebounds. Highlight stuff. Problem was, Cypress didn't have any highlight tapes. So Eaton was forced to send video from his pine-riding days at UCLA.

"I sent them a very short highlight tape from UCLA," Mark explains, with the emphasis on "short." It apparently packed a lot of punch, though, for it aroused the Jazz's curiosity. "When they looked at the tapes, they investigated me a little more. They heard some things back from some of the scouts at these games that I had played in."

So, Eaton knew that the Jazz were interested, but he wouldn't know if that interest would translate into a commitment until draft day.

"Draft day is scary," Eaton recalls as he describes watching it on TV that day in 1982. "Mostly, you sit by the phone and wait. The Jazz had a third round pick, but they drafted someone else."

After round three, the TV coverage stopped, so now Eaton had no idea what was happening. Until the phone rang.

It was the Jazz. They had drafted Mark Eaton in the fourth round. Selected ahead of Eaton that year by the Jazz was Dominique Wilkins, who was traded to Atlanta before the season began for John Drew, Freeman Williams, and money.

Being drafted did not guarantee Eaton a locker at the Salt Palace in Salt Lake City. He still had to prove himself. That summer Jazz Coach Frank Layden watched Eaton and other NBA prospects play in the California summer leagues. Apparently satisfied that Eaton could play in the NBA, Layden offered him a contract.

His high school coaches had said they wanted him, and he sat the bench.

The coaches at UCLA told him they could use him and didn't.

Would Frank Layden be different? Were the days of selling used cars and repairing broken ones finally over?

Eaton soon learned that Frank Layden, like Tom Lubin, was a coach he could trust with the use of his height.

"Frank was very good," says Eaton, with respect. "He said, 'Look, we'll make a commitment to you for a year and give you guaranteed money,' which at that time wasn't very much. But it did offer me the opportunity to come in and be able to work out and work on my game without having to worry about whether I was going to make the team. He said, 'If you come in and spend some time with the weight conditioning coaches and work out extra with the basketball coaches before and after practice, we'll give you a shot.'"

Later Layden would tell reporters, "Eaton did not come into the NBA with a lot of God-given talents. Most players were All-Americans in high school and college, and everyone paid them all sorts of attention. Mark never had that, so he came in hungry."

And Eaton responded. He played more minutes in his first two NBA games than he had his entire senior year at UCLA. He worked hard at every practice. He arrived at practice early and was the last guy to leave every day.

Off the court, a move by the Jazz helped Eaton in his progress toward permanency as an NBA player. In February of his rookie year, the Jazz traded Danny Schayes, his rival for the center's position. "I became the starting center," Eaton explains. "That was a big step for me. When Frank gave me the starting job, everything changed. All of a sudden, I had an opportunity that I hadn't anticipated. I determined to work even harder and maintain that job."

One year removed from his bench-warming lessons at UCLA, Eaton played in all 81 games for the Jazz. Immediately he began to eat up opposing players. He blocked 275 and hauled down 462 rebounds during his rookie year. He became a fixture in the Jazz defense. The next year he led the league in blocked shots with 351 and was instrumental in the Jazz's playoff success as they made their way through to the Western Conference semifinals.

It was the beginning of a long string of playoff appearances for the Jazz—a circumstance that Eaton rates as one of his most ·rewarding NBA experiences. "I think my ultimate success has been linked with the success of the team and the fact that we made the playoffs for ten straight years," Eaton says. "When I came into the league, the Jazz were looked upon as the doormat of the NBA. Yet we became a very good team within a very few years, and people began to wonder, *Why are they a good team?*

"It's a combination of things. We got some good players, but we also got some good defense."

To anyone who follows the game, the names of those good players are well-known, especially Karl Malone and John Stockton. They get the headlines and the cover stories. But they are just part of the tale of success in Utah. Another reason is Mark Eaton and his 3,000-plus blocked shots. He and Kareem Abdul-Jabbar are the only two players who have passed the 3,000 mark. That's why he gets a special feeling when those people who are trying to figure out what makes the Jazz tick say, "And you know, they've got Mark Eaton."

"Over the years, I think many fans and writers have come to appreciate what I do more. I went from being just another center to being somebody that people respected as a defensive force out there. People have been able to understand what I do out there."

During those years, Eaton was a mainstay in the Jazz lineup, playing in no less than 79 games through the 1991–92 season. But then that nagging old problem from years ago when he was an auto mechanic slowed him down. In the 1993 playoffs, he suffered a herniated disk in his lower back. It was an injury that would keep him out for the 1993–94 season and would jeopardize his career.

It wasn't Eaton's first major injury, but it was the most serious. Earlier in the 1992–93 season, he had his second knee operation. The first happened eight years earlier.

Another image surfaces: one of a man who has sacrificed his body during its best years in order to help his team become successful enough to make the playoffs ten straight times. A man who knows that a long life exists after retirement. A man who admits that "professional athletes have a tendency to live for today, and not worry too much about tomorrow, especially when you're getting on in years. You have to start looking a bit harder at what you're really doing to your body and what potential effects are going to occur at age fifty."

So Mark Eaton is looking to a future that may not include basketball. Just as he once studied auto mechanics for a future that he was certain did not include the game, so he's preparing for another future. "I've become involved in the last year or so with a company that puts on AWANA youth programs. We ran a basketball came last summer that integrated both life-coping skills and basketball. Also, we're doing wilderness camps in Wyoming with at-risk youth. I'm hoping that continues to grow, because it looks like the right thing for me."

Those post-career possibilities reveal Mark Eaton's attitude. He has proved over and over that he is willing to take the role of a servant; a helper. Even as a basketball player he has been content to excel at the end of the court most players would prefer to ignore. Instead of worrying about his scoring average, Eaton has concentrated on working hard to get the ball back to teammates for them to shoot some more.

In his role as the Jazz's player representative for four years and more recently as the vice president of the NBA Players' Association, he has again shown an interest in doing for others. This attitude comes through also as each year he donates Jazz tickets to Salt Lake area non-profit groups.

It's all a reflection of his thankfulness for God's direction, guidance, and love in his life. "I've gone through a lot of career changes, a lot of things that have changed in my life over the years, and I've always relied on the Lord to direct me, while keeping me humble the whole time. I think that's the real big thing that works in my life—the humility factor.

"I'm very grateful for everything God has done for me. If the NBA folded tomorrow, all of my investments went sour, and I would have to go and get my tool box and go to work as a mechanic, it wouldn't bother me in the least."

It may not be the right image, but as Mark Eaton has learned, image is not as important as doing what God has directed you to do.

Q & A WITH MARK EATON

Q: *What is going on with all of these huge, long-term NBA contracts? Where is all this going?*
Mark: You can't blame the players. They make enough noise and the owners give them the money. There is some talk of doing something about the rookie money. These are unproven players who may or may not work out, and they're giving them a lot of money. It hurts veteran players because you have someone coming in who takes a large amount of the salary cap. I think there may be some kind of a rookie salary cap. But the NBA has grown by leaps and bounds. The sale of licensed products alone—the hats and shirts and stuff—was pretty close to a billion dollars last year. The money is definitely out there.

Q: *Your size is a big part of the reason you have had such a successful NBA career. What drawbacks are there in being 7-feet-4 inches tall?*
Mark: The comments hurt. It never ceases to irritate me that people always think they know what I should be doing because I am tall. Stop and think about it. I don't go around telling every man who is 5 feet 10 that he should be a first baseman for some major league baseball team.

Q: *What advice do you have for kids who might be facing some kind of situation like being tall or overweight or even having a disability?*
Mark: I think the bottom line is that you have to be proud of who you are. You have to have confidence in yourself and where you're going. That's a real tough thing for young kids. Even my kindergartner comes home and says that kids don't like the pants he wore. It's a real tough deal. Kids can be extremely cruel.

Q: *What helps keep you strong spiritually throughout the long NBA season?*
Mark: The chapel program. Frank Layden was instrumental in getting that started. I started going to Jerry Lewis's church when I first came to town. He was doing some chapels for the minor league baseball team that was here, and I asked him about the possibility of doing them for the Jazz and he was very interested. I went to Frank about it, and he was very supportive of it. Since that time, we've had one of the more active chapel programs in the NBA.

Q: *You do quite a bit of hunting and fishing, and you've had some encounters with grizzly bears. What's that all about?*
Mark: Well, you have to understand that you're in their territory and for the most part, we get along very well and don't have any confrontations. I've had some bear encounters in Alaska, and it's an awesome experience. For the most part, as long as you leave them alone, they'll leave you alone. The problem is, they know the good fishing spots, just like I do.

THE NBA ROAD

1979: Selected by the Phoenix Suns in fifth round in 1979 (This was Eaton's official graduation year, since he had sat out of basketball for three years. He did not sign at this time.)
1982: Selected by the Utah Jazz in the fourth round

THE EATON FILE

Collegiate Record

Year	School	G	Pts.	Avg.	FGM	FGA	FG%	FT%	Reb.
78/79	Cypress	35	482	13.8	202	319	63.3	66.7	381
79/80	Cypress	25	374	15.0	167	289	57.8	48.2	218
80/81	UCLA	19	39	2.1	17	37	45.9	29.4	49
81/82	UCLA	11	14	1.3	5	12	41.7	80.0	22
JC Totals		60	856	14.3	369	608	60.7	59.0	599
NCAA Totals		30	53	1.8	22	49	44.9	40.9	71

NBA Record (Regular Season)

Year	Team	G	Pts.	Avg.	FGM	FGA	FG%	FT%	Reb.
82/83	Jazz	81	351	4.3	146	353	41.4	65.6	462
83/84	Jazz	82	461	5.6	194	416	46.6	59.4	595
84/85	Jazz	82	794	9.7	302	673	44.9	71.2	927
85/86	Jazz	80	676	8.5	277	589	47.0	60.4	675
86/87	Jazz	79	608	7.7	234	585	40.0	65.7	697
87/88	Jazz	82	571	7.0	226	541	41.8	62.3	717
88/89	Jazz	82	508	6.2	188	407	46.2	66.0	843
89/90	Jazz	82	395	4.8	158	300	52.7	66.9	601
90/91	Jazz	80	409	5.1	169	292	57.9	63.4	667
91/92	Jazz	81	266	3.3	107	240	44.6	59.8	491
92/93	Jazz	64	177	2.8	71	130	54.6	70.0	264
93/94	Jazz	Did not play due to injury.							
NBA Totals		875	5216	6.0	2072	4526	45.8	64.9	6939

Craig Ehlo
The Catalyst

VITAL STATISTICS

Born August 11, 1961 in Lubbock, Texas
6 feet 7, 205 pounds
College: Washington State University
Postion: Guard/Forward
1993–94 Team: Atlanta Hawks

CAREER HIGHLIGHTS

- Most assists in Pacific 10 league play, 99 in 1982–83
- Scored 37 points in his final college game at Washington State
- Was only Cleveland Cavalier to play in all 82 regular season games in 1990–91

PREGAME WARMUP

As the clock ticked its precious seconds away, Craig Ehlo drove the lane and hit a layup to put the Cavaliers ahead by one. The Bulls frantically called a time out.

The celebration in Cleveland began. Fans and players alike felt the rush of excitement, knowing that just 3 seconds separated them from a showdown with the New York Knicks for the chance to face the Pistons.

But there was one little thing in the way.

A guy named Michael Jordan.

Ehlo, who had just done the unbelievable, was now called on to do the miraculous. Stop M. J.

If he could, he would wear the hero mantle for the Cavs. A nation of hoops fans was suddenly aware of Craig Ehlo. A stop of Michael Jordan would earn him an important place of honor in the history of great NBA endings. As expected, Jordan got the ball. Ehlo waited. . .

Craig Ehlo

Craig Ehlo burst into the consciousness of sports fans across the United States on May 7, 1989, amidst a roller coaster ride of emotions.

The Cleveland Cavaliers hosted the Chicago Bulls in the fifth and deciding game in the first round playoffs of the NBA Eastern Conference, and the Cavs were looking for revenge. They had finished second in the conference behind the Pistons, and now were trying to get back at the Bulls for eliminating them from the playoffs in 1988.

And both teams wanted a crack at the Pistons, the Bad Boys from Auburn Hills. It was pretty much accepted by most basketball experts that the winner of this contest would go on to battle Detroit in the Eastern Conference finals. And the Cavs, who had tied the Lakers for the second-best record in the NBA during the season, felt that it may be their turn to climb to the top rung of the NBA ladder.

For his part, Craig Ehlo had become an integral part of the goings-on for Lenny Wilkens's ballclub. He had played in all 82 of the Cavs' regular season games and had established career bests in minutes played, field goal percentage, three-point percentage, rebounds, assists, steals, and points. His confidence level was at an all-time high.

In a nationally televised game packed with all the excitement that is expected of playoff finals, the Cavs called time out with seconds remaining. They had possession of the ball and trailed the Bulls by a point. After Wilkins set up their strategy, the Cavs put the ball back in play. Would it end up with Mark Price, who was averaging 16 points per game during the playoffs? Or how about Ron Harper, who had scored nearly 20 points a game in the series? Neither. The rock ended up with Ehlo, whose solid 12-point average against Chicago was nearly 5 points higher than his season average.

As the clock ticked its precious seconds away, Ehlo drove the lane and hit a layup to put the Cavs ahead by one. The Bulls frantically called a time out.

The celebration in Cleveland began. Fans and players alike felt the rush of excitement, knowing that just 3 seconds separated them from a showdown with the New York Knicks for the chance to face the Pistons.

But there was one little thing in the way.

A guy named Michael Jordan.

Ehlo, who had just done the unbelievable, was now called on to do the miraculous. Stop M. J.

If he could, he would wear the hero mantle for the Cavs. A nation of hoops fans was suddenly aware of Craig Ehlo. A stop of Michael Jordan would earn him an important place of honor in the history of great NBA endings. As expected, Jordan got the ball. Ehlo waited.

Ehlo describes the action. "The Bulls set him up at the top of the key, and he was just standing there. Larry Nance and I were double-teaming him, but we weren't real tight on him. We gave him enough room to maneuver, and I thought that when the play actually started, he just kind of stood there. I thought he was just basically going to be a decoy. But then 'Bam!' he went to the sidelines, caught the ball, took one or two dribbles to the middle, and before you knew it, he had a shot going up. I just tried to run in front of him and get a hand up. I was hoping to change the shot a little bit, which I did. But he still had a good shot at the basket, and it went in."

At the buzzer.

Final score: Chicago 101, Cleveland 100.

The Cleveland fans, the coaches, the cheerleaders, and Craig Ehlo stood in stunned silence. After a successful season, 87 games, and a multitude of dreams and hopes, it was over. In three game-time seconds, Ehlo had gone from hero to another in a long string of Michael Jordan victims.

To think of Craig Ehlo as a victim, though, is to do him a grave injustice.

Try thinking of him as an overcomer.

While the Michael Jordans of the world experience success after success, always leaving opponents in their dust, it is the Craig Ehlos who we can admire for their sheer determination and their continual belief that they can stop the Michael Jordans, score over the Shaquille O'Neals, and someday triumph.

You stand in awe of the superstars. You root for people like Craig Ehlo.

You enjoy his stories about his career because they sound like what happens to real people. In fact, Craig Ehlo says he never once thought about being an NBA player. Not in high school. Not in college. "Never. Not one time," he verifies. "Even through college, I never thought of the NBA."

Maybe that's why when he visited a high school friend's house one summer evening, his friend told him, "You know, when your face comes on the screen on TV, my wife and I just laugh, saying, 'That's not Craig.'"

But it is.

Craig Ehlo's basketball odyssey began in Lubbock, Texas. The two girls and one boy in the Ehlo family had a bit of a head start in basketball because of the influence of a highly successful hoops-playing mom. "My mother played high school and college basketball," Ehlo explains about Deanie Ehlo, who played for Wayland Baptist College in Plainview, Texas. "The old 6-on-6 style. She loves to tell the story of her state championship game where she scored 42 points." His mom sounds like a kind of a Michael Jordan figure who shot down the dreams of opponents.

"I always say I got my basketball talent from her and my stubbornness and work ethic from my father," Ehlo reveals. He got a good portion of each, for it took him both skill and perseverance to achieve the success he has enjoyed.

Being from Texas, Ehlo was naturally faced with a decision about football, wildly popular in the Lone Star State, seemingly since the Alamo. And at the time Ehlo was growing up in Lubbock, there was not much national interest in pro basketball.

"When I grew up, the NBA was not as popular as it is now, especially in my area of the country. Football was definitely the number one thing, and basketball was hardly ever on TV."

Craig's sports hero was Roger Staubach, and as a teen he watched the Cowboys play in many playoffs and win a couple of Super Bowls. Given those environmental factors and considering that Ehlo today stands 6 feet 7 and weighs 205 pounds, one might suspect that he would have been a pretty successful tight end in football.

"I played football," he recalls. "But I didn't like it. I was pretty skinny, and the hits kind of hurt. All through junior high I was a real scrawny kid, maybe 5 feet 5 through junior high. When I started my sophomore year, I was 5-9. By my senior year, I was 6-5. My basketball coach was thrilled."

Ehlo enjoyed what his coach had to offer him as well. "My high school coach, Joe Michalka, influenced me a lot. He taught me the game of basketball. He was a strict fundamental coach, and I really appreciate that now looking back. Also, I was fortunate to be in a big high school, so we had a couple of other bigger guys." Nobody knew it at the time, and Ehlo was the least to suspect it, but playing against those teammates gave him a chance to sharpen ball-handling skills that would later come in handy in the NBA.

Still without any great expectations in basketball, Ehlo left Lubbock to attend Odessa College, a two-year school of about 4,000 students.

Ehlo stepped right into a key role during his freshman year, averaging 12 points a game. But 1980–81 was a breakthrough year for him. En route to averaging more than 20 points a game, he attracted the attention of the right people: four-year college scouts and coaches.

"I was recruited pretty heavily my sophomore year," says Ehlo. "Some of the Southwest Conference schools were recruiting me. Then all of a sudden, they just stopped."

One of the schools that suddenly turned away from Ehlo was the one that represented the big prize for any kid from the Lone Star State. "The University of Texas stopped because they fired Abe Lemons," Ehlo explains. "He had been recruiting me pretty heavily. Growing up in Texas and having the University of Texas recruit you, that was big time."

When Texas dropped out of the picture, Ehlo was left with two options for his final two years of college: Baylor and Washington State.

"I had a lot of friends going to Baylor because I grew up in a Baptist home," he recalls, referring to the Baptist roots of the school in Waco. "I visited both schools and just fell in love with Washington and the Northwest because of the scenery and everything. I had been accustomed to mesquite, and this was so different."

So, leaving the heat, the family, and the mesquite behind, Ehlo journeyed north to play basketball for one of the game's top college coaches: George Raveling. As things turned out, it was the right move from several perspectives.

First, at WSU Ehlo, a sociology major, met the woman who would be his wife. "I met Jani at Washington State during my junior year," he explains. "We were set up by one of her sorority sisters at Washington State." They dated for several years before getting married after Ehlo had established himself in the NBA. Still today the Ehlo family, which now also includes Erica and Austin, makes its home in the Spokane area.

The second indication that Ehlo chose correctly when he became a Cougar was the success he had on the basketball court. "I had kind of filled out in my frame now," Ehlo recalls. "Instead of being 6 feet 6 and 130, I was up in the 190s. Also, I'm athletic, so I think people noticed those skills. Plus, during my senior year, we lost all of our point guards. I got to bring the ball up most of the time. My scoring average was just 12, but my rebounds were good, my assists were good, and I was active all the time."

Yet, Craig maintains that "I never thought of the NBA."

If Craig Ehlo had a big ego or a tendency to lead people on, you'd wonder how that would be possible. After all, doesn't every kid who shoots hoops and makes it beyond junior high ball dream of the NBA? But Ehlo is a realist, and he just didn't see what would endear him to NBA scouts.

Coach Raveling, however, saw something in his big guard that made him think Ehlo could play at the next level. And Raveling began to promote his big man to all the scouts. "He really pushed my name," Ehlo recalls.

"After my senior year Coach Raveling said, 'You're going to this camp and that camp. You're going to the NBA pre-draft camp.' I couldn't fathom it." It's no wonder Ehlo still looks back on those days in the early eighties and says, "I had a great coach in George Raveling."

Raveling's advice bore fruit, for Ehlo was drafted in the third round of the 1983 draft by the Houston Rockets.

"I went into rookie camp with Houston," Ehlo says of his first NBA experience. "I did well. I had a great camp, and I got a little confidence. I was thinking, *Hey, this might be easy, especially if they're going to pay me to do this.* So I went into the veterans' camp and fared very well again. But then I tore the ligaments in my ankle and had to have surgery, which may have been a blessing in disguise. The Rockets' coach, Bill Fitch, told me, 'There's no problem. You're going to make this team. But being injured, you made it for sure, because I can't release you.' He reassured me that he was going to keep me anyway."

That confidence surely came in handy during Ehlo's first year with the team. The surgery sidelined him until April, and he was limited to only seven games for Houston. During that span, he showed promise that he had the stuff to play in the NBA, especially when he scored 14 points, grabbed 6 rebounds, and handed out 3 assists in a game against the Spurs. Then during the following summer, he averaged 19 points a game in a mini-league of NBA rookies.

Yet the career never really took off in Houston. In the next two years, Ehlo played in just half the Rockets' games and scored only 185 points.

"I spent three years in Houston and didn't play very much. I was mainly the guy who came in for Hakeem Olajuwon or Ralph Sampson after they had scored 30 or 40 points and got a standing ovation. That's all I got to play.

"Then we played Boston in the NBA finals," he recalls. With 6 seconds remaining and the Celtics winning by 19 points, Ehlo drove to the basket through fans now swarming the court and "dunked on a couple of fans." It would be Ehlo's last basket for the Rockets.

"I think I got a little cocky and arrogant, not worried about it. I was always on the edge. I was thinking, *Well, we just made the finals, and they're not going to make many changes.* I probably just didn't do a lot of things I should have during the summer. Then I went to camp and just got beat out. They cut me and kept another kid that was very similar to me, Conner Henry."

So, on October 30, 1986, just days before the season was to begin, Craig Ehlo was waived by the Rockets. After three years of the NBA high life, Ehlo was unemployed.

No one would have blamed him if he had called it quits. After all, how many people can say they retired after scoring the

last basket of the NBA finals? And why not take his sociology degree and do what he often says he would do if he had not played
in the NBA: become a high school teacher and basketball coach?

That option must not have been too appealing, for Ehlo swallowed his pride and became a member of the league where you
really can't tell the players without a scorecard: the Continental
Basketball Association. It wasn't like that was on his To Do list.
Here's how it happened.

"At the time of my release, my agent said, 'Look, you came
off a championship team. There will be some teams calling you
because they know who you are.'

"But I'm 12th man. No one's going to call me."

Craig had an offer to go to the CBA right away to start the
season. But his agent told him to wait, that some team would call.
By early December, Craig was still waiting.

"I was still living in Houston, and Rudy Tomjanovich called
me one day, and said that a friend of his, Tom Nissalke, was
coaching in the CBA and he'd love to have me. My agent thought
that would be the best thing for me—get me to playing, get me
some confidence."

So Craig Ehlo, who never thought he would be in the NBA,
found himself in the CBA as a member of the Mississippi Coast
Jets, hoping for another shot at the big time. It came very soon. "I
played six games there before getting called back. I probably
would have been called up sooner if I had gone sooner."

The decision that the Cleveland Cavs made on January 13,
1987, had more than basketball implications for Ehlo. It affected
his career, for sure, but it would also eventually provide a great
friend and a new understanding of spiritual things.

"Cleveland signed me to a ten-day contract because Mark
Price had appendicitis. I always say that the Lord definitely had
plans for me about bringing me together with Mark by giving him
appendicitis and having me take his spot on the roster. He healed
pretty quickly, but I had made a pretty good impact on them [dur-
ing the ten days]. So they made a different roster move when he
came back and they kept me."

In fact, there were two Cavs injured at the time, Price and
John Bagley, a guard who was averaging in double figures. So

Ehlo was given ample opportunity to prove his worth. During one five-game stretch shortly after he was acquired, Ehlo averaged 15.4 points, 8.4 rebounds, and 5.6 assists. Less than two weeks after first donning the Cavs' red, white, and blue, Ehlo scored 26 points against Atlanta. That first year with Cleveland, in forty-four games he scored more points than he had accumulated in three years in Houston. His spot on the team was locked in.

Over the next seven years, Craig Ehlo fought his way from hanger-on status to respectability in Cleveland. And he became good friends with Mark Price. In fact, they eventually bought houses right across the street from each other.

It was because of that relationship, and Price's strong commitment to the Christian faith, that Ehlo began to reevaluate his spiritual life. When he did, he discovered that things were not quite the way he thought they were.

Craig had gone through some spiritually dry times while a college student; then as a member of the Rockets, he found himself involved in things that made him wonder where he stood with God. "I'm not knocking the city of Houston, but there's just so much to do there, so many temptations out there," he recalls. Sensing the need for help, Craig began to attend the Rockets' chapel program. "I was trying to straighten things out in my life."

Craig had thought he had gotten things right with God when he was a teenager. "When I was thirteen, I was at a Billy Graham Crusade in Lubbock. I went forward one night and thought I gave my life to Jesus, but I really didn't. I guess I just went forward because my friends did. Still, I went to church and was in the Christmas plays and did caroling and stuff like that, but I didn't study the Bible. I didn't comprehend anything that I read in the Bible.

"When I went to Houston, there were just so many things that were firing at me, and I knew I needed something else. Also, my last year at Houston was the first year of our marriage. And everybody knows what that first year of marriage is like. It's pretty tough on you if you don't have good spiritual guidance.

"At that time Jani and I started searching for something a lot stronger than just material things in life. We knew something was missing."

Despite a good relationship with the Rockets' chaplain, Craig did not make any decisions that would help him and Jani find what they were looking for. But the decision that would affect Craig and Jani's marriage the most came after the Ehlos became good friends with the player he was hired to replace: Mark Price.

"I knew about Mark, you know, all the stories about him when he was in college," Craig says. "I called him 'choir boy' and all that kind of stuff.

"Every time I got together with Mark, I was scared to death he was going to ask me about God." And they were together a lot. "We rode to practice together; we rode to the airport together. All summer after that season we played together in the gym. I thought God was going to be the whole conversation. And I didn't really have any answers if he were to ask me anything specific. I just couldn't have answered it.

"That shows you what kind of a person he is, because he never asked me. We just became friends. He knew my problems; I knew his problems.

"Then one night in November of 1987 we were over at his house with his aunt and his wife. We were just having the old cakes and cookies and talking, and I guess he felt it was on his heart to ask me if I was going to heaven if I died. I think he wanted to become friends with me before he asked me that question.

"Any other time I would have probably beat around the bush when someone would have asked me that, but this time when he asked me I said, 'No.' I said, 'I don't know Jesus. I don't know what it takes.' I gave him a confident answer, and he gave me a confident answer back.

"After that, we discussed some things about how and why God wants me to be in His kingdom. And I accepted Jesus as my personal Savior that night.

"My wife was there and she didn't know what was going on. We had a very similar background, but she just never knew how to become a Christian. She wasn't quite ready that night, but later on she and Laura, Mark's wife, prayed together and she accepted Jesus as her Savior."

Over the next six seasons, the Prices and the Ehlos remained close friends as Mark and Craig did what they could to bring the NBA title to Cleveland.

Yet it would never happen.

Ehlo continued to step up his game, finally reaching a high point statistically in 1989–90 when he averaged more than 13 points a game for the Cavaliers. Nicknamed "Mr. Everything" by a Cleveland TV reporter, Ehlo played small forward, off guard, and point guard for the Cavs, providing whatever weapon Coach Lenny Wilkens needed.

In the end, however, Craig Ehlo's tenure with the Cavs was severed by another dagger from the arsenal of Michael Jordan. In 1993, as the Cavs seemed to do annually, they faced those insurmountable Bulls on the playoff road.

The 1992–93 season had started with promise, and it was again noised around that the Cavs might have what it takes to stop the rampaging Bulls from capturing another title. Yet this time the story was worse than ever.

Chicago raced past Cleveland like they were in cement, taking all four of the playoff games. In game four, in a game that Cleveland would have given anything to win just to salvage some pride, Michael Jordan did it again.

With the score tied, and Ehlo looking safely on from the other side of the court, Jordan took on Gerald Wilkins with less than 10 seconds left. As he had done four years earlier, he fired a jumper with two Cavs covering him like a sweaty shirt. And just like before, the ball dropped through to send the Cavs home empty-handed again.

Craig recalls the fallout from the playoff loss. "There were just so many expectations from our organization and on our team because of what we had done. We had won 57 ballgames two or three times. We had gotten to the playoffs. Everybody was talking about the Cavs being the team to beat Chicago. It was almost a relief to get away from that. I think we took it upon our shoulders that we were the only team that could beat them. I think we started to believe that."

As expected, the Cavs decided that they needed new blood at the top. They fired Coach Lenny Wilkens, who was soon snapped up by the Atlanta Hawks.

At the same time, Ehlo was testing the free agency waters. "My agent researched a lot of teams and saw where I could cash in the most. Atlanta was the team where I could do that because of their spots on the salary cap. When Coach Wilkens signed there, he said, 'Go after Craig.' I was quite flattered by that."

Of Ehlo, Wilkens said, "He brings a certain amount of energy to this team. He makes things happen, he is intelligent, he knows the game, he can shoot, and he does the little things that help you win."

As it has turned out, Craig Ehlo was just the role player Lenny Wilkens and the new-look Atlanta Hawks needed. Although Seattle and Houston had sizzling starts during Ehlo's first season with Atlanta, the Hawks steadily showed the rest of the league that they had reached the top echelon. Characteristic of the Hawks' resurgence was a midseason game in January 1994 with the New York Knicks. As are all key games that involve the Knicks, the play was physical, or as John Starks says, "Our game is being physical, so it tends to get a little raucous sometimes."

This time the raucousness included Starks and Ehlo. With the Hawks leading 60-55 in the third quarter, Ehlo was blanketing Starks in the area of the three-point line. Frustrated, Starks belted Ehlo with an elbow and then when Ehlo tried to get up, he kicked at him.

Of course the benches cleared and a shoving match ensued. When play resumed, the Hawks went on a 24-12 run and put the game out of reach. It was a key win as the Hawks served notice that they too could be considered a candidate for the Eastern conference crown along with Chicago and the Knicks.

Commenting on the fracas, Ehlo said, "I think [my teammates] made some kind of statement. I liked the way we held our composure after that happened." And to show that he could handle the heat, Ehlo came up with two key steals down the stretch run as the Hawks won 114-102.

It was a typical contribution from Ehlo. Hard-nosed defense. Self-control under pressure. And smart defense. Being a catalyst and letting the other guy get the headlines.

For someone who had no aspirations to play NBA basketball, Ehlo's had an unbelievable career. And wouldn't it be only fair if the next time he scores a key basket to win an NBA playoff series he gets another chance to stop the other team's top scorer from a moment of glory? And wouldn't it be nice if he succeeds?

Q & A WITH CRAIG EHLO

Q: *When you are on the court, everything you do is out in the open. Do you think about maintaining self-control?*
Craig: In 1987 I committed my life to Christ and even a year or two after that, I argued with people on the court. I said some stupid stuff. I argued with referees. Jesus changed my life in that area. I got more self-control. I learned to hold my tongue. Even the way I talked changed, from cursing and saying stuff on the court. I don't say it anymore.

I couldn't have done it myself.

Q: *What's next for Craig Ehlo? After your remarkably long NBA career is over, what do you think you'll do?*
Craig: I've tossed coaching around. Not at the level I'm at. Not at the college level. Maybe high school. I have so much fun. My high school coach influenced me so much, and when I go to camps and I teach a third- or fourth-grader how to play basketball, the gratification that I get from that is just immense. It's a feeling that you just can't describe.

I go back to my hometown in Lubbock, and most of them know me there. Some of the kids are just stuck in there. Those are the ones that when you see them improve throughout the week, you know they are listening. And they are the ones that the first two or three days don't know that you play NBA basketball.

Q: *During the arduous NBA schedule, what do you do to keep strong spiritually?*
Craig: We had a great church in Akron. We got active in the Adult Bible Fellowship with other families with the same age kids we had. It was basically having them over for dinner and Bible study, exchanges like that. Also, going to the chapel services and listening to Newt Larson preach. We went through three or four books

with him. We try to do devotions with the kids, but it's hard because they're so little.

Q: *On the court, what is your favorite part of the game?*
Craig: I love defense. But I also love to score and stuff. That's the fun part of the game. Everybody says, what's the thrill of guarding Michael Jordan? It's the challenge of trying to stop him once or twice. Even if you're guarding someone like Clyde Drexler, it is just a thrill because he is noted so much for his offense.

Q: *When you guard guys who are quicker, how do you compensate for their speed?*
Craig: I always believe, and the way I was always taught, was to play shadow defense. The closer you are to them, the harder it is for them to move. Six or seven years ago I could do that. It's getting harder to do that now. I would rather have a jump shot taken than someone going to the basket, so I'll step off a step.

Q: *What do you think you bring to a marriage that helps your wife?*
Craig: I try to stay away from the temptations. They are all over the place, especially in my lifestyle. I just try to reaffirm her, that her love and her trust mean more to me than anything else would offer.

Q: *What dreams do you have for your children, Erica and Austin? Do you want them to be athletes?*
Craig: My parents never forced me to do anything. They just always encouraged me. Right now, my little daughter loves to hit the tennis ball. She's always asking me to go hit tennis balls to her. So just seeing her want to do something sports-minded thrills me to death. The best thing about my son is I don't have to get him a gift. He just wants a ball.

THE NBA ROAD

1983:   Selected by Houston Rockets in the third round
October 30, 1986: Waived by the Rockets
1986:   Signed by Mississippi Jets in the Continental
                          Basketball Association
January 13, 1987: Signed as free agent by Cleveland Cavaliers af-
                          ter first playing on a ten-day contract
July 2, 1993:   Signed as free agent by Atlanta Hawks

THE EHLO FILE

Year	School	G	Pts.	Avg.	FGM	FGA	FG%	FT%	Reb.
79/80	Odessa	28	352	12.6	146	300	48.7	71.4	142
80/81	Odessa	30	621	20.7	241	482	50.0	77.2	204
81/82	WSU	30	153	5.1	57	119	47.9	60.0	65
82/83	WSU	30	359	12.0	145	265	54.7	63.3	97
JC Totals		**58**	**973**	**16.8**	**387**	**782**	**49.5**	**75.4**	**346**
NCAA Totals		**60**	**512**	**8.5**	**202**	**384**	**52.6**	**62.1**	**162**

NBA Record (Regular Season)

Year	Team	G	Pts.	Avg.	FGM	FGA	FG%	FT%	Reb.
83/84	Rockets	7	23	3.3	11	27	40.7	1.00	9
84/85	Rockets	45	87	1.9	34	69	49.3	63.3	25
85/86	Rockets	36	98	2.7	36	84	42.9	79.3	46
86/87	Cavaliers	44	273	6.2	99	239	41.4	70.7	161
87/88	Cavaliers	79	563	7.1	226	485	46.6	67.4	274
88/89	Cavaliers	82	608	7.4	249	524	47.5	60.7	295
89/90	Cavaliers	81	1102	13.6	436	940	46.4	68.1	439
90/91	Cavaliers	82	832	10.1	344	773	44.5	67.9	388
91/92	Cavaliers	63	776	12.3	310	684	45.3	70.7	307
92/93	Cavaliers	82	949	11.6	385	785	49.0	71.7	403
93/94	Hawks	82	821	10.0	316	708	44.6	72.7	273
NBA Totals		**683**	**6132**	**9.0**	**2446**	**5318**	**46.0**	**68.9**	**2620**

Julius Erving
The Good Doctor

VITAL STATISTICS

Born February 22, 1950 in Roosevelt, New York
6 feet 7, 210 pounds
College: University of Massachusetts
Position: Forward
Retired: 1987

CAREER HIGHLIGHTS

- Selected to ABA All-Star team five times
- Selected to NBA All-Star team eleven times
- Elected to Pro Basketball Hall of Fame in 1992
- Played on two ABA championship teams
- Played on one NBA championship team
- Selected to NBA 35th Anniversary All-Time team (1980)
- Named ABA Most Valuable Player in 1974 and 1976
- Named NBA Most Valuable Player in 1981

PREGAME WARMUP

After his sophomore year at UMass, in which he averaged 25 points a game, Julius attended an Olympic development camp. Also there were Paul Westphal of USC and Tom McMillen from Maryland. After he led the team in rebounding and scoring, he says, "I began to think, *Hmmm, maybe*." He says he had never projected his game more than regionally, and he never thought that he could play against the nationally known players.

His teammates at the development camp spent a lot of time discussing their impending contracts in professional ball. Julius didn't even enter into the conversation because "I was completely naive about it. Pro ball? I had never considered it a reality."

Julius Erving

Julius Winfield Erving II, better known as Dr. J, received his classy nickname not from a teammate or sportswriter but a sixth grade teacher. The teacher wanted to impress on him that he could become a professional some day. Perhaps he could be a doctor or a lawyer, the teacher said.

But what if Julius really had become a doctor? What if instead of majoring in hoops and cutting out early to join the ABA he had majored in surgery and done his cutting for the AMA?

"Suture, please," says the towering Dr. Erving. Then he swoops down with those huge hands over the patient and ties the most incredible stitch anyone in the operating room has ever seen. He doesn't just stand still and lace the patient up. He does a 360, behind the back, reverse stitch with a double-pump, finishing by slamming the needle down on the table with authority. And he thinks, *That's the way all the other doctors do it.*

It's hard to imagine Julius Erving doing anything without flair.

From the time the nation first realized that the University of Massachusetts had a national treasure on its basketball team until the final time the Doctor operated on his opponents in 1987, Julius Erving has been nothing short of unbelievable.

Even as early as junior high, his coaches were noticing his exceptional skill, and one even designated him a "superplayer" before he hit high school.

On the playgrounds of Roosevelt, New York, a Long Island community, Erving worked on his game. While in high school, he considered himself small at 6 feet 3, so he felt he had to compensate with a vast array of unusual moves and by using every advantage he could muster.

And although he built up an impressive repertoire of playground-type moves, he learned how to control them and use them to his team's advantage. The fancy, in-your-face style of play, he says, "used to dominate my mind in informal game situations." But unlike the playground legends who are so fancy they serve to get in the way of the team, Erving knew how to contain his game and keep it confined to the team concept.

And he knew how to control himself when things did not go his way. For instance, when his high school coach did not start him despite knowing that Julius was perhaps the best player he had, Erving refused to get angry and quit.

It was a lesson that he seemed to learn well from a family that had a lot of love. For Erving not only displayed his cool in high school, but he later showed it in the pros.

Callie Mae Lindsey had her hands full with three kids, a job, and, by the time Julius was five, an absent father. Yet she kept on with her task, perhaps using the determination and survival skills she learned in South Carolina growing up in a family of fourteen. Her parents were sharecroppers.

Besides Julius, Mrs. Lindsey also had his older sister Alexis and his younger brother Marvin to look after. Despite her having to go to work, she was successful in teaching her children the kinds of important Christian principles that would make Julius Erving the respected man he is.

From his mom he learned that good is rewarded and bad is punished. And he recognized that his ability was not his alone. "I was given a gift," he says of his skills.

"I always had big hands and could jump, so I learned to be trickier than bigger guys. I like to experiment. I loved to watch guys and what they'd do in emergency situations."

After Roosevelt High School, Erving was off to the University of Massachusetts as a little-known kid with a lot of playground moves. He was just another student who was on his way to getting a degree and who was enjoying the college basketball experience. Then something happened to change the way Julius Erving looked at things.

In 1969, Julius Erving was a freshman at UMass. His brother was in high school. While Julius admits that he got all the athletic ability in the family, he had a high regard for the academic prowess that both Alexis and Marvin enjoyed. Of his brother, Julius once said, "I thought he would be a lawyer or a doctor."

In February of Julius's first year, Mom and Marvin visited Amherst to watch him play a game for Massachusetts. On the way back home to New York, Marvin began to complain that his arms and legs hurt. When Marvin went in for a checkup, the doctors concluded he had arthritis. Weeks later, when Julius came home for spring break, Marvin was in the hospital. As soon as Julius got back to school after the break, he got a call from Mom. Marvin had died.

He was discovered to have *lupus erythemotosus*, a disease in which deadly antibodies are produced.

What struck Julius about all of this was how powerless it made him feel as he visited his brother's grave. Julius decided that he had to give it everything he had since he didn't know how long he would have on earth. Plus, he decided, "You have to be a good person. You have to have a pure heart."

He has stated that it was a turning point of sorts, for he discovered that he couldn't control things. He knew he must give life everything he had.

After his sophomore year at UMass, in which he scored 25 points a game, Julius attended an Olympic development camp. Also there were Paul Westphal of USC and Tom McMillen from Maryland. After he led the team in rebounding and scoring, he says, "I began to think, *Hmmm, maybe*." He says he had never projected his game more than regionally, and he never thought that he could play against the nationally known players.

His teammates at the development camp spent a lot of time discussing their impending contracts in professional ball. Julius didn't even enter into the conversation because "I was completely naive about it. Pro ball? I had never considered it a reality."

As a junior, he began to get some national attention, for he was not just on the scoring charts, but on the rebounding lists as well. He was never voted higher than third team All-American, but Julius is one of only seven players ever to average more than 20 points and 20 rebounds a season in a college career.

After his junior year, and after deciding that indeed he could make some money at this game, he had no choice but to go to the ABA if he wanted to play for the pros. The NBA would not allow undergraduate signings, and Julius felt he needed the income to support his mother. Julius Erving went to the New York Nets' offices. However, Roy Boe, who owned the Nets, said no. Apparently, this Boe didn't know.

Erving then offered his services to the Virginia Squires, who said they would pay him $500,000 for four years. He signed. Once the Squires saw what they had on their hands by signing the guy with the big hands, they were ecstatic.

For one thing, he could now unveil what would become his trademark: the eye-popping dunk.

In high school and college, he was not allowed to dunk. The no-dunk rule, or as some called it, the Lew Alcindor rule, had come into existence then. So when he burst on the pro scene with his scintillating display of dunks, it was a wondrous explosion of never-before-seen showmanship.

Here's how his first NBA coach, Al Bianchi, described the good doctor's moves: "Once Julius was a wingman on a fast break and there was a bounce pass that had to be 15 feet past him. That hand came out and in one motion he took the ball in his fingers and stuffed it. It was like he stuffed the whole building through the net."

It was no fluke. All Erving did in his first pro season was to be named the ABA Rookie of the Year while averaging 27 points a game.

But he was not happy with his contract with Virginia. "The life of a pro athlete is short, and after hearing about the money that is being tossed around, I don't think my contract with Virginia is fair," he said at the time. So he signed a deal with the NBA

Atlanta Hawks for more money. But a federal court said he couldn't do that, so he returned to Virginia. They had played their first four games of the 1972–73 season and lost. After he returned, they won their next four games. Even back then, Erving seemed to be popular with everyone—even after skipping town for a while to test the courts and try to migrate to the NBA.

Before the 1973–74 season, Erving left the Squires for good. Virginia dealt him and Willie Sojourner to the New York Nets for George Carter, draft rights, and cash. Now that he was a known entity, the Nets were willing to pay big money for the man who two years before had showed up at their door with his hat in his hand. At age twenty-three, Erving signed an eight-year, $2.5 million deal. In 1973 $2.5 million was an incredible figure for a multi-year contract.

It was a good deal for the ABA because it helped establish Erving as a media star on a New York-based team. It worked well, as the Nets became a box office hit. And Dr. J helped turn the Nets, who had been 30-54 the previous year, into a winner. Behind Erving, along with newcomers Larry Kenon and Coach Kevin Loughery, the Nets went 55-29.

In the playoffs, the Nets, whose average age was under twenty-three, blew past the Virginia Squires, the Kentucky Colonels, and the Utah Stars to become ABA champions. For his efforts, the Doctor was named Most Valuable Player of both the playoffs and the season.

It was his reward for being the steadying force behind the Nets turnaround. Besides averaging 27 points a game, he helped the coach by being a superstar who cared about the team. As Coach Loughery said, "It's a lot easier when your main guy is a good guy."

Even at his young age, Dr. J had been able to survey the situation in New York and prescribe the right medicine. "The reputation of the Nets last year was that if you got up on them early, they'd start squabbling among themselves. They were losers. From the minute I knew I was coming here, I was preparing myself to stop that from happening again."

In the ABA Finals, Erving was stellar. The ABA's two New York teams had the Empire State abuzz. In Game 1, the Nets won 89-85 over the Stars, led by Julius's 47 points. In Game 2, it was no contest as the Nets won 118-94.

Game 3 was the most exciting of the Finals. In the fourth quarter, the Nets were winning by 15 with 7:56 to play. After a timeout, the Stars went on a tear, led by Jimmy Jones. They outscored the Nets by 18 to take a 3-point lead with 10 seconds left.

The Nets designed a play, which of course would have Dr. J shooting a three-pointer to tie. However, the ball ended in Wendell Ladner's hands. He shot and missed. Brian Taylor ended up with it outside the three-point line.

With just a couple of seconds left, Erving was yelling for a time out. Taylor shot anyway. The ball sliced through the net as the buzzer sounded. "I didn't realize how big the play was," Taylor said after the game. "The only thing I could think of was that I wished Julius would stop yelling in my ear. It was disconcerting." But not enough to make him miss. The Nets won in overtime 103-100.

They lost the next contest to the Stars 97-89, but then captured the fifth game 111-100 to win the ABA championship. It was
a home game for the Nets, and 15,934 fans packed Nassau Coliseum. It was the kind of excitement the new league needed.

There would be other highlights for Dr. J and his ABA team.
In one game, he scored 63 points against San Diego. In 1976 he
won the first-ever slam dunk contest with a prodigious leap that
began just inside the foul line and ended with a monster slam.
And also in 1976, the Nets won the ABA championship.

Here's all Julius Erving did to help his team beat David Thompson and the Denver Nuggets for the final ABA championship:

Game 1 in Denver before 19,034 fans: 45 points, 12 rebounds,
and a buzzer-beating jumper to win 120-118.

Game 2 in Denver before 19,107 fans: 48 points, 14 rebounds.
The Nuggets took this game 127-121.

Game 3 back home in New York: 31 points, 10 rebounds.
Erving scored 8 straight points in the final 90 seconds of the game
to secure a 117-111 win.

Game 4 in New York: 34 points, 15 rebounds. The Nets won
121-112. Trying to guard Erving for the fourth fruitless time, Bobby
Jones, who had been called the "best defensive player in the
world," had marvelous dunk after marvelous dunk slammed over
his outstretched arms. After the game, Jones said in amazement,
"To be honest, I enjoyed watching him. I know he's doing things
I'll never see again."

Game 5 in Denver: 37 points, 15 rebounds. Denver won 118-
110.

Game 6 in New York: 31 points, 19 rebounds. He also introduced his patented swooping reverse layup that has been shown
in highlight films almost as much as Michael Jordan's head-on,
hand-switching, impossible hang-time layup against the Lakers in
the 1991 finals. Erving and the Nets won 112-106.

After the 1976 season ended, the ABA disbanded, with four
teams being absorbed into the NBA. Some say it was Dr. J who
was responsible for merging the ABA and NBA. Dave DeBuss-
chere, ABA commissioner, said, "Plenty of guys have been 'The
Franchise.' For us, Dr. J is 'The League.'"

The Nets were now in the NBA, but they didn't want to pay

Erving NBA rates. His contract was worth $350,000, but Erving asked for more. Instead of paying him the big bucks, Boe shipped him to Philadelphia for cash on October 20, 1976.

It was a tough transition as Erving adjusted to his new team and new league. Instead of being the go-to guy at all times, he had to share the attack with a team with other bona fide stars. It was not something he balked at, but others took advantage of the change to criticize him. His average dropped from 29 points a game to 21, and some critics used this statistic to suggest that the ABA was a minor league and that he was just an average small forward.

That, of course, proved to be ridiculous.

Erving's second season with the 76ers, though, did have its forgettable elements. First, the Sixers' management, in either the most arrogant or most nearsighted P. R. campaign of all time, created the slogan, "We Owe You One." They knew their fans were expecting a championship, so they told them that they would give them one. Problem is, if you can't deliver on a promise, it's best not to make it.

And despite a valiant effort by the players, they could not fulfill their bosses' promise. After winning the division, the Sixers were ambushed in the conference finals by the eventual champion Washington Bullets.

As for Erving, he had what he called "a bad season." A groin injury and two bad knees led him to his lowest statistical output as a pro. The vultures started to circle overhead, claiming that The Doctor was past his prime.

He was feeling the pain of the lost campaign when he attended a family reunion during the off-season. While there, an uncle took him aside and told him that the reason he had been able to be so successful was that someone in his ancestral line had put a blessing on him. Having heard of blessings from his Bible training as a youth, his interest in the Bible was rekindled.

"At age twenty-nine, I realized I was looking good on the outside but was hitting a lot of peaks and valleys on the inside. After searching for the meaning of life for over ten years, I found meaning in Jesus Christ.

"When I gave my life to Jesus Christ, I began to understand my true purpose for being here. It's not to go through life and experience as many things as you possibly can and then turn to dust and be no more. The purpose of life is to be found through having Christ in your life, understanding what His plan is, and following that plan.

"Since I asked Christ to be my Lord and Savior, there are still some peaks and valleys. But I am operated on by the greatest Doctor of them all."

After making the change that would give him a new spiritual direction, Julius Erving had some more operating of his own to do. Although he had won two ABA crowns, the big prize that eluded him in his first few years with the 76ers was an NBA title.

Philadelphia knocked on the door in 1980 when they battled the Lakers in the Finals before losing in six games. Then in 1981 and 1982 the Sixers and the Celtics traded Eastern Conference championships: Boston winning in 1981 (and taking the NBA title) and Philadelphia in 1982. Despite the failure of the Sixers to win it all, the NBA rewarded Erving's contributions to his team by naming him the league's Most Valuable Player in 1981.

Yet it was not until 1983, seven years after he first joined the team, that Julius Erving could be a part of an NBA title winner.

Erving capped off a four-game sweep of the Lakers by scoring seven points in a minute-and-a-half to help wrap up the Sixers' 115-108 win. At age thirty-three, and with basketball mortality beginning to cast its shadow over Erving, he knew his opportunities were running out. He no longer dominated at will, occasionally having to take a backseat to Moses Malone, who came riding into town on the wings of hope and ended up riding at the front of the victory parade.

Nearly 2 million people showed up to watch the Sixers parade through town and over to Veterans Stadium for their victory celebration. After three NBA Finals losses in six years, it was a well-deserved celebration.

With the acquisition of Malone, Erving knew the heat was off him. "With our team," he had said, "we don't need a forward to dominate."

But when it was all over and the players were passing out accolades to one another, Malone was sure to pay homage to the man who had dominated for so long. "This was for the Doc. I wanted to be able to say that I played on a world championship team with Dr. J."

That he would say such a thing is no surprise. Dr. J's team-mates seemed always ready to say nice things about him. One man who leads the "Julius Erving Admiration Society" is the for-mer Nugget defensive ace Bobby Jones, who rejoined The Doctor in Philadelphia.

About his friend and teammate Jones said, "Most superstars have an attitude of 'Nobody is good enough to play with me.' Or 'I'm so much better than the rest of the team that I can be aloof.' Julius was just the opposite of that. He was the kind of guy who built his teammates up.

"I remember on particular game when one of the players had two free throws with 3 or 4 seconds to go. We had a chance to win the game if he would have made them. He missed them both. Julius was the first guy into the locker room. He went over beside the guy who missed the shots and said, 'Hey, don't worry about it. We'll get it next time.' He was an encourager. He was the kind of guy you like to have in your foxhole, and I always appreciated that about Julius. He was there for you when you needed him."

The 1983 title would be Dr. J's last, as Boston and Los Angeles captured the crown during his final four years in the league. During Dr. J's final tour of the NBA, every team in the league participated in the Dr. J Retirement Party. At each final stop of the year, he was feted by team officials and lavished with gifts. In their new home in New Jersey, the Nets displayed his retired red, white, and blue jersey. In Boston he got a plaque. In Sacramento, a tennis ball serving machine. Each stop brought more loot and more praise.

On the court, Dr. J provided some drama by scoring his 30,000th point in the next to the last game of his career, making him the third pro ever to reach that lofty mark; Wilt Chamberlain and Kareem Abdul-Jabbar were the first two. In that game, he re-minded the fans in attendance, including his wife Turquoise, his mother Callie Lindsey, and his children Cheo, Jay, Jazmin, and Cory, who he really was by scoring 38 points. How many people age 37 have scored more points in the NBA than their age?

Not many athletes are as prepared to retire as Julius Erving was. He had already established himself as a successful businessman, and his list of interests in the field is as impressive as you'll find. He serves on the boards of directors of a foundation, a bank, NBA International, and a university. His business holdings include the Philadelphia Coca-Cola Bottling Company, a television station in Buffalo, and a cable system in New Jersey. And for his civic work he has received awards from organizations such as Big Brothers, Inc., the Urban League, Boys Town, *Ebony* magazine, Easter Seals, the Salvation Army, Special Olympics, and the Lupus Foundation of America.

And in the midst of all the applause, the good doctor has maintained his relationship with the Great Physician, Jesus Christ. As Dr. J says, through Jesus he has begun to "understand my true purpose for being here." That purpose, he says, is "understanding what His plan is, and following that plan." The plan has included using his God-given talents in professional basketball, culminating in Erving's being named in 1992 to the Basketball Hall of Fame.

The remarkable thing about Julius Erving is that he has been in the public eye since the late 1960s, yet his legacy is marked by the words of Dominique Wilkins who said about him, "I've never heard anybody knock him or express jealousy. Never one negative word. I can't name you one other player who has that status."

There may be others, and there may be other players who bring similar excitement and flair to the game of basketball, but there will never be another player like Julius Erving. And just think of what he would have done if he had become a doctor, not The Doctor.

THE NBA ROAD

April 6, 1971:	Signed as undergraduate free agent by Virginia Squires of the American Basketball Association
1973:	Traded by Squires to the New York Nets for George Carter and the rights to Kermit Washington
1976:	Nets became a part of the NBA
October 20, 1976:	Sold by Nets to the Philadelphia 76ers

THE ERVING FILE

Collegiate Record

Year	School	G	Pts.	Avg.	FGM	FGA	FG%	FT%	Reb.
69/70	UMass	25	643	25.7	238	468	50.9	72.6	522
70/71	UMass	27	727	26.9	286	609	47.0	75.2	527
NCAA Totals		**52**	**1370**	**26.3**	**524**	**1077**	**48.7**	**73.9**	**1049**

ABA Record (Regular Season)

Year	Team	G	Pts.	Avg.	FGM	FGA	FG%	FT%	Reb.
71/72	Squires	84	2290	27.3	907	1810	50.1	74.5	1319
72/73	Squires	71	2268	31.9	889	1780	49.9	77.6	867
73/74	Nets	84	2299	27.4	897	1742	51.5	76.6	899
74/75	Nets	84	2343	27.9	885	1719	51.5	79.9	914
75/76	Nets	84	2462	29.3	915	1770	51.7	80.1	925
ABA Totals		**407**	**11662**	**28.7**	**4493**	**8821**	**50.9**	**77.8**	**4924**

NBA Record (Regular Season)

Year	Team	G	Pts.	Avg.	FGM	FGA	FG%	FT%	Reb.
76/77	76ers	82	1770	21.6	685	1373	49.9	77.7	695
77/78	76ers	74	1528	20.6	611	1217	50.2	84.5	481
78/79	76ers	78	1803	23.1	715	1455	49.1	74.5	564
79/80	76ers	78	2100	26.9	838	1614	51.9	78.7	576
80/81	76ers	82	2014	24.6	794	1524	52.1	78.7	657
81/82	76ers	81	1974	24.4	780	1428	54.6	76.3	557
82/83	76ers	72	1542	21.4	605	1170	51.7	75.9	491
83/84	76ers	77	1727	22.4	678	1324	51.2	75.4	532
84/85	76ers	78	1561	20.0	610	1236	49.4	76.5	414
85/86	76ers	74	1340	18.1	521	1085	48.0	78.5	370
86/97	76ers	60	1005	16.8	400	850	47.1	81.3	264
NBA Totals		**836**	**18364**	**21.9**	**7237**	**14276**	**50.7**	**77.7**	**5601**

A.C. Green
Against the Flow

VITAL STATISTICS

Born October 4, 1963 in Portland, Oregon
6 feet 9, 225 pounds
College: Oregon State University
Position: Forward
1993–94 Team: Phoenix Suns

CAREER HIGHLIGHTS

- Played on two NBA championship teams
- Named to NBA All-Star team one time
- Played in 567 consecutive games for the L. A. Lakers, a team record

PREGAME WARMUP

I enjoy the fast pace of the game," A. C. Green says. "I enjoy the game of basketball when you're playing at a very fast pace, a running game. When the team is shooting 3-pointers on you, they're running the break, and you're running the break. Then more 3-pointers, and it's just a real competitive game. That's what I really enjoy. I don't like a lot of the other types and styles and rhythms that games can be played at."

In other words, slow. A. C. Green does not like slow.

So what kind of a guy would you expect him to be—this NBA player who is stuck on full speed? This player who doesn't back down to anybody.

You might expect him to be a nasty, mean-spirited guy with a grizzled personality and a reputation to match.

Think again. A. C. Green goes against the flow.

It shows when in his thoughtful and contemplative concern for how people remember him he says, "I want to be remembered as a man of integrity. One that was not just status quo about basketball. I hope you couldn't list the stereotypical athletes and find my name in that column. My lifestyle, I believe, is totally different and contrary. I play with my heart, and I play for the heart of the Lord. And that's really the bottom line with me."

A. C. Green

Cotton Fitzsimmons, general manager of the Phoenix Suns, offers a word of advice for anybody who happens to draw the unenviable task of going head-to-head with A. C. Green: "Don't get in his way."

"Whatever he needs to do to help his team win," explains Fitzsimmons, "that's what A. C. Green does—whether it be hustling down the court to stop a fast break, whether it be to stop the No. 1 forward on the other team; whatever it takes, A. C. will do."

Watching A. C. Green play basketball is like watching a neighborhood kid heading for the ice cream truck.

Don't get in his way.

In a sense, this tendency to tackle the tough assignments in the NBA goes against the flow of what some might expect. Because offense is such a popular part of the game, you often see players expending their energy on the fun side of the halfcourt line and then dogging it a bit on the defensive end, perhaps waving at players on the way to the basket and making less-than-heroic attempts to go after the rebound.

Not A. C.

That's why Suns Coach Paul Westphal, obviously happy to have Green on his team, says, "He has a great winning attitude.

He hustles all the time when he's out there, and he's known for his defense."

There's a reckless abandon about A. C. Green on the basketball court. His rebounds are fierce. He directs the defense with gusto. He runs the court with grace.

"I enjoy the fast pace of the game," Green says. "I enjoy the game of basketball when you're playing at a very fast pace, a running game. When the team is shooting 3-pointers on you, they're running the break, and you're running the break. Then more 3-pointers, and it's just a real competitive game. That's what I really enjoy. I don't like a lot of the other types and styles and rhythms that games can be played at."

In other words, slow. A. C. Green does not like slow.

So what kind of a guy would you expect him to be—this NBA player who is stuck on full speed? This player who doesn't back down to anybody. This player who would, as even his friends say, never let you come into a lane he is guarding without your paying the consequences.

You might expect him to be a nasty, mean-spirited guy with a grizzled personality and a reputation to match. Perhaps a street-brawler who is mean to little children and who snaps at sportswriters. Perhaps a recluse who stashes his money in high risk ventures and high-powered sports cars.

Think again. A. C. Green, remember, goes against the flow.

It shows when in his thoughtful and contemplative concern for how people remember him he says, "I want to be remembered as a man of integrity. One that was not just *status quo* about basketball. I hope you couldn't list the stereotypical athletes and find my name in that column. My lifestyle, I believe, is totally different and contrary. I play with my heart, and I play for the heart of the Lord. And that's really the bottom line with me."

Not words you often hear from hard-nosed, look-out-below power forwards in the National Bashing Association.

The combination of tough play on the court and tender words off describe perfectly the heart and soul of A. C. Green during the past few years. Someone of weaker constitution and less resolve might crumble under the criticism that has resulted because of his stand on one of the hot topics in our world today: sexual abstinence before marriage.

Even more than how he separates himself on the court from many of his colleagues, A. C. has separated himself from the popular voices in society on the subject of sex.

He is going against the flow. And he can take it.

Through his own Athletes for Abstinence organization, the Suns' forward has come out in a big way for abstinence from sex outside of marriage. In a video production called *It Ain't Worth It,* Green has placed his view of sexuality squarely against that of many of today's most influential people and institutions.

Taking such a stand in the sexually free 1990s may seem as tough as A. C. protecting the basket as mighty Shaquille O'Neal goes coast-to-coast against him. In that instance, A. C. Green would hold his territory and attack the Shaq.

Green knows what he is up against when he sets out to tell kids to stay away from sex. "The media states—as well as professional athletes or entertainers or just people in general—that when you want to have sex, to try to do it safe. But I want to say how reasonable it is to wait until you get married before you start having sex—or stop having sex now. Just wait out the period of time until you choose to get married, and then marry an uninfected partner. And then practice faithfulness inside of that marriage. This is nothing more than developing self-control as opposed to learning so much about birth control."

Of course, he knows people are going to disagree. That's what going against the flow always leads to. But A. C. is sure he has the right stuff in his message, and he's not about to change. "I'm sure there are those who disagree," he acknowledges. "People say it's just not for today or that it doesn't relate to kids. People say 'It [abstinence] is one of the best things, but not many kids are going to listen' or 'They're already having sex' or 'They're going to continue having sex; at least do it safe.' And that's normally what I hear as far as feedback. These are just untruths about the condom itself, that it's an invincible shield. That's the thing that really scares me. They're putting so much confidence and trust in it, and it's so fallible."

Green's video includes a rap song featuring David Robinson and football stars Barry Sanders and Darrell Green. It's part of the Athletes for Abstinence project sponsored by A. C.'s umbrella organization: A. C. Green Programs for Youth.

Describing this venture, which is at the heart of his off-season activities, Green says, "It's a nonprofit foundation in downtown Los Angeles. "We are working throughout the Southern California area, but also in other states, so it's more of a national foundation, as far as our programs and projects. But L. A.'s probably going to be the place where I'll reside once I'm finished playing basketball. I still have a strong presence in the L. A. area."

That strong presence is what Green is trying to use to give hope to the young people of Los Angeles and beyond. Through his foundation, he feels confident that he can provide the answers that they are searching for. "Young people are seeing that they're not getting answers on [key issues]. You know, they're not getting any answers about relationships. They need to have a boyfriend or a girlfriend, and there is nothing wrong with that, but at the time and place and when young people are getting involved with sex, society is obviously not giving them the answer.

"They're not finding the answers inside of their own roofs, because they're not having the communication that they really need at home. So they're seeking out answers from a boyfriend or girlfriend. They're looking for comfort. They're looking for love. They're looking for something to identify with and consider to be a part of the family. Like everyone else, they want to be identified with something, and consider it theirs, or consider them to be a part of it.

"When you don't find it under your own roof, you sometimes go and look elsewhere, and that's where you see a lot of kids running with the gangs, because there seems to be a strong sense of family there. People want to be committed to one another—not being embarrassed and not being sheltered by how someone might think or feel. I want to be a part of something that intrigues them and captivates them."

To captivate the kids, then, Green has established a program that gets into their lives and provides answers. The program, neither a baby-sitting time for young people, nor simply a time to

play basketball, has several elements. Essential to its success, argues Green, is his effort to build up the family structure. The program offers courses and techniques to strengthen family ties and reinforce family values. "We want to assist with parenting skills, help kids work through sibling rivalry, and build up parent-child relationships."

A. C. himself had strong relationships with his parents and with his high school coach. "I had a great basketball coach and I had some really solid teachers who cared for me as a person, so they tried to push me to excel. I went in with very low expectations my freshman year—not really wanting to succeed much in school from an academic standpoint—but by the time I got to my junior year, my greatest goal was to be on the honor roll. I wanted my name listed on our school board that was right by the front main door. I wanted to bring my parents in to see my name on the board. It was the greatest goal that I had, and the desire that I had, to see my name there, made me work harder, and to keep it there for a whole year."

At Benson Polytechnic in Portland, Oregon, A. C. kept his name on the board throughout his senior year.

When A. C. started high school, it appeared more likely that he would get on a scholastic honor roll than he would find his name on any all-anything basketball lists. In the ninth grade, he was 5-feet-11 inches tall—not exactly the size that would suggest he would someday be a powerful forward in the NBA. Yet by the time he reached his senior year at Benson, he had added nine inches to his stature. He soon was all-everything, including All-State, All-American, and Player of the Year in Oregon. While his name stayed on the honors board at the school's front door, recruiters now were knocking at his home door.

Green was pursued most heavily by Oregon State, Washington State, and UCLA. Having enjoyed the advantage of a loving home and a caring community, the talented senior chose nearby Oregon State. "I just wanted to be at a place where I would be close to home, and be where my parents could see me play a lot. And it was a big thrill for me to be on TV and have my parents be able to watch me play."

A. C. looks back on 1981 with fondness, for he not only signed a letter-of-intent to play major college basketball, but he also did something that has affected everything he has done since. In fact, it's the main reason he is a man who goes against the flow. That summer A. C. Green became a Christian.

"I was very religious growing up," A. C. says as he begins to tell about his spiritual turnaround. "But I was much a man-pleaser, one who lived according to what people wanted me to do. Even though I went to church consistently, it was nothing personal. I was seeking after religion, but I was not looking forward to having a relationship with Jesus."

"I lived according to what my friends thought or what they wanted me to do. I was very insecure, very empty." He was seventeen, bound for college with a full-ride basketball scholarship and his own car, a gift from his parents. He was an All-American player, as well as the Oregon Player of the Year. He was very popular.

"I had a lot of things going on from the external, but at the same time, I was very empty. Something was wrong. I considered the most important thing for me to do would be to find out what it took to go to heaven and understand more about this Jesus person that I heard about. I was at a church in Hermanston, Oregon, and the amazing thing was that God really spoke through the minister. He had a sermon that day, in which he asked, 'Do you want to go to heaven or do you want to go to hell?' He spoke from what I understand now to be the gospel. I had to make a decision whether I wanted to trust Jesus and live by the standards He set or be someone who seeks to please man."

A. C. was at church with ten of his best high school friends. "God by His grace made me separate myself from them," A. C. says. "I was the only person that went down that Sunday; my ten friends stayed behind. The devil was lying and trying to bombard my mind—trying to tell me 'They're going to be laughing at you, they're going to be joking, calling you all kinds of crazy names.' As I was going down to the altar, everything he said was going to happen, didn't happen. It was a lie. He was trying to keep me from the true blessings and the true fortunes of understanding who Jesus is and the relationship that can come from knowing Him.

"Well, that day, August 2, 1981, I really got born again, as John 3:3 says every man should be."

The young man who was on his way to Oregon State was a new man. Besides his scholarship to go to Corvallis, he now had the assurance that he would be going to heaven someday.

A. C. Green had learned that it was important not to be a man-pleaser but to be a God-pleaser. That belief rankles some people, for they think that kind of philosophy would lead an athlete not to care as much and to be less aggressive in his sport.

But one look at A. C. Green's college career shows that thinking to be as uninformed as a player without a playbook. In his first year with the Beavers, he was selected to the Pacific 10 All-Rookie team on the basis of his 61.5 percent shooting and his work around the basket. As a sophomore, he was All-Pacific 10 and led the team in rebounding. By the time he was a junior, he had improved to conference player of the year. His shooting average, 65.7 percent, was the fourth best in the country.

As he led the Beavers to two straight NCAA tournament bids during his last two years, he got the attention of the NBA, especially the Los Angeles Lakers, who eventually picked him 23rd in the 1985 draft.

Soon Green became one of the valuable supporting players for a new brand of NBA basketball called *Showtime*. The cast featured stars Kareem Abdul-Jabbar, James Worthy, and Magic Johnson, and the show played well at the Forum, not far from Hollywood. Green went from a team that had dropped their first-round NCAA games in his junior and senior years to a team that was tantalizingly close to being World Champions.

In his first year with the Lakers, the purple and gold won 62 games and reached the Western Conference finals. And their rookie from Oregon State was a major cog in the wheel. He and Michael Cooper were the only Lakers to play in all 82 regular season games, and A.C. Green was the first rookie since 1962 to do that.

For the next four years *Showtime* was a hit at the Forum. With dapper coach Pat Riley and a sizzling fast break, the Lakers were one of the hot tickets in town. Green helped the Lakers win two more NBA championships. Eventually, though, the old guard that A. C. Green represented was gone. Jabbar had retired. Riley had stepped down. Magic had contracted the AIDS virus. It was not the same any more.

So, when Green's contract expired after the 1993 season, he had a decision to make. "I had some great years with the Lakers," Green says as he explained how he ended up in Phoenix. "I had a lot of fun. I developed so many relationships there. I had planned on continuing with the team. But it did not turn out to be the case for me."

So, after eight years with the Lakers, Green moved east to Phoenix in search of another NBA championship ring.

The move created a unique setting for A. C., for on this team he was far from a Lone Ranger as a man of faith. From the owner of the team, Jerry Colangelo, to the coach, Paul Westphal, to the point guard, Kevin Johnson, the Suns had people who were committed to Jesus Christ.

Playing for a Christian coach was not new to Green, for he had done that under Randy Pfund of the Lakers. As for Westphal, the Suns' forward knew he was in for a special relationship. "It's great to have a person who has values, who has a love for Jesus. It's something that you really can't take for granted. I have played for coaches or known coaches who weren't Christians, but I still had a high level of respect for them because the Bible teaches me to respect those in authority—even if I do not agree with the patterns they've chosen to live for their own life. It is good to be playing for someone such as Paul Westphal right now.

"He really loves God. It's something I've noticed being here talking with him and asking other players about him. He can stand on his own and on his own merit as far as his own beliefs, and that's really comforting to see. It's not something that he does for show; it's something that he personally believes. The head coach of the Phoenix Suns or not, I know it's the conviction that he has."

As he was in Los Angeles for so many years, A. C. Green is on a team that has taken center stage in the world of basketball. Some of it is because of the flamboyant style of Charles Barkley, who came to town and gave the Suns the chance to hope for a title. Some of it is because of Kevin Johnson, who is a fan favorite and a catalyst for success. Some of it is because of Thunder Dan Majerle, who came to town unheralded by the media and unwanted by the fans but has become wildly popular.

And as in L. A., some of it can be attributed to A. C. Green. Not as a superstar who commands all the attention. But as a support player, one who goes in and digs out the loose balls, hustles down the floor, and cleans up the messes made by others with his swooping rebounds. One who cannot stop doing whatever it takes to win, even if no one much notices.

So A. C. Green is not looking to be remembered as the highest-paid player nor the most photographed nor the one with the most endorsements. He would prefer that fans think of him as "the very best player I possibly can be. That's always a goal I keep before myself. I know when I'm out there playing, I put everything on the line for Jesus. I don't really compromise or lower my standard or my expectation of what I can do out on the court. I really want to develop as a basketball player, just as much as I want to develop as a strong Christian."

And through his A. C. Green Programs for Youth, he wants youth to develop as young men and women. After he retires, he plans to continue Programs for Youth, offering the many activities now available, including an extracurricular after-school program, where children can come in and work on their homework or take computer classes.

And he will continue to emphasize important family ties. Programs for Youth requires that participants bring their parents with them, "just to get the two back together again, or just to continue the strong relationship between the two in a non-home environment," Green explains.

He may continue to offer the popular summer basketball camp, which has operated since 1990. More than one hundred children attend the free week-long camp, where Green and friends teach them basketball in the mornings and afternoons. Time is included for field trips to various companies, to make children more aware of "what jobs are out there, what they can possibly become in life if they put their mind to it." The week concludes with "an honoring banquet. We honor the kids and give them trophies and medals. We invite the parents. We invite someone inside of their home to come with them and see them being honored and appreciated. It's something that we also want to do for the family structure, so it's very important to try to keep these together. We want to build a sense of communication between the two."

His goal is a united family, where teens and young adults learn to stand against the flow. For it is the family that allows a boy to become a man, a girl to become a woman. In fact, says Green, the idea of going against the flow has its roots in a Portland family whose parents knew the value of putting down strong roots and caring for one another. "My home was one where there wasn't a lot of money, but there was a real strong presence of love in one another. I've got two older brothers and an older sister, and both of my parents are still living.

"What really got my family through was the environment I grew up in. There wasn't a lot of finances, but there was definitely a lot of love. We valued the dollar. We always used to take family outings to California, to see our relatives there, then went to Arizona to see relatives there. We did little things like that to really help keep our family structure very strong. We weren't a Christian household, but we were one that was built on trying to care for one another, and really sticking together, which is very contrary to what we find today.

"We find a lot of turmoil inside the family," Green observes, "and a lot of reasons for the family to split up." For the kids who go through the doors of the A. C. Green Programs for Youth, one of the common problems in their own homes is that there is either no dad or if there is he isn't interested in their life.

And Green admits that growing up in his own family, "We had a lot of turmoil, but back then you were together and it wasn't an option to leave. It wasn't an option to separate at all. So my family was very precious for me—something I thoroughly enjoyed." He remembers his dad, A. C. Sr., "had a strong work ethic. Whatever it took to get the job done—if he had to work two or three jobs—he was going to do it just to make sure we had food, a home." His mother, Leola, taught him "a lot about love and just being sort of caring for people; she was a hard worker herself, and she really cared for people."

So does A. C. He cares about his teammates, his family, and the school children of Los Angeles. And he cares about his God. In fact, it is because of that faith in God and His Son, Jesus Christ, that A. C. Green continues to go against the flow.

Q & A WITH A. C. GREEN

Q: *What was it like to move from the Lakers to the Suns?*
A. C.: It takes some getting familiar with the situation. You're in new surroundings because God has taken you from one place and placed you in another. You have to step out in faith. You're out there in the water, so to speak. You got off the boat and you're there. You have to allow all the surroundings and the other elements out of your control to filter down. Those elements include where you're going to live, understanding the chemistry of the team, developing your relationships, and establishing personal relationships with the guys on the team.

Q: *How do you keep spiritually strong during the season?*
A. C.: It really comes down to having a strong covering. I have a good relationship with my pastor back in Los Angeles, and two or three other gentlemen that are very close to me. We have a solid relationship and inside of that relationship there is a sense of being held accountable to one another. We pray for one another.

When I was with the Lakers for eight years, I had a great relationship with our team chaplain. We became very good friends; he was not just the chapel service person only. So the main thing is you need people to stand with you.

Q: *At the* A. C. *Green Programs for Youth, what kind of facilities do you have for the kids?*
A. C.: We are looking to acquire our own facility. We're waiting for the funds to come in so we can do that, but that's something we are looking into. What we have been doing in the past four years, as far as the basketball camp goes, is using a high school gym on the west side of L. A. and running the program out of there. We have had local businesses sponsor the lunches, so the lunches are completely free for the kids. The foundation itself may be a key sponsor, for instance, to develop the funds for the clothes the kids might need. So we haven't got our own center, but it's something I want to do. I also want to get our own home for single mothers and expectant mothers.

Q: *When people ask you why they should bother considering the claims of Christ, what do you tell them?*
A. C.: Well, I always say, 'Why don't you?' My question is 'Why shouldn't you?' Why should a person want to remain or stay in the current position where they don't even consider themselves very happy or life seems to be such a roller coaster emotionally?

Only you can speak from a personal experience. Your greatest ministry tool, your greatest sermon is your own life, your personal testimony. I can always relate to anyone when they come up and talk to me about why they should really think about being a Christian.

THE NBA ROAD

1985:   Selected 23rd by the Los Angeles Lakers
September 28, 1993: Signed as a free agent with the Phoenix
                           Suns

THE GREEN FILE

Collegiate Record

Year	School	G	Pts.	Avg.	FGM	FGA	FG%	FT%	Reb.
81/82	Ore. State	30	259	8.6	99	161	61.5	61.0	158
82/83	Ore. State	31	435	14.0	162	290	55.9	68.9	235
83/84	Ore. State	23	409	17.8	134	204	65.7	77.0	201
84/85	Ore. State	31	591	19.1	217	362	59.9	68.0	286
NCAA Totals		**115**	**1694**	**14.7**	**612**	**1017**	**60.2**	**69.6**	**880**

NBA Record (Regular Season)

Year	Team	G	Pts.	Avg.	FGM	FGA	FG%	FT%	Reb.
85/86	Lakers	82	521	6.4	209	388	53.9	61.1	381
86/87	Lakers	79	852	10.8	316	587	53.8	78.0	615
87/88	Lakers	82	937	11.4	322	640	50.3	77.3	710
88/89	Lakers	82	1088	13.3	401	758	52.9	78.6	739
89/90	Lakers	82	1061	12.9	385	806	47.8	75.1	712
90/91	Lakers	82	750	9.1	258	542	47.6	73.8	516
91/92	Lakers	82	1116	13.6	382	803	47.6	74.4	762
92/93	Lakers	82	1051	12.8	379	706	53.7	73.9	711
93/94	Suns	82	1204	14.7	465	926	50.2	73.5	753
NBA Totals		**735**	**8580**	**11.7**	**3115**	**6156**	**50.6**	**74.7**	**8580**

Hersey Hawkins
No Longer the Center

VITAL STATISTICS

Born on September 29, 1966 in Chicago
6 feet 3, 190 pounds
College: Bradley University
Position: Guard
1993–94 Team: Charlotte Hornets

CAREER HIGHLIGHTS

- Selected NBA All-Star one time
- Holds NBA record for highest free-throw percentage in playoffs at 93.8 percent (120 for 128)
- Selected College Player of the Year in 1988
- Named to 1988 U.S. Olympic team
- Led NCAA Division I in scoring in 1988 (36.3 points a game)

PREGAME WARMUP

While the other talented kids in Chicagoland dreamed of NBA stardom and while many of them took off to the prestigious basketball camps to be ogled by major college scouts, Hersey Hawkins didn't seem headed anywhere big. "In high school I played center," Hawkins explains, "and I have always thought I was good. But I had no idea how good I could become. I knew I was not Kareem Abdul-Jabbar. I was thinking, *I'm a senior in high school. I'm not going to grow much more. I'm 6 feet 3*."

Six feet 3 is almost small for a guard these days, so Hawkins saw little future in basketball.

Bradley Coach Dick Versace was blunt, indicating that a 6-feet-3 center was not on his shopping list. But he accepted the Westinghouse coach's invitation to watch a practice, where Hawkins's coach then put his star player at guard. The center-turned-guard showed Versace that he could handle the ball and shoot from outside, and that was enough for the curly-haired coach. He knew Hawkins could play in Peoria.

"I think the reason I ended up going to Bradley," Hawkins says, "was that the coaches were good friends and I knew I'd have an opportunity to play." In addition, Hersey wanted to be close to home so his family could see him play.

Of course, at Bradley, Hersey was no longer the center. But soon he would be the center of attention.

Hersey Hawkins

Hersey Hawkins still gets a chance to post up now and then. Although he stands only 6 feet 3 and would be not a match physically for the tall timber in the NBA, there are still sporadic chances for him to reprise the old days of high school and play with his back to the basket.

It happened in a game during the winter of 1994, for instance, with respectable results. At the time, the Charlotte Hornets were in the throes of a horrid streak. With both Alonzo Mourning and Larry Johnson on the injured list, the Hornets had lost their stinger.

On that February night the Golden State Warriors were in town, bringing with them a torrid Latrell Sprewell and a cool Chris Webber. Without Mourning and Johnson, the Hornets didn't figure to be buzzing throughout the game.

But that wasn't the way Hersey Hawkins looked at it. He knew it was time for a career night.

He started hot and then warmed up. From the guard position, he hit everything. Then to fill in for some missing artillery, he moved inside. The results were the same.

Finally, Hawkins found himself posting up in the lane. Just like he had done in high school. And he kept scoring.

It was the Sprewell-Hawkins show on TNT and an impressed cable TV audience watched both players hit shot after shot. When the Warriors and Hornets had stopped attacking each other and the final tally was added up, it read like this: Warriors 126, Hornets 116. Sprewell: 34, Hawkins: 41.

For Hawkins, it must have been like old times. Especially because at one point the Hornets' lineup was no bigger than many high school lineups. The Hornets had 6 footer Tony Bennett and 5-feet-3 Muggsy Bogues at the guards, a couple of 6-feet-5 forwards in Dell Curry and David Wingate, and Hawkins playing in the center post.

Hersey Hawkins was first at the center spot in the early eighties while a student at Westinghouse Vocational High School in Chicago. But not because he wanted to. He didn't. In fact, he didn't want to play basketball at all. So he quit.

During his freshman year of high school, Hersey Hawkins, future Player of the Year in the NCAA, quit.

It was the early-morning practices that did him in. "I simply did not want to play," Hawkins recalls about those days. "In my particular high school, we had practice in the mornings and we had practice in the afternoon. When you're young, that's a lot of commitment. We had to get up at 6 o'clock in the morning to go to practice, then go to classes, and then stay afterward to practice again. My days were from 6 to 6. At that time, I wasn't willing to make that commitment."

It wasn't as if he had decided to be a great scholar instead. "At the same time, I wasn't really doing much in school. My grades weren't all that great."

"The year I quit," Hawkins adds, "I was doing nothing but hanging out of the streets. My grades were struggling. Nothing was happening—nothing positive." That's when Mom stepped in. *I'll make him play basketball, it'll keep him off the streets,* Laura Hawkins figured.

"My mom just sort of made me go back," Hersey explains. "I had quit my freshman year, but she made me go back my sophomore year."

And Westinghouse High, Bradley University, the Philadelphia 76ers, and the Charlotte Hornets are all pretty happy she did.

Of course, Hersey Hawkins has benefited from his return to basketball too, but for much more than just the sport. As with so many struggling youngsters who finally choose the hardwood over the streets, Hawkins knows what a powerful influence basketball can become in a man's life. When this middle kid of a working class family of seven finally decided to move back inside the gym, lots of positive things began to happen.

During Hawkins's sophomore year, Westinghouse won the city league championship. During his senior year the team was ranked first in the state and Hawkins was named Player of the Year in Chicago.

Yet while the other talented kids in Chicagoland dreamed of NBA stardom and while many of them took off to the prestigious basketball camps to be ogled by major college scouts, Hersey Hawkins didn't seem headed anywhere big. "In high school I played center," Hawkins explains, "and I have always thought I was good. But I had no idea how good I could become. I knew I was not Kareem Abdul-Jabbar. I was thinking, *I'm a senior in high school. I'm not going to grow much more. I'm 6 feet 3*."

Six feet 3 is almost small for a guard these days, so Hawkins saw little future in basketball. And the lack of attention he garnered from major college scouts probably verified his feelings. "I didn't make any All-American teams," Hawkins remembers almost wistfully, recognizing where that might have led as far as recruiting goes.

"A lot of Division II and Division III schools wanted me," he begins as he describes the recruiting non-war that followed his high school career. And as far as Division I schools, he recalls, "there was Bradley, Illinois State, Northern Illinois, and Marquette."

As it turned out, it was probably best that way. Perhaps if one of the big dogs had come hunting around the Hawkins home, Hersey would not have made the decision he made. And perhaps he would not have benefited from the wisdom of Dick Versace, the Bradley coach.

Versace was a friend of Hawkins's high school coach, so he had the inside scoop on Hersey. But Versace was blunt, indicating that a 6-feet-3 center was not on his shopping list. But he accepted the Westinghouse coach's invitation to watch a practice, where

Hawkins's coach then put his star player at guard. The center-turned-guard showed Versace that he could handle the ball and shoot from outside, and that was enough for the curly-haired coach. He knew Hawkins could play in Peoria.

"I think the reason I ended up going to Bradley," Hawkins says, "was that the coaches were good friends and I knew I'd have an opportunity to play." In addition, Hersey wanted to be close to home so his family could see him play.

Of course, at Bradley, Hersey was no longer the center. But soon he would be the center of attention. First, though, he had to gain confidence in his new role. Coach Versace inserted his fledgling guard into the starting lineup right away, trying to build that confidence. Yet such assurance didn't really come to Hawkins until Versace did something that has affected his game ever since. In a move that was reminiscent of what his high school coach did, Versace gave an entire practice over to building Hawkins's confidence. He told him that every time he touched the ball in the corner, he was to shoot it.

"From that point on, I told myself, 'Hey, I can play!'"

It was a turning point, for it proved to Hawkins that his coach cared. "Dick was instrumental in making sure my confidence didn't waver too much."

In his first two years at Bradley, Hawkins established himself as a more-than-adequate performer in the Missouri Valley Conference, averaging 15 points as a freshman and 19 as a sophomore. Included in that sophomore year was Hawkins' initial trip to the NCAA tournament. The Braves had won the Missouri Valley Conference championship and had a remarkable 31-2 record. In the NCAA first round, they whipped the University of Texas at El Paso 83-65.

From No. 20 UTEP to No. 7 Louisville was a huge gap, though, and the Braves were outgunned by the Cardinals 82-68. If that loss was not enough, Dick Versace, the man Hawkins would call his "father away from home," left the Braves after the team was put on probation for recruiting violations.

How would Hawkins respond to the new man, Stan Albeck? Albeck, a graduate of Bradley, had recently been in the NBA

coaching the Chicago Bulls. During his final season at the helm of the Bulls, Michael Jordan had missed 64 games and the team had lost 52 times. Now he looked forward to joining Bradley's improving program with a proven scorer. But because of Versace's desertion, Hawkins contemplated taking his deadly jump shot to Villanova.

However, Albeck, who had coached such notable scorers as George Gervin, Otis Birdsong, and Jordan, convinced Hawkins that he was just what was needed to pave his way to the NBA. And Albeck showed he meant it by installing a pro-style offense.

"Stan ran an NBA-type of offense where he basically highlights one guy and everybody has to go out and get their own," Hawkins explains. "And I was the guy that he said, 'Hey, you're going to get a lot of shots.' Anybody wants to get the opportunity to know that anytime you come down court, the offense is going to run through you and you're going to have an opportunity to shoot it."

Shoot it he did.

With the big guys setting screens on both sides of the lane, Hawkins would come down court, curl around the picks, and be open for his jumper. As a junior, Hawkins's scoring average shot up to 27 points a game.

Early in his senior year, people watching Hersey started recalling college basketball's great scoring machines, players such as Pete Maravich and Johnny Neumann. In the first game of the year, Hersey tallied 42 points against New Orleans. Then against Colorado, he raised that a notch to 44 points. A few days later, against U. C. Irvine, Hawkins poured in 51 points, a school record for Bradley. The topping on the scoring cake came against the University of Detroit on February 22, 1988, when he poured in 63 points against the Titans, the tenth best individual effort ever in Division I history.

Just as he had done in his sophomore year, he led the Braves to the NCAA tournament, this time with a 26-4 record. This time, however, they dropped their first round game, 90-86 to Auburn, and Hawkins's college career was over.

The kid from Chicago, who was recruited by only four major colleges, had accomplished what few ever do. He was the nation's leading scorer, averaging 36.3 points a game. His 1,125 points as a senior ranks him seventh on the all-time list for single season scoring. And he was just the fifth player in Division I history to break the 3,000-point mark in career scoring.

Now people knew who Hersey Hawkins was. "When you score, people will find you," he says of the recognition. "All of a sudden I found myself being asked for stories wherever I went. *Sports Illustrated, The Sporting News,* and all of these things. It was a little odd—going to this smaller school and all of a sudden having all of this national recognition." In addition to his scoring honors, Hawkins was named the College Player of the Year by almost everyone, including the Associated Press, United Press International, the United States Basketball Writers Association, and *The Sporting News*.

Other high-powered scorers have made it to the NBA, only to get lost in the shuffle of dozens of other players who could score. So the ultimate test for Hawkins would be how he would adjust to the league where everybody is All-Something.

Drafted by the Los Angeles Clippers, Hawkins was immediatedly traded to the Philadelphia 76ers, where he would get a chance to show his wares. He had a modestly successful first year as a Sixer, even breaking the team record for points by a rookie with 1,196.

Another highlight occurred that year off the court, yet it was not something that Hawkins took all that seriously at the time. It was a luncheon with 76ers team chaplain Bruce McDonald. "Bruce and I we went to lunch one day in Philadelphia during my rookie year. He talked to me about becoming a Christian and the importance of Jesus in my life. At that particular point, it didn't really concern me a lot."

Yet as the years went by, there was an uneasiness in Hawkins's life, and he would remember that conversation. The uneasiness may have begun after his first year in the NBA, when marriage changed the way he looked at things. He had married Jennifer, "the first love of my life." They had met in high school and continued to date through college. "People say that when you see the right person, you know they're right for you," Hersey says, "and I think that's how it was for Jennifer and me."

Having a family of his own gave Hersey "a different perspective. It makes you realize that basketball and sports and whatever comes up in life isn't all that important. It's important to a certain degree, but you know that as long as you have good health in your family and you try to make them happy, that's what is important."

Perhaps that realization was behind the troubled spirit that began to afflict Hawkins as his career wore on. "I was frustrated with basketball," Hersey recalls. "I was frustrated at taking the game home with me and not being able to communicate and talk with my wife. I was not really feeling satisfied, and I was just worried about a lot of things. The only thing that came to me was that this was becoming too big of a burden to take on by myself. I was worrying about basketball rather than my family, and I was being grumpy all the time. That was the reason I decided that it's time to let the Lord handle it."

The feeling that something was missing seemed to mount each season, but the 76ers chaplain had remained a good friend to Hawkins. "Bruce was always there to make sure things were going well with me. He's always seemed to have a sense when things weren't going well. I would receive a letter in the mail from him saying, 'Keep your chin up, and we're praying for you.'

"I attended the chapel from time to time. You know, he never burdened me about accepting Jesus. It's not his style. He wanted me to make the decision myself."

During his fourth season with the Sixers, Hersey Hawkins finally heeded McDonald's earlier words and put his faith in Jesus Christ. "Bruce was pleased that I had made the decision myself—without the influence of my wife, and without his influence. It was something that I wanted to do."

Both the chaplain and Hawkins's wife had prayed for Hersey to join them in faith in Jesus. Jennifer had provided a positive witness in the home. "She studied the Bible and stayed in her walk of faith," Hersey recalls. Now Hersey and Jennifer would be working together to instill within their children, Brandon and Corey, the importance of matters of faith.

"That is very important as we raise our kids," Hawkins says. "This way, it's a lot easier. It would have been difficult if she were a Christian and I wasn't—wanting to raise them a certain way. It would have been a battle with everything. This way, we raise them according to what the Bible says."

When Hawkins became a Christian, he calmed at least one frustration that had troubled him as a 76er. Yet the matters on the court were still there to trouble him. Gone for Philadelphia were the glory days of Dr. J. Yet Hawkins plugged on.

"In the beginning, it was good," Hawkins says about the early days of his career in Philly. "But as you start to lose games, I think the crowd starts to get down on you. You have a tendency to get down on yourself." When that happens the fun departs.

And so do some of the players. "I think it was a situation where we really weren't going to be going anywhere in the next two or three years, so they made a decision to rebuild. If you're going to trade people," Hawkins explains, "you're going to have to get rid of your most valuable people, and I just happened to be one of those guys."

And indeed Hawkins had proved himself to be of immense value to the Sixers. One of the most exciting elements he brought to the game was his deadly three-point shooting. Although his college stats from beyond the arc were definitely not anything to get drafted about, his proficiency increased when he got to the more distant line in the NBA.

At Bradley, despite his remarkable scoring average, his 35.9 percent shooting from long range was not record-breaking. Yet with the Sixers his accuracy from downtown increased. In his five years with Philly, Hawkins buried more than 40 percent of his long-range bombs to become the all-time Philadelphia standard-bearer in attempts, in three-pointers made, and in percentage.

His value in the City of Brotherly Love in 1992-93 is clear in these facts:

• Captain of the team
• Scored 20-plus points 40 times
• Led the team in minutes played
• Scored 40 points in one game and 39 in another
• Registered a triple-double for scoring, rebounding, and assists
• Missed only one game

Hersey Hawkins had proved that he was a valuable member of the team, and if the Sixers wanted to get some blue-chippers in a trade, he was the one to go.

Therefore, on September 3, 1993, the Sixers shipped Hawkins to the Charlotte Hornets. Hawkins was pleased with the deal. "I was going somewhere where we had the potential to do something. Going to a younger team. Plus I think they were getting something good. I enjoyed myself in Philadelphia. I think the organization treated me well."

After two years of being the go-to guy at Bradley and five more years of getting the ball a lot in Philadelphia, things were about to change for Hawkins in Charlotte. He knew it and was not terribly upset about it. "It was a little unusual for me, being in Philly the last five years, I was always the number one or number two guy on the team. I knew I was going to get a lot of shots, and I knew I was going to score my 20 points a night. But all of a sudden to be on a team with Larry Johnson and Alonzo Mourning and Dell Curry and Eddie Johnson—all of a sudden you may have been the third or fourth option, maybe the fifth option if somebody gets hot. That was a little odd for me, and that took a lot more getting used to than anything else—being out on the court and knowing that you could go for a while without getting the shot."

Of course the 1993-94 season did not turn out the way the Hornets had hoped, mostly because of injuries to Mourning and Johnson. That opened up the court on several occasions for Hawkins to reprise his high-scoring act, including the 41-point performance against the Warriors. The night he also brought back his post game.

Besides the injuries to his Charlotte teammates, Hawkins wishes other aspects of the game could change. One is the travel, as most players attest. The other aspect of the game that concerns him is the image some people have of his fellow players. "The perception of NBA players from other people bothers me," Hawkins says. "I think everybody thinks NBA players are just out there looking for women. They've got a lot of money. They're materialistic, and that's all they think about. That bothers me a lot. They think we're dumb jocks. Without really knowing anyone, I don't see how they could have come to that conclusion."

As for this NBA player, who is happily married and who says, "My number one priority when I'm not playing basketball is my family and making sure they're happy," those are indeed misconceptions. Even in regard to the money monster that seems to have consumed so many athletes, Hersey says, "We don't put a lot of emphasis on worldly possessions. I know a lot of people say that's crazy, but you have to realize that this is only a small part of life. The goal is eternal life and to be with the Lord Jesus Christ. That's what our family is looking to do."

As a certified family man, Hawkins has an idea of what kind of husband and father he wants to be. "I want to bring to my family some stability and some peace of mind. Hopefully they know that I'll always be there for them, and when I go on the road Jennifer doesn't have to worry about me doing anything. She can trust me. With the boys, I want them to be secure that I'm their daddy. They can talk to me. They can have fun with me. I'll be there for them."

To help with the spiritual side of his life as he makes his way through the NBA, Hawkins has a plan. "I try to read the Bible as much as I possibly can and surround myself with people who are also in the Word. It's always nice to get other people's opinions. People can read the Word and get different ideas. We had great Bible studies in Philly. I miss that."

Whether Hersey Hawkins misses those days of posting up in the middle in high school or those days of fighting around picks for his patented jumper at Bradley or those early days of getting established in Philadelphia, he alone knows.

But it is clear that he does not miss those pre-salvation days of bringing his frustrations home and not knowing what to do with them. Spiritually, he has the solutions to those problems.

What lies ahead still is the challenge of contributing to a young basketball team that many think has a bright future. For Hawkins that could mean getting back into the playoffs as the Sixers did when they reached the Eastern Conference semifinals in 1989–90 and 1990–91. "I hope we can do the same in Carolina," he says.

But no matter what lies ahead, he has the right attitude. "I thank Jesus Christ every morning and every night for giving me the strength to go out and continue to play basketball and continue to be confident, because people are watching. When things are going bad, you have a tendency to not do the right things—to be negative. You have a tendency to shy away from your faith. The good thing about it is that Jesus Christ has a plan and as bad as it may look now, we know that there's a brighter picture tomorrow."

No matter where Hersey Hawkins plays: whether in the paint or beyond the 3-point arc; whether in Philadelphia or in Charlotte or someplace else; he'll continue to succeed. He may no longer be the center, but he's still very much in the middle of things—both on and off the court.

Q & A WITH HERSEY HAWKINS

Q: *What kind of impact did your parents have on you as a kid?*
Hersey: They were a positive influence on anything I wanted to set my sights on—anything that I wanted to go after. They gave me the support that I needed and always were there when things didn't go well. They were always there to pick me up with encouraging words.

Q: *Who, other than your parents, played a key role in your youth?*
Hersey: My high school coach had a big part in developing me as a basketball player and as a person. If you spend that much time around people, they sort of become your second father, and I think that's what my high school coaches became. Coaches have a big influence on kids. I don't think most coaches realize what a big impact they have on kids.

Q: *What do you have planned for your sons? Do you want them to play ball?*
Hersey: Whatever the Lord has in His plans for them, that's what they'll do. I'm not going to push them to play basketball. They love it because they're around it. They're going to learn stuff about it.

THE NBA ROAD

1988:	Drafted by Los Angeles Clippers in first round (sixth pick). Clippers traded rights to Hawkins with 1989 first-round draft choice to Philadelphia 76ers for draft rights to Charles Smith.
September 3, 1993:	Traded from Philadelphia to Charlotte for Dana Barros, Sidney Green, the rights to Greg Graham, and a draft option

THE HAWKINS FILE

Collegiate Record

Year	School	G	Pts.	Avg.	FGM	FGA	FG%	FT%	Reb.
84/85	Bradley	30	439	14.6	179	308	58.1	77.1	182
85/86	Bradley	35	656	18.7	250	461	54.2	76.8	200
86/87	Bradley	29	788	27.2	294	552	53.3	79.3	195
87/88	Bradley	31	1125	36.3	377	720	52.4	84.8	241
NCAA Totals		**125**	**3008**	**24.1**	**1100**	**2041**	**53.9**	**80.6**	**818**

NBA Record (Regular Season)

Year	Team	G	Pts.	Avg.	FGM	FGA	FG%	FT%	Asst.
88/89	76ers	79	1196	15.1	442	971	45.5	83.1	239
89/90	76ers	82	1515	18.5	522	1136	46.0	88.8	261
90/91	76ers	80	1767	22.1	590	1251	47.2	87.1	299
91/92	76ers	81	1536	19.0	521	1127	46.2	87.4	248
92/93	76ers	81	1643	20.3	551	1172	47.0	86.0	317
93/94	Hornets	82	1180	14.4	395	859	46.0	76.8	216
NBA Totals		**485**	**8864**	**18.3**	**3021**	**6516**	**46.4**	**85.7**	**1580**

Avery Johnson
The Little Warrior

VITAL STATISTICS

Born on March 25, 1965 in New Orleans
5 feet 11, 175 pounds
College: New Mexico J. C., Cameron, and Southern University
Position: Guard
1993–94 Team: Golden State Warriors

CAREER HIGHLIGHTS

- Distributed 18 assists in one game at Denver
- Increased his NBA scoring average six consecutive seasons
- Led NCAA Division I in assists in 1987 and 1988 (10.47 and 13.3 per game, respectively)
- Selected Southwest Conference Player of the Year two consecutive years

PREGAME WARMUP

Avery Johnson is an intense competitor, an intense person, and an intense Christian. It's not hard to see how he has defeated all kinds of obstacles to make it in the NBA.

Take, for instance, his senior year at St. Augustine High School in New Orleans. We often hear of NBA players who didn't make a junior high team, or, like Michael Jordan, didn't make the varsity team at first. But not many have to endure the kind of senior year Johnson had.

As he puts it, he was so far from the starting lineup that "the coach had to use a bullhorn to reach me" at the end of the bench. And it wasn't like he was some great big behemoth who was just waiting to develop. He was 5 feet 3 inches short.

Just think of how many guys there are like that in any given year in the United States. Short guys who don't get to check into the game until it is out of reach. Guys who don't have to shower after the game. Guys who might be better off putting their time in at McDonald's rather than at basketball practice.

But Avery Johnson was not sitting down there by the water container thinking about flipping burgers. He was sitting there with determination in his heart. He had put in the hours of practice, and he was sure he could do the job. He was just waiting for the chance.

Avery Johnson

Everything seemed to be going Avery Johnson's way in 1993. He had put together his finest season as an NBA point guard during the 1992–93 campaign, as he improved his scoring average for the fourth straight year. His old friend and coach John Lucas had rescued A. J. from obscurity (and unclaimed free agency) and handed him the starting job as point man on one of the best teams in the NBA. He was teamed with a guy who could single-handedly give you 5 assists a game with no sweat—David Robinson.

Off the court, he and his little family of three were enjoying each other's company. And his growing fame in the San Antonio area had given him increased opportunities to do what Avery Johnson loves to do: Tell people about his Savior, Jesus Christ.

So what was he doing playing chess with his career as the 1993-94 season started? Why was A. J. playing games before the opening night of the year?

Avery Johnson had been a no-show at the San Antonio Spurs training camp. Some thought he was burying his NBA career, throwing away a chance to contribute to a contending team's success. Not so, Avery answered. He was simply asking to be paid the kind of salary he figured he deserved.

And to Avery's way of thinking, that does not mean just being paid for the 1992-93 season. In a somewhat unorthodox way of figuring net worth in the NBA, Johnson says, "What people have to realize is that we are not getting paid for what we are doing now. We're getting paid for when we were eighteen years old out there in the rain and the snow playing basketball 365 days of the year all day long after school. Your mother pulling you by the ear to get you to come in and eat. Then you're running back [to practice].

"That's what you're getting paid for. You're not getting paid for what you are doing now. You're only practicing an hour or two a day."

Cynics might wonder how the NBA owners are responsible for hours in the driveway, and most basketball wanna-bes who end up being accountants or used car salespeople would like to know where they can get paid for all the hours they practiced in their unsuccessful attempts at reaching the pros. But besides all that, A. J. has a point.

Avery Johnson is a warrior. He was never handed anything. He has had to work hard for everything he has accomplished. And if somebody's going to pay you some big dollars for your effort, why not look around for it?

After his 1992-93 season with the Spurs, during which he established himself as a valuable point guard, Johnson figured the team would be glad to move him up the salary ladder. When they weren't, Avery held out. Eventually the little warrior got a call from the Golden State Warriors, who needed a replacement for injured Tim Hardaway. Once again it was time for Avery to prove his worth.

Avery Johnson is an intense competitor, an intense person, and an intense Christian. It's not hard to see how he has defeated all kinds of challenges to make it in the NBA.

Take, for instance, his senior year at St. Augustine High School in New Orleans. We often hear of NBA players who didn't make a junior high team, or, like Michael Jordan, didn't make the varsity team his first try. But not many have to endure the kind of senior year Johnson had.

As he puts it, he was so far down from the starting lineup that "the coach had to use a bullhorn to reach me" at the end of the bench. And it wasn't like he was some great big behemoth who was just waiting to develop. He was 5 feet 3 inches short.

Just think of how many guys there are like that in any given year in the United States. Short guys who don't get to check into the game until it is out of reach. Guys who don't have to shower after the game. Guys who might be better off putting their time in at McDonald's rather than at basketball practice.

But Avery Johnson was not sitting down there by the water container thinking about flipping burgers. He was sitting there with determination in his heart. He had put in the hours of practice, and he was sure he could do the job. He was just waiting for the chance.

"I rode the pine my senior year," Johnson recalls. "I thought I should have been starting naturally, but the coach chose somebody else. Just didn't get no time."

As he sat there, the team took off, playing through the entire regular season without a loss. "We were rolling real high," A. J. recalls.

Then, as the state tournament competition began for St. Augustine, Johnson got the break he needed. "The guy who was playing in front of me, a good friend of mine, got put off the team for one reason or another. The coach inserted me into the lineup at the beginning of the playoffs and my game took off. Everything was clicking at the right time. We finished the senior year 35-0 and won the state championship. I played pretty much the whole game in the state finals. That's how that one scout got a look at me."

The scout was from New Mexico Junior College, and he was the only scout who ever talked with Avery Johnson. It was his only shot at college basketball. And A. J. went for it.

A. J. just needed one shot, and he made the most of it.

Looking back at his growing-up days, Johnson knows why he is so motivated. He knows why he never gave up on high school basketball and was able to turn one junior college opportunity into a professional career: his dad, Jim Johnson.

"My father taught me everything. He was my role model. He was my example. He taught me how to be a husband, how to be a father, how to work. He worked sixty years without a vacation. He just taught me about working hard and being the best you can be and putting that extra effort into things. A lot of self-discipline stuff. My dad was not an athlete. He only had a sixth grade education. But He knew stuff about the Lord and just life in general."

Looking at the list of things Jim Johnson taught his son shows what kind of man he was. And considering the fact that Avery was the ninth of ten children indicates what kind of heart his father had for the children. Even down to the next-to-the-last child of a big brood, Jim Johnson had time to teach what was important.

On October 16, 1992, Jim Johnson died. With his wisdom and instruction he had helped his son reach the NBA. Today Avery Johnson still feels the influence of his father. "I can just feel his presence. We had a great relationship, just what a father-son relationship should be. He taught me how to be a man—how to be a godly man. Those are things I could never repay him for."

Avery also credits his mother for who he is today. "My parents were both Christians, so I came up pretty much in a God-fearing family where God was the main attraction. My father was a hard-working man, a construction foreman, and my mother stayed home and took care of the kids. God was always first in our household. After God, our parents instilled stuff in terms of hard work and confidence and 'you reap what you sow.' Those types of values—biblical values."

He calls his parents "prime-time examples. My dad taught me how to be a man and how to provide for my family. My mother taught me patience and kindness and understanding. They were great examples, and they were always there for me. They were always there for each of their kids."

His mother, Inez, has seen three of her children complete college, including Avery. "She's proud of me for what I do on the basketball court," he notes, "but she is most proud of my degree from Southern University."

The road to Southern in Louisiana had to go through New Mexico. That, of course, is where he had to go to get the only basketball scholarship he was offered. After playing for New Mexico Junior College and coach Ron Black for one year, it was off to Division II Cameron University in Lawton, Oklahoma. There John-

son competed for a year in the Lone Star Conference against such schools as Central Oklahoma and Abilene Christian. At Cameron, Johnson averaged an unimpressive 4.3 points a game in 33 contests.

Next, it was off to Southern University, a Division I school in the Southwestern Athletic Conference. After sitting out the 1985–86 season as a transfer student, Johnson began to play some serious minutes for the Jaguars. During his two years in Baton Rouge, Johnson averaged more than 36 minutes of playing time a game. As a true point guard, he didn't get much of an opportunity to score, taking only 453 shots in 61 games.

But it wasn't his scoring that helped this unknown kid from New Orleans make a name for himself. It was his passing. In those 61 games, Johnson dished the ball off 732 times for teammates' baskets. He became everyone's favorite assists man. To put that number into perspective, only two NBA guards had that many assists in 82 games during the 1992-93 season.

Johnson led the nation in assists both of those years. "It was definitely a big thrill," he recalls. "It wasn't just leading the conference that I was playing in, but it was the whole nation. So I was out there competing with guys from Duke and Georgetown and all the schools, so it was a great accomplishment."

A. J.'s unselfishness with the ball not only got him the immediate recognition of leading the nation those two seasons, but it also got him a spot in the record books. His 1987-88 average of 13.3 assists per game still stands as the best in NCAA history, as does his career average of 8.9 assists per contest (including 106 assists at Cameron).

For the first time in his career, Avery Johnson was beginning to get noticed for his basketball exploits. Yet it wasn't enough to get the attention of the right people. And Johnson is the first to recognize why. "I definitely had to improve on my shooting."

Not that he couldn't score. He still recalls fondly his highlight college outing, 21 points and 20 assists against Texas Southern. "It was just one of those games when everything was just going right." Yet those 21-point nights were not frequent enough for the scouts. And a 7.5 points per game average in college doesn't get very many people a congratulatory handshake from David Stern at the NBA draft.

And then there was the small matter of Avery's body. It was certainly bigger than that of the Charlotte Hornets' Muggsy Bogues, but that's about it. "I was very weak. I needed to get stronger physically to be able to go through 82 games in a season with all that wear and tear on your body. I was about 166 pounds."

So who does a short, thin point guard with a questionable jump shot but great court sense depend on for help? For Avery Johnson, the help he got came from above. He went undrafted in the 1988 draft, but he still ended up with a chance at the bigtime with the Seattle Supersonics. "When I look back on it, God was definitely in on it because I got a chance to go to a team that I thought I could make it with.

"I went to a free agent camp with Seattle in July 1988," Avery recalls. "I played really well there. At the L. A. summer league, I was on the team with veterans like Sedale Threatt, Olden Polynice, and Derrick McKey. And we had a pretty good team for the Sonics. I led the team in scoring and assists that summer."

The young man from New Orleans was in awe, but he was not so awestruck that he couldn't show the Sonics that he belonged. "We played against Byron Scott and Terry Porter. But I held my own and that really gave Bernie Bickerstaff a reason to look at me. He felt for me, and he thought I could be a good player down the road. They didn't need anybody to play immediately because they already had three point guards: John Lucas, Sedale Threatt, and Nate McMillan."

For the first two years of his NBA career, Avery Johnson must have felt like he was back in high school, trying to prove himself. And, in a sense, he was in school. Even now he says, "I was a weak undrafted player. I had to develop my game." And that meant more pine time. In fact, during those two years at Seattle, Johnson played 866 minutes out of a possible 7,872. So, it was a lot of learning by watching.

One of the players Johnson got to watch a lot was John Lucas. It was the beginning of a friendship that would pay off for both men a few years later. "It seemed that John just took a liking to me," Johnson remembers. "He saw a lot of himself in me as a young player. So he helped me a lot, both on and off the court. He had made a lot of mistakes in his career and he didn't want Avery Johnson to fall into some of the same pitfalls."

After Seattle, Johnson floated between Denver, San Antonio, and Houston, never really establishing himself as a key player. He improved his scoring average, steals, assists, and field goal shooting percentage each year, yet he just couldn't carve out a niche. A sporadic starter, he did prove his value, though, as his teams were 14-7 with him in the starting lineup.

When the 1992-93 season began, however, Avery was a player without a team. Having fulfilled his obligations with the Houston Rockets, he was looking for a new place to play. After the season was a couple of weeks old, the Spurs signed Avery to a second tour of duty with them.

For the next month or so, Avery languished at the end of the bench, again reprising his performances in high school and Seattle. "It wasn't an ideal situation when I came to the Spurs," he recalls. "Coach Tarkanian was not in favor of me."

Then, in a flash of insight, the Spurs ownership made a move at Tark's end of the bench. They fired Tarkanian, who had the Spurs playing at an unacceptable 9-11 pace. In his stead, the team hired John Lucas, the same John Lucas who had befriended Avery Johnson in Seattle several years earlier.

Suddenly it was a whole new ballgame for Avery. He now had someone who knew him and trusted him at the helm of the Spurs. Lucas quickly inserted Johnson into the lineup to run the Spurs' offense.

He responded in amazing fashion. Avery started the next 28 games, during which time the Spurs were 21-7. Avery averaged 11 points and 10 assists a game during that run.

By the time the regular season had rolled to a halt, Johnson had put up some impressive numbers. He finished fourth on the team in minutes played and scored 656 points to increase his scoring average for the fourth straight season. In addition, he finished fourth in the league among guards in assist/turnover ratio, and he averaged 7.5 assists a game.

Then, in the playoffs, he had the fourth best assists-per-game average, 8.1, including two 15-assist games against the Suns.

And A. J. knew that it was John Lucas who made it possible. "The main thing he did was allow me to go out and be the leader of the team and play to the best of my ability. There are a lot of intangible things, but that's what he did. He's like my friend. That allows Avery Johnson to be the best he can be. What more can I ask for from the Lord?"

For Avery, everything in his life seems to go back to his relationship to God, whether he is talking about basketball, his family, or his off-the-court activities. As he clearly explains when he talks about his background, he grew up in a Christian family, and he had put his faith in Jesus at an early age. But it was not until just a few years ago that he began to take his relationship with Jesus Christ seriously.

It was July 16, 1989, during the first summer after his rookie year in the NBA. "That's when I gave my life to the Lord," Avery begins as he explains the significance of that day. "I mean committed, fully committed to Him every day. I heard a sermon at my church, and the minister was talking about being fully committed.

He talked about the Lord coming back like a thief in the night for those who were committed to Him. He said, 'If you can't walk out of here and say you are going to heaven if you die, you had better come up here and dedicate your life to the Lord on a full-time basis.' I was the only one who went forward."

As with everything else, Avery Johnson is intense about his commitment to Jesus Christ. His intensity as a person has allowed him to succeed in basketball, and his intensity in faith has allowed him to become a strong witness for his faith. "Perseverance would definitely describe me, with faith in parenthesis," he explains. "I've had to persevere through a lot of different things, both on and off the court. I had to walk by faith and not by sight in a lot of situations, and I thank God for developing that type of quality in me because it's made me a better person in every area of life."

During the heat of the basketball season, it is difficult for players to keep the perspective that helps them improve as people. Constant travel, pressure to win, and continual exposure by the media can make life less than conducive to personal improvement. To combat the negative factors, Avery has a three-point attack: "Number one, I stay in the Word. Number two, I stay on my knees; I stay in prayer. And number three, I stay in right fellowship with friends, with guys who will build me up. Don't get me wrong, I'm eating dinner with the sinners. I'm talking to them all the time. I was there one time. I go out to dinner with the guys, but that's it. That's where it stops.

"Sometimes I share with them about my faith, sometimes I don't. The Lord lets me know when to share. You don't want the guys to say, 'Oh, here he comes! Here he comes with that Bible stuff again.' But there is a time and a place. You want to do everything as the Lord says in the Bible: in decency and in order. You do your part. You can't change people anyway. Only God can change them. I just plant the seed."

In addition to staying in a good relationship with God, Johnson knows how important it is to keep things going smoothly at home. For Johnson, the home team includes his wife, Cassandra, and his daughter, Christiane, who was born in 1992.

Cassandra and Avery met during her senior year of college at Southern University, soon after he had graduated. She was in nursing school. The two of them dated for a couple of years until, as Avery says, "I finally got the nerve to ask her to marry me."

It sounds like it was a good move, if his description of Cassandra means anything: "My wife is just awesome. She's everything. A business partner, an accountant, my fitness partner, Bible partner, and friend. She has grown tremendously in faith since we met."

For his part, Johnson wants to be the right kind of man in the relationship, which is a tribute to his father. He says the main quality he brings to the marriage is leadership. "My dad taught me to be a leader in the home. Just to be an example. A lot of people, whether they're pastors or deacons or regular people, they're in that Word of God and they're in the church, but they're not good examples at home. So I think I'm a good example at home. I want to be an even better man of God than he was.

"It gets a little difficult trying to manage this type of lifestyle in your home, but God has given me unique skills of trying to balance it, and I think my wife would say I'm doing a good job. Sometimes I mess up, sometimes I'm untimely, but my heart is there. My heart is right. I get a lot of invitations to do a lot of different things, but God is first, family is second, and then my job."

One of the invitations that Avery Johnson accepted while still a member of the San Antonio Spurs was to an event that he considers one of the most life-changing in his life. He participated in Jammin' Against the Darkness, a two-day event that was held at the San Antonio HemisFair during the summer of 1993. It was a joint effort led by then-fellow Spurs David Wood and David Robinson.

"When we say, 'jammin' against the darkness,' we basically mean beating the devil," A. J. explains. "We mean jamming against anything that the devil stands for: drugs, gangs, depression, divorce, racism, sexual immorality. It was a very successful event. We had 800 people give their lives to the Lord the first night and 900 the second night. I've never been a part of anything for the Lord like those two nights. He really used our team. At the time I didn't know if I would be with the Spurs the rest of my career, but I know one thing: God brought me here to be a part of that."

As things turned out, Avery Johnson never played another game for the Spurs. As training camp wore on before the 1993-94 season, Avery held out for what he thought he was worth. He loved John Lucas. He loved his teammates. He loved his new job as starting point guard. But what he wanted from the Spurs and what they wanted to give him to play were figures that were too far apart.

It seemed foolhardy. Sure, he had been just what the Spurs needed last season, but what if they refused to budge? What if no one else needed a point guard? What if after all the sweat and aggravation and effort to make it to the NBA, he ended up without anywhere to play?

Those questions did not need to be answered. During the preseason, the Golden State Warriors' All-Star point guard Tim Hardaway blew out his knee. Suddenly, the door of opportunity opened for Johnson. He may have felt unappreciated in San Antonio, but when the Warriors called within an hour after Hardaway went down, he knew he was needed.

So, on October 25, 1993, Johnson became teammates with Chris Webber and Latrell Sprewell.

The little warrior showed his value during opening night against his former teammates when Golden State traveled to San Antonio to play the Spurs at the Alamodome, the Spurs' new arena. An NBA opening night record crowd of 36,523 fans watched their former hero play well, as the Warriors lost a close game, 91-85.

Another game a few weeks later showed the value Johnson brought to Golden State. The Warriors repelled the Dallas Mavericks 103-91, as Johnson scored 12 points in the third quarter to help break the game open. In all, Johnson scored 19 points during the game, which was the Warriors' fourth straight victory.

Within the bigger game that night was a mini-contest that again demonstrated Johnson's determination. In the fourth quarter, he got tangled up with 6-feet-8 Popeye Jones in a jump ball situation. Jones towered nine inches over Johnson as the referee prepared to throw the jump ball.

"I'd been working on my jump ball in my dreams," Johnson would say later. "I just tried to steal the jump ball. I don't think he thought I would jump with him."

Johnson did jump, and he controlled the tip, showing again that perseverance and self-confidence can help a player overcome all kinds of disadvantages.

The little warrior who loves to compete showed his fire during a rematch with San Antonio in early 1994 when the Warriors hosted the Spurs. This time, the Warriors came out on top, and the difference seemed to be at guard. "The thing that won the game for us," Golden State coach Don Nelson said after the game, "was the turnovers." San Antonio had 26 of them. Golden State had 8.

With A. J. at the controls, Golden State had the advantage. Besides handling the ball, Johnson had 13 points and 8 assists.

It is often the little thing that wins. And as a little guy in a world that is mostly dominated by people far larger, Johnson has learned how to both survive and flourish. He has parlayed an almost nonexistent high school career into a starting job in the NBA, despite being among the ten shortest players among the more than 300 players in the league.

And he has done so with his heart on the right object: his faith in Jesus Christ; his appreciation for the right people: his parents; and his affection for the right group: his wife and child.

It's a combination that you don't see very often in the NBA. But then, you don't see many people like Avery Johnson come along very often anywhere. He's a true warrior.

Q & A WITH AVERY JOHNSON

Q: *Who were your sports heroes as you were growing up?*
Avery: Nate Archibald was one. Tiny Nate Archibald: he was left-handed, he was short. He led the NBA in scoring and assists one year. Also Pistol Pete Maravich.

Q: *Who were your heroes outside of sports?*
Avery: Martin Luther King, Jr., and all the black achievers: Booker T. Washington, Bethune Cookman, people like that. Naturally for

me, those were my role models outside of basketball. Of all the role models, I've really had only two main models in my life. Even though back then I wasn't living for the Lord every day—I was pretty much a Sunday Christian—Jesus has always been a number one role model. And my father.

Q: *When you get a chance to talk to kids, what message do you give them?*
Avery: My whole thing is about putting Christ first. No matter what you do, just put God first. Be strongly committed to Him, because without Him we are nothing. And I don't want Jesus to think that what He did on the cross was in vain for me. I want to continue to do all that I can while I'm on this journey. That's pretty much what I try to share with kids: putting God first and just striving for excellence.

God sent His best gift in Jesus, so whenever you're in the classroom or whenever you're participating in sports or whatever it is, do it to the best of your ability and just strive for excellence.

Q: *How did you get started playing basketball?*
Avery: When I was eleven, I was playing on a playground, and a guy named Joe Almont, who I'm friends with now, came and asked me if I wanted to come and join an organized team at a recreational center. That helped get me off the streets and play basketball. It helped get me into something organized, which was something we had never seen before. Most of the inner-city kids, we weren't involved with that. We played street ball. So I finally got into organized basketball, and I think that was another big step in my heading in the right direction.

Q: *On the court, how do you maintain self-control and your testimony? Do you think about that consciously?*
Avery: I just go out there and play. If I elbow somebody, and if I say something that is unChristianlike, then God will correct me later. I'm out there doing a job for the Lord and for my team second. I try to keep everything in perspective. You want to play and play to win, and to play by the rules, but if I mess up out there, God will correct me afterward.

I'm not out there to let them just run over me anyway, especially being just 5 feet 11. I'm out there, I'm fighting. I'm fighting
for my team, and I have to do whatever I got to do to help us win
the game. Now, I'm not going to hurt anybody and nobody's trying
to hurt me. But I'm going to be physical. It is a physical game.
Whatever I've got to do, if it's going to bring glory to the Lord for
us to win, that's what I want to do.

People don't understand that. I get questions all summer
about A. C. Green, about why he plays so physical. He's out there
trying to 'kick butt.' That's what it's all about. We're not passive
sissies for the Lord.

I have friends all over the league, but they understand that
within the 48 minutes of that game, I've got a job to do. If the
other player doesn't do his job, then shame on him. I'm definitely
going to do mine. Then afterwards we can forget about it and go
have dinner. I have a couple of great friends, Kenny Smith of the
Rockets and Rickey Pierce of the Sonics. We work out all summer. But hey, when they come down that lane, I'm going to stop
them. That's just a part of the game.

THE NBA ROAD

1988:	Signed as a free agent by Seattle (was not drafted by the NBA)
October 24, 1990:	Traded by Seattle to Denver for a 1997 second-round draft choice
December 24, 1990:	Waived by Denver
January 17, 1991:	Signed by San Antonio as free agent
December 17, 1991:	Waived by San Antonio
January 10, 1992:	Signed by Houston to two consecutive ten-day contracts; subsequently signed by club
November 19, 1992:	Signed by San Antonio as free agent
October 25, 1993:	Signed by Golden State as free agent

THE AVERY JOHNSON FILE

Collegiate Record

Year	School	G	Pts.	Avg.	FGM	FGA	FG%	FT%	Reb.
83/84	NMJC		Statistics Unavailable						
84/85	Cameron	33	142	4.3	54	106	50.9	61.8	31
85/86	Southern		Did not play; transfer year						
86/87	Southern	31	219	7.1	86	196	43.9	61.5	73
87/88	Southern	30	342	11.4	138	257	53.7	68.8	84
NCAA Totals		**94**	**703**	**7.5**	**278**	**559**	**49.7**	**64.1**	**188**

NBA Record (Regular Season)

Year	Team	G	Pts.	Avg.	FGM	FGA	FG%	FT%	Asst.
88/89	Sonics	43	68	1.6	29	83	34.9	56.3	73
89/90	Sonics	53	140	2.6	55	142	38.7	72.5	162
90/91	Nuggets/Spurs	68	320	4.7	130	277	46.9	67.8	230
91/92	Spurs/Rockets	69	386	5.6	158	330	47.9	65.3	266
92/93	Spurs	75	656	8.7	256	510	50.2	79.1	561
93/94	Warriors	82	890	10.9	356	724	49.2	70.4	433
NBA Totals		**390**	**2460**	**6.3**	**984**	**2066**	**47.6**	**71.4**	**1725**

Kevin Johnson
Bright Spot for the Suns

VITAL STATISTICS

Born March 4, 1966 in Sacramento, California
6 feet 1, 190 pounds
College: University of California, Berkeley
Position: Guard
1993–94 Team: Phoenix Suns

CAREER HIGHLIGHTS

- Selected to All-Star team three times
- Holds NBA Finals record for most minutes played in one game: 62, set in Game 3 of 1993 Finals against Chicago
- Named to All-NBA second team three consecutive years (1989-91)
- Placed second in NBA in assists in 1992
- Holds all-time assists record for Phoenix Suns

PREGAME WARMUP

The biggest life-changing experience in my life was becoming a Christian," Kevin Johnson says. "There's no way around it. It happened in my junior year of high school when I accepted Jesus Christ in my life."

And his journey to Jesus started in, of all places, math class.

"I was in geometry class," K. J. begins. "And needless to say, it was a tough class, so I wasn't listening to what the teacher was saying. I had a friend on the basketball team, and he started talking to me about Jesus. Growing up, I had always heard about Jesus, though I didn't grow up in a Christian household.

"I was always curious, but not curious enough to ask anybody. I felt comfortable enough with this friend, so I asked him about Christ and going to church and what this is all about.

"After going to church a couple of times and hearing about Jesus, I said, 'This seems right. There has to be something more to life than getting up every day, going out there and having five good days and five bad days.' It just seemed like there should be something else. He introduced me to Christ, and that was the start of it.

"The things that used to be boring and dull now . . . [became] exciting. In college I started appreciating things I didn't appreciate before. I was able to quit going out and partying and chasing all the girls and all that carousing. I was able to focus on some things that were more important and really slow up my lifestyle. I discovered that people will always let you down. But Christ never contradicted Himself. . . . He is the ultimate person we should try to be like."

Kevin Johnson

Kevin Johnson is glad to be employed by the Phoenix Suns for several reasons. He appreciates the leadership of Coach Paul Westphal and General Manager Jerry Colangelo. He enjoys the comfort of the sparkling America West Arena. He likes the success of playing in the NBA championship against the Bulls in 1993.

But the primary reason K. J. is glad to be a Sun is because of what it means he isn't—like a resident of Cleveland. Not that Johnson has anything against the city itself or the people or the team. It's the weather. Having grown up in California, K. J. likes weather that matches with his personality: bright and warm.

Yet for half of his first NBA season, Johnson was a member of the Cleveland Cavaliers.

He calls getting drafted "the most memorable moment of my basketball career," though he adds that winning an NBA title would easily become an even greater moment. "I was the seventh pick, and to be drafted in the first round was something that I was hoping for, but I never anticipated going as high as I did. Being drafted is more than getting your foot in the door. It's getting in the door."

However, when K. J. arrived at Cleveland, he discovered that it was a revolving door. "I don't think my teammates in Cleveland really thought I was going to amount to much of a basketball play-er. As a rookie, I made a lot of mistakes, and I had to learn the ways of the game."

At the same time, a fellow player by the name of Mark Price was beginning to come into his own, averaging 16 points a game during K. J.'s rookie year.

So on February 25, 1988, the Cavs packed up Tyrone Corbin, Mark West, and K. J. and trundled them off to Phoenix in ex-change for Larry Nance and Mike Sanders.

Not that Johnson was too upset about it. "When the initial trade occurred with Cleveland, I thought instantly it was gonna be a great trade for me. I knew I was going to get an opportunity to play."

And there was the small matter of the weather.

"To be quite honest, I was very thankful to be leaving the Midwest and Cleveland, where the sun didn't shine very often, to go to Arizona where the sun shined on a regular basis." That, of course, was a long time ago. "Looking back at the trade today, it's hard to believe that I was even in Cleveland. But I am still thankful for Cleveland drafting me seventh. God has His ways. I think I learned a lot from Mark Price in that situation."

Now the situation is that Mark Price and Kevin Johnson are arguably the best two point guards in the NBA. One is happy in Cleveland and one is happy to be in the land of the Suns.

Besides Cleveland, another place Kevin Johnson used to be from is Sacramento, California. Oak Park, to be exact. And just as K. J. returns to Cleveland periodically to play a little hoops, so he goes back to Oak Park to do a lot of good.

Back home in Sacramento, Kevin Johnson has established himself as more than a basketball player. He has proved to be an intelligent, caring young man who is familiar with what Oak Park was and has a vision for what it can become. "Back in the fifties, Oak Park was a suburb of Sacramento," K. J. begins as he traces his neighborhood's past. "But as the city expanded, its metropoli-tan area encompassed Oak Park. The dynamics of Oak Park changed. It used to be a suburb with a lot of affluent people. As the sixties and seventies came, the rich people moved farther out-side the city. Oak Park became pretty much a ghetto area."

Growing up in that part of Sacramento, K. J. knew a side of life that people expect when they hear of the inner city. "Drugs run rampant, there's high unemployment, the drop-out rate is unfortunately very high. There's a lot of crime. It's unfortunate that young kids have to grow up with that."

Kevin Johnson was there, "hearing the gun shots, listening to the sounds of police cars patrolling the streets at 3 in the morning." Yet K. J. was not swallowed by the mean streets. He knows why, and he wants to try to give today's kids a chance to succeed as he did.

"I was raised by my mom and my grandparents. What I appreciate most was that my grandmother was always at home. As a kid, what that did was to make me a very secure individual. I knew that every day when I came home somebody was gonna be there to greet me. That did a lot for my self-esteem."

That confidence was a huge advantage for Kevin as he stood up and stood out among his friends. And it helped him live with his mom's advice that in basketball and in life he had to be different to succeed.

K. J. was Georgia West's only son as he was growing up (although K. J. now has an eleven-year-old brother), and he thinks that may account for the competitive drive that has helped him use his difference to an advantage both on and off the court as he was growing up. "I was an only child, and by being the only child you always kind of want your way. So when I participated in sports and in school, I was very competitive. I always wanted to be the best. I always wanted to challenge myself.

"I can remember that whatever sport we were doing or whatever assignment we were working on in class, I wanted to be one of the best. I wanted to be different. I wanted to be special. I realized that if you work hard and really commit yourself, you always set yourself up to being pretty good.

"It wasn't until I was in the seventh grade that I realized how good my athletic abilities were. We started competing on a citywide basis, and I realized that I was still able to compete successfully and be one of the best in baseball and basketball. That's when I thought that perhaps this particular athletic ability and talent could open a door for Kevin Johnson to go to college—to pay for a college education."

It would do that and so much more.

K. J. was kind of the baseball/basketball version of Bo Jackson while growing up in Sacramento, playing both sports well. "I've always felt that I was probably a more natural baseball player than a basketball player," the All-Star NBA point guard confesses. "That was something that came easily to me, and I really loved the sport."

Today he's the object of awe by young basketball fans across the country. As a kid, he knew about that kind of hero worship, but K. J.'s admiration was reserved for baseball players. "My favorite team was the Oakland A's in their heyday of the early seventies. All those players were my idols. I would go in the backyard and create my own baseball games. I would throw the ball against the wall and I'd be the shortstop, Bert Campaneris. Or I'd hit a long ball like Joe Rudi or Gene Tenace or Reggie Jackson. When I pitched, I was Vida Blue or Catfish Hunter. I got a chance to become all my heroes.

"But the one person who really was my role model and the person I tried to emulate growing up played for the Los Angeles Dodgers. That was Steve Garvey. I remember that people disliked him because he was too nice. I thought that was the ultimate compliment."

As a baseball player, Johnson was All-City in high school and after his third year of college was drafted by his favorite team. That summer K. J. journeyed to Modesto, California, to play two games as shortstop for Oakland's single A team. He batted twice, scored a run, got two assists, and made one error in his brief stay at Modesto. That would be the beginning and the end of his pro baseball career.

"I had to make a firm decision," he explains. "Do I want to pursue both sports or do I want to make a decision to go one way or another? I felt for me to reach my maximum potential, I had to devote myself to one sport. At that point, I felt that basketball was my best opportunity."

He had good reason to think so. In his senior year of high school, Johnson led all California high school basketball players in scoring with a 32.5 points per game average. In one game that year, Kevin had his career game when he scored 56 points.

But a fine baseball career and an even better basketball career were not the highlights of Kevin Johnson's high school days. "The biggest life-changing experience in my life," he says, "was becoming a Christian. There's no way around it. It happened in my junior year of high school when I accepted Jesus Christ in my life."

And his journey to Jesus started in, of all places, math class.

"I was in geometry class," K. J. begins. "And needless to say, it was a tough class, so I wasn't listening to what the teacher was saying. I had a friend on the basketball team, and he started talking to me about Jesus. Growing up, I had always heard about Jesus, though I didn't grow up in a Christian household. I hadn't been to church since I was five or six.

"I was always curious, but not curious enough to ask anybody. I felt comfortable enough with this friend, so I asked him about Christ and going to church and what this is all about.

"After going to church a couple of times and hearing about Jesus, I said, 'This seems right. There has to be something more to life than getting up every day, going out there and having five good days and five bad days.' It just seemed like there should be something else. He introduced me to Christ, and that was the start of it."

That meant that his first years of college were also his first years as a believer in Jesus. Both were adjustments for the kid from Oak Park.

In basketball, he obviously adjusted well. His eye-popping high school stats were good enough for the University of California at Berkeley, who snatched him up and gave him the scholarship that he had worked so long and hard to earn. At California, Johnson made All Pacific-10, but he didn't impress himself. "I wasn't a dominant player," he says of those days during which he averaged 14 points a game. He might not have been dominant, but he did establish school records at Cal for career points (1,655), assists (5,321), and steals (155). And he achieved the first triple-double in Pac-10 history when he scored 22 points, grabbed 10 rebounds, and handed out 12 assists in a game against Arizona.

The university must have been impressed, for they retired K. J.'s number 11 on October 21, 1992. K. J. was pleased too, for he had successfully fulfilled his boyhood dream, and he had earned his degree.

The adjustment to his new life as someone who wanted to follow Jesus Christ may have been harder than his adjustment to college basketball. "For the next three years while I was in college, I wasn't perfect, but I was learning what it took to be a good Christian. I don't mean one of those Christians who are 'holier than thou.' I needed to know what my responsibility was and what I was supposed to do as far as emulating and following my ultimate role model: Jesus Christ.

"I discovered that when you make a change in life, the things that you used to find fun and exciting will no longer have that same thrill. And the things that used to be boring and dull will now take on a whole different meaning and be exciting. In college I started appreciating things I didn't appreciate before. I was able to quit going out and partying and chasing all the girls and all that carousing. I was able to focus on some things that were more important and really slow up my lifestyle. I was able to give up drinking. I discovered that people will always let you down. But Christ never contradicted Himself. He was never hypocritical. He never failed. He is the ultimate person we should try to be like.

"When I was a junior, I took the New Testament and said, 'I don't know what it really is to be a Christian. I don't know enough about what I'm supposed to do or how to act. I don't think I'm totally fulfilling my responsibility.' I made up my mind that I was going to read one chapter of the New Testament every night. I read it all the way through. That's when my true conversion to Jesus Christ came.

"It just turned my life upside down, and from then on life has been fun. Every day, for the most part, I've been able to have joy in my heart."

That joy has been enhanced with the happiness of a successful pro career. After a slow rookie season playing little with the Cavaliers, Kevin was named the NBA's Most Improved Player during his second season. Since then he has been selected to the second team All-NBA team three times and has played in three All-Star games.

His teammates feel little jealousy as they heap praise on a key team player.

"He's been our leader since the day he arrived and that continues to be his function—in the locker room and on the floor," says center Mark West.

"He brings a lot to the team," adds center Oliver Miller. "He's a good shooter, a good passer, and he's a great defensive player. That's where leadership starts. We are focusing on defense, and it all starts with K. J. He's a great leader all around."

That recognition of his talents gives Johnson some leeway with others in the league as he lives in a way that is sometimes contrary to what is expected of pro athletes.

"As long as you don't try to hit them over the head with your beliefs, I think players have a tendency to respect you. I think that's the beauty of the NBA. We respect the individual rights of others. Of course, any time we get a chance or somebody wants to know something about what I believe, then it's a great opportunity to share."

When Kevin Johnson says "we" as he talks about sharing his beliefs, he is probably talking about himself and guys on the team like A. C. Green. When A. C. joined the Suns in 1993, Johnson was not afraid to express his happiness about it. "Having a brother in Christ always feels great. But he's not a normal brother in Christ. He's very exceptional. I think his presence has made a big difference in my approach to basketball and life. He is somebody who takes a stand day in and day out. He is confident in who he is and what he believes, and I think that sort of devotion and confidence and faith permeates the team."

And it's not just off the court that Kevin is glad to have A. C. "He's a very hard worker. He knows how to win. Day in and day out he's going to do some of the garbage tasks, some of the little things other people don't want to do for the overall sake of the team. Any time you get a player that unselfish, that blend is going to be dynamic for the team."

Those characteristics also apply to K. J., as he showed vividly in 1993 when the Suns and the Chicago Bulls battled for the NBA title. Throughout the series it was clear that as K. J. goes, so goes the Suns. Sure, Sir Charles Barkley had to be there, but it often was the playmaking and the backcourt work of Johnson that made the Suns shine the brightest.

Consider the third game of the Finals. The first two games had become the Disaster in the Desert. The Suns had lost both games on their home court. It was the first time in the league's 47-year history that the home team had gone in the tank so quickly.

And for many, much of the blame was laid at the quick feet of Kevin Johnson. He had indeed had a miserable first two games, scoring but 15 points and handing out only 8 assists combined. It was time for K. J. to radiate. He had to light it up or the Suns would sink in the West.

So it was that in the third game, in one of the most remarkable contests in NBA championship history, the Suns beat the Bulls 129 to 121 in triple overtime. Led by a rejuvenated (and after the game very tired) Kevin Johnson, the Suns refused to go down.

Johnson set an NBA Finals record by playing 62 minutes, as he scored 25 points and dished out 9 assists.

He knew he was up against the wall when he showed up at Chicago Stadium for the game. After his vital performance, he told reporters, "I'd like to thank my teammates and coaching staff for standing by me. It was the law of averages. After two games, I was due for a good one."

The Suns lost game 4, but in game 5—the final game at Chicago—K. J. nearly matched his game 3 performance, again scoring 25 points and passing out 8 assists. The Suns won 108 to 98 to send the series back to Phoenix. There, however, John Paxson's killer three-pointer with less than 4 seconds left gave the Bulls the 99 to 98 win and their third NBA crown.

One of the most memorable images of that series was a little set-to between two of the "initial kings" of the NBA: K. J. and B. J. Kevin and B. J. Armstrong had a bit of a difference of opinion during the Finals, and they ended up squaring off against each other, although neither landed a damaging punch.

Anyone who has ever played sports knows how the intensity of the game can lead to such extracurricular activity, and in a basketball championship series, the pressure is magnified.

Kevin Johnson has thought about what is behind such action. "I think it's important for people to understand that Christians are going to get into situations they would prefer not to be in. It's all part of being competitive and holding your ground. There's no way I condone violence or try to say that you should get into fights and shoving matches. But I think by the nature of sports, things are going to happen like that, and you have to hold your ground.

"Then, after that incident is over, you have to leave it there and apologize." Which is exactly what K. J. did.

"It was unfortunate that my Christian example wasn't ideal to what I would have wanted it to be, especially for the kids. But I'm not perfect and those times are going to come.

"The Bible tells us that God doesn't give us a timid spirit. He gives us a spirit to compete and to work hard—to stand your ground and to take initiative. But, you always have to do that with the right context."

This whole idea of physical play and how players feel toward each other in the NBA is an ongoing controversy. It was brought to the forefront during the Suns-Bulls series in 1993 when player-turned-TV-commentator Magic Johnson kept contending that the players could not really play their best against each other unless they had an intense hatred one for the other. Behind his argument were references to players on opposing teams getting together as friends during their free time between games of the series.

K. J. has heard the argument, but he does not completely agree. "What he meant by that," he says, "was that you don't necessarily have to hate your opponent. But it's harder to do whatever it takes to win if you are fraternizing with him before the game. Take A. C. If he and I were playing against each other in the finals and we happened to be great friends, I couldn't hang out with him. I wouldn't spend time with him while those finals were going on."

Now, of course, as teammates A. C. Green and Kevin Johnson are good friends. K. J. also has admiring friends outside basketball. Scores of children throughout Sacramento call K. J. their friend through an organization the All-Star player founded called St. Hope Academy. Seventy-five children participate year round in the core program, and many more kids come to the summer programs. "We try to say yes to every kid that wants to be a part of it," K. J. explains.

St. Hope deals with educational and spiritual issues. "We take their school curriculum and build on that and teach them some of the values and characteristics we think are important." One of the most important programs is called a "rites of passage" and deals with building character.

"By character," K. J. explains, "I mean we teach biblical principles; we memorize Scripture. We spend a lot of time as it relates to the Christian aspect of living. Treat people like you want to be treated. Always try. Always do your best. Know the difference between right and wrong. Try to be an upstanding citizen. Try to help those who are less fortunate or perhaps more disadvantaged than you. It's been very exciting.

"Also, we try to teach them a lot of African-American facts in history, because it's important for them to know who their ancestors were and where they came from."

Because K. J. knows where he came from and is willing to go back there to help the kids who are left behind, it is easy to slap on him the label that Kevin's friend Charles Barkley made so controversial not long ago: role model. And because he is viewed as one, Johnson has some definite ideas about what it means. "What he was trying to say was that the ones who are going to have the biggest and most lasting impact on our young people are parents and the people who are in contact with kids on a day-to-day basis. Not athletes they just see on TV. In my case the role models happened to be my grandparents, my next door neighbor, my mom, and a couple of my teachers."

Still, as a sports star, Johnson has been acknowledged as a role model for kids. K. J. has won the Walter J. Kennedy Citizenship Award from the NBA and was given the Good Sport Award by *Sports Illustrated for Kids*. Former President George Bush once named Johnson a "Point of Light" for his work with young people at St. Hope's.

With his skills for guiding the offense and his improving defensive intensity, Johnson is one bright light any team needs to have success on the court and respectability off it. Coach Paul Westphal describes his ace guard in fitting terms when he says Kevin is both a great player and "great citizen. He's really concerned with helping kids. He's very true to his beliefs in all that he does and he's somebody that everyone can look up to. Kevin is a great guy to have on any team, both for his basketball ability and for who he is."

Q & A WITH KEVIN JOHNSON

Q: *What is your favorite part of the game? Offense or defense?*
K. J.: During the first 5½ years of my NBA career, offense was the most fun. We've been an offensive team. We try to win a lot of our games with offense. But in the last year or so, as we have tried to get to the top level and win a championship, we've realized that defense and rebounding have to be our focal point. So I've taken a new responsibility in taking pride in my defense. That has been a great challenge because night in and night out you go out there

and fight with all your might and hold and push and do everything it takes, and it's all legal.

In the 1993 finals, I got the unfortunate responsibility of guarding Michael Jordan. That wasn't easy. There was a lot of pain involved in that because he's an amazing athlete. Yet it was a challenge that I took pride in and that I'm thankful I had.

Q: *Are you going to miss facing Michael Jordan? Is his retirement kind of a downer for you and your team?*
K. J.: I'm not going to say it's a downer, but I mean sports aren't the same. That guy was just so unbelievable in the things he was able to do on the basketball court. This is probably the greatest compliment: We would all run home after our games to watch ESPN to see the highlights and see what he did. Because he was always doing something amazing and is an unbelievable person. He doesn't talk about his Christianity a lot, but I think God has a role in his life.

Q: *With the busy schedule and road trips making going to church so difficult during the season, how do you maintain your spiritual health during the NBA wars?*
K. J.: I think there are seven things you have to do on a regular basis to keep your relationship with Christ strong. You have to pray on a regular basis. I mean the power of prayer is awesome. So I try to do that regularly. Second, you try to read. I think that the more I can read and understand different people's perspectives on Christianity and faith and prayer and forgiveness, the stronger I'm going to be.

You have to be able to study the Word. You have to take the Bible and study it. You have to try to study what Christ and his disciples were trying to tell the people. You have to take those messages and make them applicable in your everyday life. You have to memorize Scripture and meditate on the Word. You have to hear the Word, and you have to go to church.

Q: *If you hadn't become a basketball (or baseball) player, what do you think you'd be doing today?*

K. J.: I think I would have been a teacher. I like teaching and sharing with kids. I think that's important. I draw from kids. They give me a lot of energy, and I hope that I have a few things to share with them that would be helpful.

Q: *The NBA has tried to tighten up on the trash talk that goes on during the games. How does the trash talk affect you? [We note that "trash talk" does not mean profanity or obscenity; it means challenging the other player with a comment like: "Don't bring no weak stuff down the lane or I'll put it back in your face."]*

K. J.: You take Larry Bird, Magic Johnson, Michael Jordan, Charles Barkley. These are the best players that ever played the game, and they talk trash. But I don't think they do it in a bad manner. I don't think they ever try to disrespect somebody. I don't think they ever threaten anybody or try to hurt somebody. I don't think they ever say anything that's too insulting. It's all the nature of the game, and that's part of sports.

Personally, I don't talk trash that much unless somebody talks to me first and then I might react a little bit. You've got to hold your ground.

If talking leads to tempers flaring and emotions getting out of hand, then it's not necessarily trash talk. That's provoking. Then it's not good. I think the officials have a really tough job of trying to distinguish between friendly and sportsmanlike trash talk versus trash talk that can end up in violence.

Q: *Who are some of the toughest people you have to guard?*

K. J.: One of the toughest I have to guard is Mark Price. He's a Christian too, so he's probably got the extra support that most players don't have. He's such a great perimeter shooter, and his big men do a good job of setting a lot of picks to get him open. And if he's open for one split second, that's gonna cost you 2 or 3 points.

Another former teammate, Jeff Hornacek of the Jazz, is a very tough player to guard. And last but not least is Tim Hardaway of the Warriors.

THE NBA ROAD

1987:   Selected by Cleveland Cavaliers in round one
                        (seventh pick)

February 25, 1988:   Traded to Phoenix along with Tyrone Cor-
                        bone, Mark West, 1988 first-and second-round
                        picks and 1989 second-round picks for Larry
                        Nance, Mike Sanders, and a 1988 second-
                        round pick

THE KEVIN JOHNSON FILE

Collegiate Record

Year	School	G	Pts.	Avg.	FGM	FGA	FG%	FT%	Asst.
83/84	Cal	28	271	9.7	98	192	51.0	72.1	N. A.
84/85	Cal	27	348	12.9	127	282	45.0	66.2	74*
85/86	Cal	29	451	15.6	164	335	49.0	81.5	99*
86/87	Cal	34	585	17.2	212	450	47.1	81.9	100*
NCAA Totals		118	1655	14.0	601	1259	47.7	75.7	423

NBA Record (Regular Season)

Year	Team	G	Pts.	Avg.	FGM	FGA	FG%	FT%	Asst.
87/88	Cavs/Suns	80	732	9.2	275	596	46.1	83.9	437
88/89	Suns	81	1650	20.4	570	1128	50.5	88.2	991
89/90	Suns	74	1665	22.5	578	1159	49.9	83.8	846
90/91	Suns	77	1710	22.2	591	1145	51.6	84.3	781
91/92	Suns	78	1536	19.7	539	1125	47.9	80.7	836
92/93	Suns	49	791	16.1	282	565	49.9	81.9	384
93/94	Suns	67	1340	20.0	477	980	48.7	81.9	637
NBA Totals		506	9424	18.6	3312	6698	49.4	83.7	4912

*Assists are for only 18 conference games per year.

Bobby Jones
The Quiet Man

VITAL STATISTICS

Born: December 18, 1951 in Akron, Ohio
6 feet 9, 212 pounds
College: University of North Carolina
Position: Forward
Retired: 1986

CAREER HIGHLIGHTS

- Selected to NBA All-Star team four times
- Named to NBA All-Defensive first team eight consecutive years (1977–84)
- Played on the 1972 U.S. Olympic team
- Received NBA Sixth Man Award (1983)

PREGAME WARMUP

From all appearances, Bobby Jones would probably prefer to be known simply as a quiet man who loves his family and wants to serve God with his life.

In one of the paradoxes of basketball and life, Bobby Jones, the player who irritated opposing players with his tough, tenacious defense for nine NBA seasons, is a soft-spoken man who cherishes the solitude of home and the contemplative moments that family time brings over the blaring sounds and fame that pro basketball has given him. Bobby Jones seems to be the kind of person who would prefer a bike outing with his wife Tess and his children over public appearances.

Yet when Bobby Jones was a college student at the University of North Carolina, making it to the NBA was his only goal. "My goal was to play basketball and to be as good as I could be. I really had no desires in my life other than that. I majored in psychology, but my goal was to make it in the NBA."

One of the reasons Jones was able to even dream of such a lofty goal was that after his sophomore year as a Tar Heel, he made the U.S. Olympic team. That experience, which not only gave him the exposure and experience he needed to get the attention of NBA scouts, also gave him one of the most bittersweet moments of his basketball career.

Bobby Jones

When basketball fans think about Bobby Jones, any one of several images may come to mind:

- There's Bobby Jones, NBA champion—for he and his Philadephia 76er teammates won it all in 1983.
- There's Bobby Jones, successful high school basketball coach —for he led the Charlotte Christian High School to the state championship in 1992.
- There's Bobby Jones, Olympic silver medalist—for he and his 1972 Team USA teammates won at least second place in the most controversial of all Olympic basketball final games.
- There's Bobby Jones, epileptic—for his professional basketball career was threatened by the disease.

But from all appearances, Bobby Jones would probably prefer to be known simply as a quiet man who loves his family and wants to serve God with his life.

In one of the paradoxes of basketball and life, Bobby Jones, the player who irritated opposing players with his tough, tenacious defense for nine NBA seasons, is a soft-spoken man who cherishes the solitude of home and the contemplative moments that family time brings over the blaring sounds and fame that pro basketball has given him. Bobby Jones seems to be the kind of person who would prefer a bike outing with his wife Tess and his children over public appearances.

Yet when Bobby Jones was a college student at the University of North Carolina in the early seventies, making it to the NBA was his only goal. "My goal was to play basketball and to be as good as I could be. I really had no desires in my life other than that. I majored in psychology, but my goal was to make it in the NBA."

One of the reasons Jones was able to even dream of such a lofty goal was that after his sophomore year as a Tar Heel, he made the U.S. Olympic team. That experience, which not only gave him the exposure and experience he needed to get the attention of NBA scouts, also gave him one of the most bittersweet moments of his basketball career.

Along with future NBA players Doug Collins, Tom Burleson, Tom McMillen, and Ed Ratleff, Jones and the Hank Iba-coached American team traveled to Munich to take on the world. The United States had won every medal ever awarded in Olympic basketball, and this team was expected to be no exception. In basketball, the world was catching up with the Americans, but no one thought they were ready to beat the United States at its own game.

On September 10, 1972, the championship game pitted the Americans against their old nemesis, the Soviet Union. At halftime, the Soviets held a 5-point lead, and the Americans' perfect record in the Olympics was in jeopardy. As the game wore on, the USSR maintained its lead. With just 6 seconds left, the Soviets had the ball and a one-point lead.

Then Alexandr Belov, the Soviet star, threw a bad pass that Doug Collins picked off. Collins was fouled, and he hit both free throws to put the Americans in the lead 50-49 with just 3 seconds on the clock.

That's when things really began to unravel for the Americans. The Soviets threw the ball inbounds, but the pass was knocked down. The buzzer sounded and the Americans began to celebrate.

But wait. Officials ruled that the Soviets had been interfered with and they let them try it again.

Same result. Errant pass. Buzzer. Pandemonium for the good guys.

Not yet. R. W. Jones, an important basketball official with no official duties in this game, interceded and ordered 3 seconds restored. The ball went back to the USSR.

This time, a long pass went to Belov, who shoved Americans Kevin Joyce and Jim Forbes out of the way and scored.

This time the team celebrating was the Soviet one. The Americans were stunned beyond words. After 62 straight Olympic wins, they had fallen.

Bobby Jones still recalls the feeling that swept over the team. "It was frustrating knowing we had won the game but wouldn't receive the gold medal. I realized it wouldn't change and that the situation was political." The players were so demoralized by this turn of events and the way the result of the game had been taken out of the players' hands, they refused to receive their silver medals.

"They're supposed to be in some vault in Switzerland," Jones says. "But I don't discount that possibly someday we may get the gold medal."

Still these many years later, that loss is a bitter memory for the men who were on that team. Jones, though, has an advantage in working through the loss. "Things like that could turn your outlook on life sour," he says. "But the longer I am a Christian, the stronger my faith is, and the more I see God working in my life."

It was about the same time that Jones was going through his Olympic experience that God began to work in his life, for it was when he was a student at North Carolina that he gave his heart to Jesus Christ.

This is not the story of a dramatic turnaround for a guy who was headed down worldly paths of sin and degradation. In fact, his wife Tess recalls that when she first met Bobby while both were students at North Carolina, "He was not a drinker and he didn't use bad language in front of me. And I don't think he did on the courts. He was basically what you would call a good guy. He was not a partygoer by any means. He was just satisfied with himself."

And this isn't the story of a guy who never darkened the door of a church. "I grew up in a Southern Baptist church," he says. "I heard the Word, but I never applied it to my life."

Therefore as he made his way through North Carolina and as he pursued his NBA dream, Bobby Jones was typical of so many people who are morally good and have a church background. He didn't realize he was lost.

"I had grown up in the church, but in my first year at North Carolina, I did not go to church. I really didn't feel the need to go. I felt that I was a pretty good person, not a troublemaker, not a bad person, and I felt that I was OK. I didn't really think about spiritual things or heavenly things. I had no idea that a decision had to be made. I didn't know what being a Christian was. My faith was in myself and my basketball ability."

A couple of things happened to Jones at North Carolina, though, that began to change his perspective.

The first wake-up call for Bobby came when he attended a Fellowship of Christian Athletes summer conference in Arkansas. "For the first time, I was confronted with the truth of the Scripture. I saw the Scripture being applied by young men my age and with my athletic ability. I came back from that conference and did some thinking."

The second situation that changed his thinking was meeting Tess. A typical Southern belle with beauty, poise, wisdom, and a radiant personality, she would prove to be the perfect match for the somewhat withdrawn basketball star.

"Tess was from Charlotte also," Jones says, "but she went to a different high school. We met on a blind date. She was a senior and I was a sophomore at North Carolina. Her roommate was dating my roommate. In fact they were engaged. He was a ballplayer and she was a cheerleader. So, we went out on a blind date. I took her to watch my high school's state championship basketball game. We really had a good time. We really enjoyed each other. I've always been real quiet, but she's outgoing and very talkative, so she really carried the conversation, and I enjoyed that. I didn't date anyone else after that."

Neither of them were Christians when they first met. Tess tells the story of how her own journey of faith helped Bobby in

his. "Bobby and I had dated for a year, and then I met the Lord that summer through a Bible study that I belonged to. Before I was saved, one of my friends made the comment, 'I just can't date unbelievers because dating leads to marriage, and I can't marry someone who is not saved.' I didn't understand that because I was not saved. But then after I did ask Christ into my heart to be my Savior, I realized that I was dating an unbeliever."

Of course from his perspective, Bobby was now where Tess had been before—unable to understand that dating restriction. "I wanted to get married," he recalls. "I said, 'Look, why don't we get married next year after I graduate?' That was right before my senior year in college. She said, 'I don't think I can marry somebody if I don't know they are a committed Christian.' That really stuck with me, and I began to think about what it means to be a committed Christian."

But as much as he loved Tess, and as much as he wanted to please her, there was something that was holding Bobby Jones back from trusting Jesus as his Savior.

Basketball.

"My concern was that if I had faith in the person of Jesus Christ, as Tess did, then I couldn't do what I wanted to do. I wanted to go to the NBA, not to some foreign country to be a missionary."

"My thinking was, *I'm a pretty good person. I know God will let me into heaven and all that.* But I came to the understanding through Tess that that's not what it is. It's transferring your trust from yourself to Jesus Christ and asking Him to forgive you of your sins. Not only to be the Savior of your life, but also to be Lord of your life, to guide you and make the decisions in your life that will lead you to a closer walk with Him. That was scary for me because I didn't want to give up my basketball. But then I contemplated eternity, and I compared that to how long I could play in the NBA. It really was no contest.

"I got on my knees and asked the Lord to come into my life, to forgive me, to change my life, and to show me how to live as a Christian every day."

After he became a Christian, though, he still failed occasionally. "In Carolina that last year," he admits, "it was in a lot of ways the same old Bobby. One time in practice, Mitch Kupchak elbowed me in the back of the head. I don't know whether it was on purpose or not, but I gave him one back. Then I proceeded to curse him up and down the floor. I remember when I did that, that one of the things I had said to myself before was that as a Christian I should not curse. I had picked swearing up in college just because everyone else did. Then I go ahead and do that, and I remember it so vividly because I was so disappointed with myself. I said to myself, *How can you do this?*

"I don't remember who it was—I think it was a Bible study leader—who shared with me, 'Man, you're trying to do this by your own strength. You need to let God work in your life.' I remember I prayed that He would take that away from me."

Over the years since those early days as a Christian, Jones has discovered how great God's plan is compared to what he had wanted to do on his own. He and Tess were married. He got to play in the NBA. He prevailed in pro basketball for twelve years despite having epilepsy. And he became a missionary. "He allowed me to be a missionary, not to South America somewhere, but to be a missionary in the NBA."

During the four years at North Carolina, Bobby and his teammates were in the National Invitational Tournament three times and the NCAA tournament once. They won the NIT one year and placed third another; in 1972 they lost in the NCAA semifinals to Florida State 79 to 75. As a senior, Jones led UNC to a 22-6 record and another NIT berth. For his efforts, Jones was named second team All-American.

On draft day, Jones was selected by both leagues, the NBA and the upstart American Basketball Association. The Denver Nuggets of the ABA and the Houston Rockets of the NBA both picked Jones. As his fellow North Carolinian David Thompson would do the following year, he chose Denver.

It would be a four-year stint for Jones in Denver—two in the ABA and two in the NBA. After the 1974–75 season, the National Basketball Association decided to absorb the four top franchises of the American Basketball Association. Along with Denver, the New York Nets, the Indiana Pacers, and the San Antonio Spurs became members of the older league.

But before he could reach any level of success, he had to get over a fear of failure that could have killed his career. "On occasion early in my career," he recalls, "I would be nervous. I remember one time in Utah we were playing in the playoffs. I was hiding in the corner because I didn't want the ball. They knew how bad a free throw shooter I was. And they threw it to me, and a player for the Stars fouled me. They called time and I had to sit there. I remember going to the line, praying to the Lord, 'Please don't let me shoot an airball.' I made them, but they rattled in. They weren't pretty, but they went in. I remember thinking about that. My wife told me later that she was in a Bible study and they were all praying for me."

Fear or no fear, in his first year as a pro, Jones led the league in field goal percentage by hitting on more than 60 percent of his shots. He also finished sixth in the league in rebounds per game, fifth in blocked shots per game, and eighth in steals per game. The Nuggets finished the year with a record of 65-19.

As a sophomore in the ABA during 1975–76, Jones again enjoyed a fine season as the Nuggets went 60-24. Again he led the league in field goal percentage and was in the top ten in several other categories.

But his joy in his ABA success was tempered by two incidents that occurred while he was with the Nuggets. He had two puzzling seizures.

It wasn't the first time, though. He had suffered a seizure during his sophomore season at North Carolina. Doctors were uncertain, but they diagnosed the condition as pericarditis, an inflammation of the heart sac. Bobby was hospitalized for almost a week. "Right after that I made the Olympic team, so I figured it was just a once-in-a-lifetime thing."

It wasn't. In his first season with the Nuggets, he endured a rapid heartbeat during the first five minutes of each game. His arms and legs felt weak, and he had to come out of the games. Doctors prescribed Inderal after they discovered a problem with his heartbeat.

"In our heart we have a primary pacemaker and seven secondary pacemakers," Jones explains. "One of my secondary pacemakers takes over, so the medication was there to control it. It did a pretty good job."

With that problem licked, Jones sailed through his first year. But at the beginning of his second year, he had another seizure like the one he had suffered at North Carolina. "The first seizure I had was at 2 o'clock in the morning. The second one was at the exact same time. Almost to the minute."

Doctors prescribed Accutain, an anticonvulsion medicine. However, Jones was allergic to it and had a really bad reaction. Next, they tried Dilantin. "I was allergic to it too," says Jones. "I was allergic to the two main medicines."

At this point, Bobby Jones still did not know what was ailing him. "I think the doctors knew I had epilepsy, but they didn't tell me," he recalls. "That way I could play. No news is good news."

So he continued to play. Until it hit again.

In his fourth year at Denver, he felt sick with a fever just hours before a game against the Bulls. "I went in and told the Nuggets that I was sick, and then I went home. While I was at home, the phone rang. I answered it, and it was for Tess. As I started to hand her the phone, I collapsed."

As Jones fell, his head struck a butcher block table. He had a seizure for almost five minutes. In the hospital, doctors ordered extensive tests on the athlete but were unable to prove that it was epilepsy.

Not satisfied with the local doctors, Jones sought a second opinion. "On my own I went to the Duke University hospital, and the doctors there diagnosed it as epilepsy."

The medicine they prescribed for Bobby packed a big punch. They ordered phenobarbital, a barbiturate that acts as a sedative to depress body functions and relax the nervous system. That plus the Inderal for his heart affected his play.

"Those two drugs made me a zombie," Bobby recalls. "For a guy who is skinny and doesn't shoot very well and gets by on reactions, that was taken away."

It was a scary time for Bobby and Tess. "I remember one time I almost got sick on the court," Bobby says. "I was real white and pale. Larry Brown was our coach, and he said, 'I want you in the locker room.' So I just staggered to the locker room. I thought I couldn't play anymore. Those were the saddest days of my life.

"As young Christians, we could only trust in the Lord that this was part of His plan for our lives to grow us in our faith and to make us stronger to face this adversity. One thing I tried always to do was to thank the Lord for the wins and the losses, so I tried to apply that to this situation."

Although it might not have been what the Joneses would have designed for their lives, they look back on it now with appreciation. "I believe the Lord allowed me to have epilepsy so that I could bear witness not only in the Christian world but also in the secular world. What I share is that my strength comes from Christ. I really believe that through my career, people prayed me through it. As I look at it, I'm 6 feet 9, 210 pounds at the most, and out of 1,000 games I missed maybe twenty games. Nothing serious. The epilepsy was serious, but I didn't miss many games with it. There is no way by myself I could have done that.

"We thank God for it," Jones says about the illness. "We didn't really want it. We didn't really understand it. But we know that it was for our good, so I think He really blessed us through that."

In fact, it was, Bobby feels, the illness that eventually led to his wearing an NBA championship ring. He feels God was interceding for him. "He got me traded to a really good team and allowed me to continue to be effective in the game." In August 1978, the Nuggets shipped Jones off to Philadelphia, where he would join Julius Erving and others who were in the hunt for an NBA title. "The trade was billed as the longest trade in the NBA," Jones says, "because they announced it in June but it didn't happen until August because both George McGinnis [whom the Sixers traded to Denver for Jones] and I had no-trade clauses."

When Jones went to Philly, he felt that the Lord allowed him, in an almost miraculous way, to continue to play his slashing, aggressive style despite the conflicting medication that he took. "I asked my doctor, 'How was it that even under this medication my stats went up instead of going down?' He couldn't explain it. He said, 'That would be a case study to look into.' But I know that the answer was the Lord. The Lord allowed me to do that so I could give Him the honor and the glory."

In Philadelphia Bobby knew he would make adjustments not only to new players but also to his game and his faith. "I was living a good Christian life when I was traded, but I had been kind of laid back about my faith. But when I got sick and then when I went to Philadelphia, I realized why I was here. So that got me moving a little bit.

"Sometimes when you say you're a Christian, people hold you to a higher standard, and some people will doubt. When I got to Philly, I felt a bit of uneasiness from my teammates. They were kind of saying, 'This guy is different from us. He doesn't mess around on the road and he doesn't do some things that we want to do.'

"But I didn't go into Philadelphia to judge those guys. I just tried to be a teammate, tried to be a friend, and tried to be there when tough times hit. I got involved in the chapel services and let them know I was praying for them. I think that was somewhat effective. It's a hard lifestyle to travel and to endure the physical nature of the game, but the Lord allowed me some opportunities to be a witness."

Besides a new dedication, Jones decided to play with a new approach to his illness. "When I got to Philadelphia, I decided I wasn't going to take the Inderal because during the summer I didn't take it at all. I was noticing that I was really feeling good, I didn't think I needed it. The rapid heartbeat disappeared. I think it might have had something to do with the altitude in Denver."

Once Bobby Jones had come back down to earth in Philadelphia, it seemed to be only a matter of time until he would be part of an NBA championship team. After all, the Sixers already had Julius Erving, Darrell Dawkins, Doug Collins, Maurice Cheeks, and enough depth to make Jones a sixth man. Things seemed to be falling in place for Philadelphia to start thinking title.

Yet the first year ended in a second-place finish as guard Doug Collins played only 47 games because of a foot injury. All Bobby Jones did was to establish himself as one of the top defenders in the league, making the All-Defensive first team.

The next season was 1979-80, and it looked as though the new decade might bring in the Sixers era as the team compiled a 59-23 mark, only two games behind the Celtics. The two Atlantic Division rivals went at each other in a series of pitched battles as the new kid on the block, Larry Bird, took on the established pro, Julius Erving. During the season, the teams split their six meetings, and they met again in the Eastern Conference finals.

After trading the first two games, the 76ers swept the last three, earning the right to face the Lakers in the finals. There the Lakers beat the Sixers in six games. In the memorable sixth game, Magic Johnson stole the show, filling in for an injured Kareem Abdul-Jabbar at center and scoring 42 points. Jones and the 76ers were again forced to go home and wait again for next year.

The 1980-81 season proved to be another toe-to-toe battle between the Celtics and 76ers. Again they split their six regular season games, and after 82 games they both had records of 62-20.

People were beginning to think that this was the year for Philadelphia. That finally the team with the potential would grab the ring. They were so strong that Bobby Jones, who didn't even start for the 76ers, made the All-Star team. At the time, Jones said, "Every guy on this team can play. It seems like all eleven guys are having their best year."

Yet it all came down to the annual showdown with the Celtics in the Eastern Conference Finals. This year it was the Celtics' turn as they edged the Sixers in seven games, winning 91-90 in the last contest.

They would do it all over again in 1981–82, with the 76ers taking their turn at the NBA Finals. Again, as they had done in 1980, the Lakers beat them in six games.

It was beginning to seem that Bobby Jones and the Sixers would never get their turn at the top. For three years they had climbed to the precipice, only to have their hand stepped on in the end by either the Celtics or the Lakers.

Yet the Sixers were not done. They signed free agent Moses Malone in the off-season as they prepared for the 1982–83 season and went to work to fashion a remarkable 65-17 record. Then they breezed through the playoffs like they were playing Moses's old high school team. They swept the Knicks 4-0, nailed the Bucks 4-1, and swept the Lakers 4-0. When it was over, the Sixers had won 77 games and lost but 18. Finally, they were NBA champs.

When you talk about the stars of that remarkable team, you gravitate toward Moses Malone, Julius Erving, Andrew Toney, or Maurice Cheeks. But you cannot ignore the value of a player like Bobby Jones, a role player whose job it was to defend, box out, set up his teammates, and sweat a lot. Sixth men, even ones who make the All-Star team, don't get the headlines and don't get the ink.

"One of the things that helped me when I was a ballplayer," Jones says in reflection, "was that I never really worried about what others thought or what I wanted to do, that I wanted to score a lot of points. That never concerned me. I wanted to win the game and get my paycheck, go home, and be with my family."

Yet don't get the idea that he didn't want to win that NBA title, because he did. Even that, though, pales in comparison to what he thinks is really important. "If you think winning a championship is very important, my question would be, 'Who won the NBA title twelve years ago? Or fifteen years ago?' When I say that, my perspective is, that's one sport in one country over one short period of time. Really, when you compare that to God and His Word and eternal promises—life with Him forever—seeking to honor Him and say 'Thank you, Lord' is much more important than winning a ballgame or a championship.

"The great thing about my Christian faith is that God loves me no matter what I do, no matter what level I achieve, or don't achieve. I am accepted in His sight because of His Son, Jesus Christ, who stood before Him and said, 'He's forgiven because of what I did on Calvary's cross.'"

Bobby Jones is a winner. He won the state championship as a player in high school. He won ACC titles and the NIT in college. He won an NBA title with the Sixers. And now as the athletic director and basketball coach at Charlotte Christian High School, he has led a high school team to the 1992 state championship.

He is proof that you don't have to be a egomaniac to be a winner. You don't have to pat yourself on the back and brag to everyone about your accomplishments. You can work hard. You can make it despite physical setbacks. You can contribute without being the star.

It boils down to this. When you live for Jesus Christ, keep your priorities straight, and give it your best shot, you can be a quiet man because there will always be lots of people who will be willing to say good things about you.

THE NBA ROAD

1974:   Drafted by Denver (ABA) and Houston (NBA).
                    Signed with the Denver Nuggets
August 16, 1978: Traded to Philadelphia

THE JONES FILE

Collegiate Record

Year	School	G	Pts.	Avg.	FGM	FGA	FG%	FT%	Reb.
71/72	UNC	31	316	10.2	127	190	66.8	65.3	195
72/73	UNC	33	496	15.0	206	343	60.1	65.6	318
73/74	UNC	28	452	16.1	189	236	58.0	61.7	274
NCCA Totals		**92**	**1264**	**13.7**	**522**	**859**	**60.8**	**64.1**	**817**

ABA Record (Regular Season)

Year	Team	G	Pts.	Avg.	FGM	FGA	FG%	FT%	Reb.
74/75	Nuggets	84	1245	14.8	529	876	60.3	69.5	692
75/76	Nuggets	83	1235	14.9	510	898	56.8	69.8	791
ABA Totals		**167**	**2480**	**14.9**	**1039**	**1774**	**58.6**	**69.7**	**1483**

NBA Record (Regular Season)

Year	Team	G	Pts.	Avg.	FGM	FGA	FG%	FT%	Reb.
76/77	Nuggets	82	1238	15.1	501	879	57.0	71.7	504
77/78	Nuggets	75	1088	14.5	440	761	57.8	75.1	636
78/79	76ers	80	965	12.1	378	704	53.7	75.5	531
79/80	76ers	81	1053	13.0	398	748	53.2	78.1	450
80/81	76ers	81	1095	13.5	407	755	53.9	81.3	435
81/82	76ers	76	1095	14.4	416	737	56.6	79.0	393
82/83	76ers	74	665	9.0	250	480	54.3	79.9	344
83/84	76ers	75	519	8.3	225	432	52.3	78.4	323
84/85	76ers	80	600	7.5	207	385	53.6	86.1	297
NBA Totals		**704**	**8419**	**12.0**	**3223**	**5851**	**53.0**	**78.0**	**4087**

Clark Kellogg
The Class of '83

VITAL STATISTICS

Born July 2, 1961
6 feet 7 225 pounds
College: Ohio State University
Position: Forward
Retired: August 12, 1987

CAREER HIGHLIGHTS

- Led Indiana Pacers in scoring and rebounding three consecutive years (1983–85)
- Runnerup to Terry Cummings for Rookie of the Year in 1983
- Named Most Valuable Player of Big Ten Conference in 1982

PREGAME WARMUP

One of the events that made Kellogg stand out, besides his stellar pro career, was his performance in his last game of high school.

St. John's Arena in Columbus. In Ohio, it is the mecca of high school sports. Every boy dreams of racing up and down the scarlet-and-gray decorated floor that once was home for greats such as John Havlicek and Jerry Lucas. For most it is the culmination of a dream. For others like Kellogg, it is a step on the way to something bigger.

For Clark Kellogg, the trip to the state finals included a meeting with Granville Waiters of Columbus East High School. Both players were All-State. Both were on their way to Ohio State and then the NBA. It was a classic matchup.

When the final horn sounded, Columbus East had won yet another state championship. And all Clark Kellogg had was a new state finals scoring record. Long before the NCAA approved the 3-point shot, Kellogg had ripped the St. John's nets for 51 points in the biggest game of his career.

Clark Kellogg

The comparisons came early for Clark Kellogg. Comparisons to some of the best players in the game.

Playing his prep basketball as he did in the late seventies in the Midwest, and playing as he did a versatile game that included superb ballhandling and powerful, fluid moves inside, one name that kept coming up was Earvin "Magic" Johnson.

The Magic man from Michigan had set new standards for big men in basketball by becoming the biggest point guard known to man. Yet he also knew how to make things go when he was under the basket. He was the prototypical player of the eighties. Long before anyone wanted to be like Mike, they all wanted to be like Magic.

Then along came Kellogg. First name of Clark. As in Superman.

For the people at Cleveland St. Joseph High School, he must have seemed like the man in the blue and red suit. During his junior and senior years, he was an All-American. The subject of heated recruiting wars, Clark had basketball people around the country licking their chops to see what kind of magic he could perform in college.

Even then, Kellogg knew he was in the basketball stratosphere. "Coming out of high school, I was mentioned in the same

breath—even ahead of—guys like Wilkins, Cummings, and Worthy."

It was an incredible group of basketball players that graduated from high school in 1979 and was part of college basketball's
marvelous Class of '83. The group included guys like Isiah Thomas, Ralph Sampson, Sam Perkins, Dominique Wilkins, Terry Cummings, James Worthy, Antoine Carr, and, of course, Kellogg.
Looking back, he notices one sign of the success of that class.
"Of the twenty-five who played in the McDonald's All-American
game that year, sixteen of us played in the NBA for at least a year.
Another nine or ten have been top-notch players, with a handful
of those guys being perennial All-Stars."

One of the events that made Kellogg stand out, besides his
stellar career, was his performance in his last game of high
school.

St. John's Arena in Columbus. In Ohio, it is the mecca of
high school sports. Every boy dreams of racing up and down the
scarlet-and-gray decorated floor that once was home for greats
such as John Havlicek and Jerry Lucas. For most it is the culmination of a dream. For others like Kellogg, it is a step on the way to
something bigger.

For Clark Kellogg, the trip to the state finals included a meeting with Granville Waiters of Columbus East High School. Both
players were All-State. Both were on their way to Ohio State and
then the NBA. It was a classic matchup.

When the final horn sounded, Columbus East had won yet
another state championship—their fifth. And all Clark Kellogg
had was a new state finals scoring record. Long before the NCAA
approved the 3-point shot, Kellogg had ripped the St. John's nets
for 51 points in the biggest game of his career.

A couple of years earlier, Magic Johnson had gone to the
state finals in his final high school game. Although a buzzer-beating shot had sent the game into overtime, Johnson's Lansing
Everett team had won.

It would be the beginning of a charmed existence in basketball for Johnson. Within the space of four years, he would win his
high school state championship, the NCAA national championship at Michigan State, and the NBA title with the Lakers. Time

after time after time he had the right situation, the right team-mates, the right circumstances to come away the champion.

When people compared Clark Kellogg to Magic Johnson, they did so on the basis of so many factors. Their ability. Their size. Their statistics. Their knack for taking over in game situations.

Yet for some reason, Clark Kellogg wasn't allowed to walk the smooth path to mega-success that Magic Johnson walked. Whereas Johnson stayed home to go to Michigan State and became a legendary college hero, Kellogg stayed home to attend Ohio State and become part of a huge disappointment.

It would have been tough for Kellogg to do anything but stay home. "There was tremendous pressure," he says. "I had a basket full of letters from all kinds of people all over Ohio."

The decision to stay came down to a choice among two schools: OSU and Michigan. "After evaluating everything and recognizing that I was going to have a chance to play right away, it boiled down to being part of a rising program in my home state. Basketball had gone through a bit of down period after the glory years of the sixties, and it had been somewhat stagnant through the early seventies. Then Eldon Miller came and recruited Herb Williams, Carter Scott, and Kelvin Ramsey. Then I came along in 1979."

Yet things didn't work out exactly as planned. There was no dramatic turnaround with the Ohio State Buckeyes as Jud Heathcote and the Michigan State Spartans had experienced with Earvin Johnson. But there was improvement.

"Kelvin Ramsey was a senior when I was a freshman," Kellogg recalls. "Then Herb Williams, Carter Scott, Jim Smith, Todd Penn, and Marcus Miller were part of the big-time recruiting class in Eldon's second or third year. I was foreseen as kind of the missing piece to help us win some Big Ten championships. But it never happened. We were always there, but we never were able to actually win one in the three years that I was there."

For Kellogg, it was a major disappointment. "It is especially bad now that time has gone on and you look back and see that you were never part of a championship team, and we had the talent to do that. Especially in my freshman year. Three of us ended up being first-round draft choices: Kelvin Ramsey, Herb Williams, and me. We were part of a starting team in 1979–80, and we still ended up finishing second in the Big Ten to Indiana. It was tough."

It is an ambivalent Clark Kellogg who reflects on those years in Columbus. "When I was there, it was well-chronicled that Coach Miller and I often didn't see eye-to-eye on how we were playing and how I ought to be played. When I look back on it, I see that I was seventeen, eighteen, nineteen years old and I had some ideas about what I thought my skills were. Coach Miller had some ideas. On occasion those ideas did not mesh. I felt harnessed a bit while I was here. I know I grew as a player from a fundamental standpoint, but still I felt somewhat restricted in terms of what I thought I could bring to the club and what I could make happen on the floor. It can be bumpy, but I grew through it.

"I think if I had to do it over again," he says, displaying his diplomatic skills, "I still would choose Ohio State. The basketball wasn't what I had hoped it would be in terms of style of play and championships. But there was so much else here. I'm thankful that I met my wife here. I've got a number of friends that I met through school who are lifelong friends, so the overall experience was good. I wish the basketball part could have been a little better."

No, Clark Kellogg could never be the Magic Johnson of Ohio. And perhaps he never cared to be.

Yet there is something about Clark Kellogg that sets him apart. Call it class. Call it sophistication. Call it a result of his parents' fine work. Call it a matter of faith.

He has something that no championship ring can bring.

A lot of the credit goes back to his parents in Cleveland. It was a home that could not help but breed success. "The greatest impact on my life has been my mother and father," Clark reveals. "There really wasn't anybody else outside that had a great influence on me."

It was a two-parent home. Dad was, and still is, a policeman in Cleveland. He worked the beat for eighteen years until a knee injury forced him to take a desk job. The younger Clark's namesake, Clark Sr. was what his son proudly calls, "a really great

athlete. He was a track star in high school. As a matter of fact, he held the state shot put record up until I was a freshman in high school. I was a freshman in 1975–76 when it was broken by somebody else. Later, he played some semipro football. He was a very good basketball player as well. He was a great athlete, but he just didn't have a chance to go on to play professionally."

Because of his dad's interests, and because of the basket his dad nailed to a tree in the back yard, Clark got started playing at an early age. "It was football initially, but by the time I was nine years old and started hanging out at the Y, basketball became my sport of choice."

Mom was a homemaker until the last child started school. There were five Kellogg children—Clark, a younger brother, and three younger sisters. "Mom's solid," he says. "She made the house a home. Whenever dad was working, she brought stability and security."

The thing Clark and Mattie did that their son appreciates the most was sending him to Cleveland St. Joseph High School. "It was a great experience for me. My first eight years of schools I went to a public school. Solid schools. I got a nice background academically, socially, and athletically.

"But when I went to St. Joe's, it was a predominantly white school, all male, and I was a little apprehensive because it wasn't in my neighborhood. I grew up in primarily an all-black neighborhood. I went to St. Joe's with some apprehension in terms of fitting in and being among all males.

"Those four years were probably the greatest four years of my life—not only from the standpoint of what I could accomplish as a basketball player, but academically it was challenging. Socially it prepared me to operate in the real world." There Kellogg became a two time All American in basketball and was a member of the National Honor Society.

Then followed those bittersweet years as a Buckeye. Kellogg never accomplished the goals he wanted to achieve on the court, yet his OSU years were good enough to earn him a shot at fulfilling a boyhood dream, to be an NBA player.

As Kellogg had worked his way through the ranks from YMCA ball to high school and to college in pursuit of his lofty goal, he discovered some NBA role models to pattern his own playing style after. But it wasn't just their ability to shoot and rebound that attracted Clark to the players he would emulate. It was their style and grace.

"As I got older," he explains, "I watched as many games on television as I could. Lew Alcindor [of UCLA, later to be Kareem Abdul-Jabbar] was a guy who seemed like a good athlete and a great basketball player, but he also seemed to me a pretty intelligent guy. He seemed to handle himself well. Julius Erving was much the same way. Any time I had a chance to see him interviewed, he seemed to handle himself in a classy manner. Marques Johnson, who played at UCLA, was one of my favorite players because I liked his style and he seemed to have a grace about him off the floor. I tried to look at guys who were not only great basketball players, but guys who were articulate. Guys who seemed to be more than just good basketball players. Of course, this was from a distance, so I didn't know for sure what these guys were like, but the impression I got was that these guys were solid in their sport and also outside of it as well."

It was the kind of model that would serve Kellogg well as he developed his own on and off the court persona, one that can be described in the same ways he described Alcindor, Dr. J, and Johnson.

But first there was the matter of fulfilling a dream so he would have the professional platform from which to display his classy demeanor. For Kellogg, hope became reality in June of 1982, when he joined with seven other talented underclassmen to stake their claim on their part of the NBA dream. Members of the Class of '83 who left college a year early, they supplemented a rather mediocre senior class of 1982 to become truly the class of the draft.

Picking eighth in the draft, the Indiana Pacers chose the boy next door from neighboring Ohio.

"It was a tremendous feeling," Kellogg recalls about that eventful day in 1982. "The Pacers picked me eighth. The NBA had flown me and my parents in. Rosey and I weren't married yet, but she was there. Just to know that I was drafted and just to go through that process of being interviewed and dealing with the media and then flying into Indiana a day or two later to meet the press there. It was an exciting time; I wished I would have documented it more in terms of keeping a diary. It was a great moment to know that something I had aspired to since I was eight years old had finally happened. I thought about the things I could do to help my family financially."

So now it was time for the youngster from Cleveland (he was twenty years old when he was drafted) to grow into a man. And it was time, perhaps, to fulfill those expectations that many felt were not realized at Ohio State. There were still no championships in Clark Kellogg's résumé as there were in Earvin Johnson's. It would only be fair for him to get one now.

But as anyone who has lived long knows, life is not always fair. Things don't even out. Some people just seem to end up in the right place at the right time. If Clark Kellogg wanted an NBA title ring, though, Indianapolis in the early eighties was not the place to be. There was no *Showtime*. There was no Jabbar-like man in the middle. There was no chance of an NBA title.

There was only Clark Kellogg putting together an incredible rookie season on a bad team. "We just didn't have enough NBA talent to be very competitive," Kellogg says about his first year. "The team was in turmoil in terms of ownership and stability. We weren't drawing very well, but my whole approach that initial season was to establish myself as a solid NBA player and do the best I could for the team."

Although he toiled in the outback of the NBA with Indiana, he drew rave reviews from those who saw him play. And although he was the eighth player chosen, by the mid-point in the season he was considered the second-best rookie, behind Terry Cummings and ahead of such notables as James Worthy and Dominique Wilkins. And even then, Maurice Lucas of the Phoenix Suns said Kellogg had an advantage over the Clippers' top rookie from DePaul: "He's smoother than Cummings." And speaking of accolades, one of Kellogg's coaches said, "Clark is a little bit like Moses Malone. He'll shoot, miss, and go right back up. He has an incredibly quick second jump, which is why he's such a good offensive rebounder." Indeed, Kellogg finished behind only Moses Malone and Buck Williams in offensive rebounds in his first year.

Oh, and by the way, the Magic Johnson thing—the comparisons. Remember? They started in high school for Kellogg, but kind of tailed off when things went sour at Ohio State. Now finally in the same league playing the same teams, their statistical records are worth comparing. Here's their statistical line in 1982–83, Kellogg's first year and Johnson's fourth:

	G	Pts.	Min	FGA	FGM	FG%.	DReb	OReb	Reb.	Stl.
CK	81	1625	2761	1420	680	47.9	340	520	860	141
MJ	79	1326	2907	933	511	54.8	214	469	683	176

Clearly, Clark Kellogg had arrived among the top players in the game. His incredible talent was allowed to shine in Indiana, and he was fast becoming an NBA superstar.

However, Indiana was struggling in a big way. Despite Kellogg's efforts, the Pacers won only 20 games in his rookie year. The next year was pretty much a carbon copy as Kellogg again led the team in most categories while the Pacers could win only 26 games. Ditto for 1984–85 as the team slipped to 22 wins. Sixty-eight wins in three years. To put that into sad perspective, the Boston Celtics won 67 in the 1985–86 year alone.

Yet things were not all bleak. "We were starting to become a better as a team and the ownership was a little more solid in 1985–86," Kellogg recalls. "I was really excited. I was starting to do a lot of the little things that take you to the next level as a player. Not only was I compiling the numbers, but the guys around me were looking to me as a leader. I was embracing the role and enjoying it."

And indeed the Pacers were beginning to amass some top NBA talent. Kellogg's former OSU teammate Herb Williams was improving every year. Then the Pacers picked up first-rounder Wayman Tisdale in the draft. Vern Fleming was maturing at guard. And fellow Class of '83 alum Steve Stipanovich was realizing some of his college promise.

The Indiana Pacers, long the NBA doormat, appeared ready to step over the threshold into the land of the playoffs.

That's when Clark Kellogg's knees went bad on him. It happened just a few weeks into the 1985–86 season. "We were playing in Indianapolis against Cleveland when I twisted my left knee midway through the game. I continued to play because I didn't think it was that serious. It wasn't until I got home that night that it began to swell. It was torn cartilage."

When he went into the hospital to have his knee repaired, Kellogg figured he would respond as most athletes do. "I thought I would be back in six to eight weeks, as good as new. I didn't think it was career-threatening. I figured I'd be ready to play in January."

But he wasn't. Every time he tried to play on his repaired knee, it would swell up and get very sore. After resting it for the remainder of the 1985–86 season, Kellogg tried to made a go of it when the next season rolled around. The knee just would not respond. More surgery did no good, and in August of 1987, Clark Kellogg had to call it quits.

He was twenty-six years old, on the verge of superstardom with a team on the rise. In his final two years as an active Pacer,

Kellogg would play in just twenty-three games. And in 1986–87, as their once graceful, explosive, high-scoring forward sat and watched, the Pacers made the playoffs.

Never would Kellogg again have the chance to show a basketball-crazy nation how skillful and powerful he was. At age twenty-six, even before he could reach his peak as an athlete, the game was over. There had to be a lingering sadness as he contemplated the loss in the state championship, the disarray at Ohio State, and the lack of support at Indiana. There had to be an intense sadness that would need something special to wipe it away.

Then that something special came to Clark Kellogg.

"I was going through my second knee operation. A guy was showing up to conduct chapel services that winter. His name was Brian Chapman. I found out later that nobody had led him to the Pacers. He was just led by the Spirit of God to start conducting chapel services for the guys."

It wasn't that Kellogg was looking for anything spiritual to happen to him or anything. Indeed, what this man brought was a new idea to Kellogg.

"I grew up in a home where there was pretty much some God-consciousness. There were Judeo-Christian values that our parents tried to raise us by, but there was no real talk or understanding of a relationship with God through faith in Jesus Christ. There was no real pattern of activity that placed God at the center of our lives. So basically I had an idea about religion and about God, but I had no idea as to how you could have a personal relationship with God or how it impacted your life—if in fact you were obligated to God to know Him and live according to what the Bible says. Even though I had gone to a religious school and religion classes were mandatory, I looked at it as something on the periphery; it wasn't something that you built your life on. It was OK in my mind just to be a decent guy, to treat others the way you want to be treated, not to be big-headed when you were successful, to think about others before yourself. Just some basic rules to live by.

"But then Brian Chapman started showing up in November of 1985, and because I was recovering from knee surgery, I wasn't traveling with the team. I started thinking about what this guy was offering and what the Bible might have to say about how we should live.

"My wife and I had been married for two years, and she was a little curious. She was sensing that there may have been a little something missing in our lives. Having gone through a church wedding and not having been part of a church or even in a relationship with God left both of us uncomfortable. We were both sensing that there was a piece in our puzzle that was missing.

"Because of my knee injury, I was not in the hectic fast lane which is pro basketball, so I had a little bit more time to sit and think. My wife was nudging me a little bit about finding a church home. I was kind of trying to resist it, but this guy showing up for chapel for every home game was a reminder.

"My own spirit was wondering about what God might have to say about how we should live, and I realized that I should have a sense of gratitude. Even though I was injured, as I look at my life and the choices I had made and how things had unfolded, I had an awful lot to be thankful for. Sure, I had done my part, but certainly it couldn't all go back to what I had done."

All those thoughts coursing through Clark's mind caused him to sit down with Chaplain Chapman one spring day in 1986 for a one-on-one talk. After their talk Clark decided he and his wife, Rosey, should talk to Chapman together. As they listened, their curiosity piqued and they asked questions. They would continue to meet with the chaplain at least weekly through the fall.

"We let him unfold the gospel before us. He just kind of laid it out, and we were spiritual blackboards that had been erased. There was no preconceived baggage. There were no real hindrances to our hearing the gospel clearly presented. By the winter, both my wife and I were ready to give our lives to Christ."

And it was not too many months later that Clark Kellogg also had to be ready to give something very important over to God. His basketball career. "I was able to handle giving up basketball a lot more easily than people thought I could, because of my relationship with Jesus Christ. It was a matter of knowing that God's picture and plan are far superior to any of the things that I'll do. Once I turned myself over to Him, then He's in control, guiding and directing my path and giving me direction and purpose. He gave

me the opportunity to recognize that yes, this is tough and disap-
pointing, but it's not the most devastating thing that can happen
to me."

A lot of people would think that the story should go like this:
Clark Kellogg injures his knee. Clark Kellogg turns to God. God
heals Clark Kellogg's knee and he becomes the greatest player of
all time. Yet Kellogg and anyone who is familiar with the work-
ings of God knows that He doesn't have to work that way for people to keep their faith in Him. Although Kellogg was able to have
one more career highlight during 1985–86—a last-second buzzer-
beater to knock off the Celtics at home before a sellout crowd—
there would be no miracle return for Kellogg.

Yet there would be hope. "There's more hope in what's
ahead because my life is being controlled and governed by the
Word of God, and that's allowed me to excel in not only trials and
tribulations, but also the triumphs and the blessings and the perspective that God wants me to take on everything that comes
about in my life.

"I realized that my significance to God was not as a player,
but as a person. I think the Holy Spirit was challenging me to seek
Him. Romans 8:28 began to come alive to me."

That verse, highlighted by the apostle Paul's declaration that
"all things work together for the good to those who love God,"
was manifested in how God worked the next stage of Kellogg's
life. Out of the devastating news that his playing days were over
came another opportunity: broadcasting.

Starting on a station in Cleveland, doing Cleveland State
games, Kellogg has progressed to doing TV announcing for the
Pacers, ESPN, and CBS. Ironically, he is again chasing the same
dream as that guy he was compared with long ago: Magic
Johnson.

Two players with incredible basketball skills. Two players
whose careers were suddenly cut short. Two players who now
wear the headsets and provide expert analysis of basketball action. The comparisons could continue, but perhaps they should
not. Because while we cannot know how Magic Johnson is handling his own tragic turn that ended his playing career, we can
know that Clark Kellogg is handling his with his usual class.

To Kellogg, the key elements of his life now are his faith and his family. His faith he bolsters by "applying the same discipline I gained as an athlete to my quiet time, my prayer time, and my reading," he says.

And the family he protects by making sure his wife and children are a top priority. "Rosey and I celebrated our tenth anniversary in July of 1993. We have three wonderful children: Kelisa, Alexander, and Nicholas. I try to align my life and my manhood with the example that Christ has given us. Through that, I have a greater desire to know my wife better—to be sensitive to her needs and her desires.

"This is totally contrary to what the world looks at in manhood. Biblically when you talk about manhood, especially when you talk about a husband and father, then you've got some clearcut distinctions about what God requires of us and what the world may consider OK. I think the responsibility you have as a father and husband is tremendous when you take it from a biblical perspective. You are responsible for the salvation of your family, for their spiritual nurturing, and for modeling that to them on a consistent basis. That's major league work. I'm trying to allow God's Word to really dwell in me. This has helped my perspective and attitude toward Rosey and the things she has to deal with based on my unique job situation."

It's not the job Clark Kellogg probably figured he would be doing in his late twenties and early thirties. He must have envisioned doing what Terry Cummings, Dominique Wilkins, and James Worthy were still doing as they neared middle age—still playing NBA hoops. But although it didn't turn out that way for Kellogg, he continues to show that he was—and is—one of the classiest people in the classy Class of '83.

THE NBA ROAD

1982:   Drafted in the first round (eighth pick) by the Indiana Pacers

August 1987: Retired

THE KELLOGG FILE

Collegiate Record

Year	School	G	Pts.	Avg.	FGM	FGA	FG%	FT%	Reb.
79/80	Ohio State	29	335	11.6	136	313	43.5	79.7	232
80/81	Ohio State	27	468	17.3	190	345	48.1	78.6	324
81/82	Ohio State	30	462	16.1	213	404	52.7	72.7	316
NCAA Totals		**86**	**1285**	**14.9**	**539**	**1112**	**48.5**	**71.2**	**872**

NBA Record (Regular Season)

Year	Team	G	Pts.	Avg.	FGM	FGA	FG%	FT%	Reb.
82/83	Pacers	81	1625	20.1	680	1420	47.9	74.1	860
83/84	Pacers	79	1506	19.1	619	1193	51.9	76.8	719
84/85	Pacers	77	1432	18.6	562	1112	50.5	76.0	724
85/86	Pacers	19	335	17.6	139	294	47.3	76.8	168
86/87	Pacers	4	20	5.0	8	22	36.4	75.0	11
NBA Totals		**260**	**4918**	**18.9**	**2008**	**4041**	**49.7**	**75.7**	**2482**

Brent Price
A History of Success

VITAL STATISTICS

Born December 9, 1968 in Shawnee, Oklahoma
6 feet 1, 165 pounds
College: University of South Carolina and University of Oklahoma
Position: Guard
1993–94 Team: Washington Bullets

CAREER HIGHLIGHTS

- Led the Bullets in steals 14 times during rookie season
- Scored a career-high 22 points against Orlando
- Scored 56 points in one game at University of Oklahoma
- Set a school record in that game with 11 three-pointers

PREGAME WARMUP

One of the things Brent Price proved he could do at Oklahoma was to light up the scoreboard. Especially in a contest with Loyola Marymount during his junior year. It was December 15, and it was no secret that this game would be a modern version of the OK Corral—a real shootout. Loyola Marymount finished second in the nation in scoring throughout the year, averaging 103 points. Oklahoma wasn't far behind, scoring 96 points a game on average.

For a shooter such as Price, it was a game made in basketball heaven. And Price was angelic. "I had 56 points that game. I was so tired after the first half, just getting up and down the court. I had 11 three-pointers. I was in a rhythm and everything seemed to fall. I remember my tenth three-pointer was from the corner. It hit off the backboard and went in. You know you're having a good night when that goes."

Brent Price

When the final game of the Washington Bullets' season ended and the team had put away their uniforms for the last time, Brent and Marcie Price were ready for a vacation.

After all, it had been a long season for Price—his longest ever. He had been used to the 30-game schedule of college, but the NBA had rewarded him with a tiring seven months of countless plane trips, an endless string of hotel visits, and, including the preseason, 90 basketball games.

In the supposedly glamorous world of pro basketball, the relentless schedule is one recurring theme when players are asked what takes the gloss off the glitz. Brent Price puts it like this: "I think you'll hear every player say the traveling is hard to adjust to. It is tough getting used to spending so much time in hotels and [moving] in and out of places. It's very tiring."

But now the season is over. Price has successfully negotiated the potholes and struggles of his rookie season. You can almost hear an off-camera voice asking, "So, Brent Price, you've just completed your first year in the NBA. Where are you going next?"

"I'm going to Williamsburg," might have been Brent's reply.

For Brent Price, the sights of the nation's capital and American history sure beat Disney World. It was time to study some history.

"We've really enjoyed being in the Maryland area, because we get to see all the history stuff," Price recalls. "Right after the season, we took a month, and we just took off and became tourists. We went to Mt. Vernon and we went to Williamsburg. We saw a lot of the history that is around here. We really enjoyed that."

Brent Price has good reason to appreciate history. His family has its own long history in basketball, and he and his brother Mark Price of the Cleveland Cavaliers are just now writing the latest chapter in it.

It's a history that started way back in the sixties when both his mom and his dad embarked on their own basketball careers. Mom played high school basketball. "She's very intense and competitive," says her husband, Denny, of his wife, Ann.

"She probably knows the most about the game of any of us after sitting through as many games as she's had to watch," Brent says. "She married my father when he was playing at Oklahoma, and you can imagine how many games she has seen. So she is quite the expert on it."

Denny Price proved his value as a high school basketball player when he scored a record 42 points in one game in the state tournament. From there he moved on to the University of Oklahoma.

"He was quite a competitor," Brent Price says of his dad, echoing his dad's comments about Mom. "I know just from watching him now and from hearing other people tell me about what a competitor he was."

Although Denny Price didn't reach the level of his sons Brent and Mark, he did play for several years for the touring Phillips 66ers, a semipro team based in Oklahoma.

This was a family that was creating its own string of historical landmarks as basketball marched toward popularity—a mom who played by the old 6-on-6 rules and a dad who was part of a popular semipro team that flourished before TV began bringing the NBA to every home in America.

After his playing days were over, Denny Price moved into coaching. That move would provide for his three sons a traveling road show of exposure to basketball.

When Brent Price was born, Papa Price was coaching in an Oklahoma high school. Next he became an assistant coach at the University of Oklahoma. After that his dad served two years with the Phoenix Suns (1974–76) as an assistant to Jack MacCleod. Then Denny Price served as head coach at Sam Houston State University in Huntsville, Texas. "From there," Brent says, "we made our way back to Oklahoma. We made it back to Enid, where Dad got out of coaching for about seven years and went into the oil business. The oil boom was big. But after that started to go down, he bailed out and got back into coaching. So we moved around quite a bit when I was younger. We finally settled in Enid, which is what I call my home town. That's where I went through all my junior high and high school years."

Brent Price was only six when his father joined the Suns staff, but Denny Price's little boy got a taste of some exciting history as the Suns made it to the NBA Finals. Brent especially grew to appreciate Dick Van Arsdale and Paul Westphal, and he became a Suns fan because of the experience.

There seems to be quite a need for a knowledge of geography to follow this family. If you think following Dad from one coaching job to the next was tough, imagine parents Ann and Denny chasing to keep up with Mark, who went to school in Atlanta, Matt, who traveled to North Carolina to play ball at Appalachian State, and Brent, who played his first two years of college hoops at the University of South Carolina.

Add to that the boys' first full-time jobs in Cleveland (Mark), Chattanooga (Matt), and Brent (Washington, D.C.), and you have a family that had better know how to use a map.

With a family history like Brent's, it was no surprise that he would be a hoopster. "I was naturally brought into the game of basketball because of my father and brothers," Price says. "I just came up playing. I remember that my dad always would take us to the gym during practice and let us run around. We probably bugged everybody—three little kids running around—but we were always in the gym.

"Being the youngest in the family, I looked up to my older two brothers. Because Mark and Matt were older, I was always getting dragged around to watch their games. And so whatever they did, I was doing because I wanted to do the same things as they.

"When I started getting up into grade school, I played every sport. But when I got up into junior high, I was just naturally better in basketball than any of my friends. And that probably was just from being in the gym all the time and always having a basketball in our hands. Basketball was always first nature for us. We were always just naturally better in that sport just from being around it and being around Dad and the games."

By the ninth grade Brent realized his basketball skills could lead to other things, perhaps college ball or even the pros. So he turned his focus to basketball alone, concentrating on the sport year-round.

Looking at the growing basketball focus of the Price family, it would be easy to form the wrong impression. The natural conclusion would be that this is an incredibly one-dimensional bunch of people. Is basketball all they thought about as those boys were growing up? The historical evidence suggests otherwise.

There were two other great loves among the Price Five: faith and music.

Matters of faith were easily and naturally discussed in the Price household. "I was raised by godly parents," he says proudly, "and they were a great example to me. I'm fortunate. There are very few who are as fortunate as I, that were raised in the church and with parents who not only set an example by their words but by their actions. I just followed in my parents' footsteps and in my brothers' footsteps.

"When I was nine, I went to my parents and told them that I wanted to accept Jesus Christ as my Savior. I remember that night. I had gone to church, had gone down in front, and afterward visited with the preacher. That night I knelt by my bedside, and my mom and dad led me in a prayer of salvation. It's been continually a growing experience ever since. I've never doubted my Christianity from that moment because it was so real at that time."

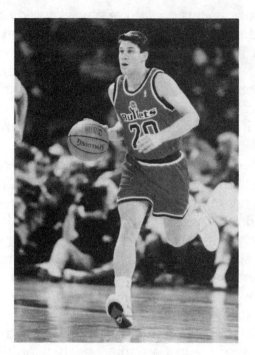

"A family that goes to church together grows mature together" could be the Price family motto. According to Dad Price, "It was mandatory that when it was time to go to church, the boys would go to church. There were no excuses that we really expected. Even when we heard, 'Dad, I don't want to go,' we felt that as long as we were responsible for them, we made the final decisions. The boys were involved in youth group, choir, and personal Bible study with their leader."

The music side of things began at home. "We began when they were very young with getting around the piano, singing," Denny Price continues. "My wife is an excellent piano player and we would get the boys around the piano. We would spend time in the evening around the piano. We had a good time enjoying each other. As a result, we had the opportunity to witness as a family. We went to different churches to sing and share with people our idea of what Christian families should be like."

Just as the family times that centered around basketball resulted in Brent's having a love for the game, so did those family times of singing give him an appreciation for music. In fact, he says, "My first love is music, and I've always loved Christian music —all kinds and all types. My family grew up singing gospel quartet since I was five years old, and we continued all the way up through college. I was always in show choir and musicals. I've always had aspirations of getting into Christian music in some form or fashion. That's kind of been my dream. So if that is where God leads me, if he opens the door, then that's something I'd like to do."

With his background in both basketball and music well established by the time he had finished high school, it was time for Brent to strike out on his own. And wouldn't you know it, when it came time for Brent to go to college, history repeated itself.

About five years earlier, a man named George Felton had made himself well-known in the Enid, Oklahoma, area. As a scout for Bobby Cremins at Georgia Tech, Felton had watched Brent's big brother Mark play seventeen times before snagging him to play for the Yellow Jackets.

Now, in 1987, Felton was back. He now was the head coach at the University of South Carolina, and he wanted Brent Price. "He really came after me hard," Price remembers. "After looking at all my options, after praying about it, and after visiting the school, I just felt like I was led to go to South Carolina."

As college is for everyone, it was a learning experience for Price. And it was not all related to basketball. "I had never been away from home," recalls the coach's kid who had hobnobbed with the Phoenix Suns as a child. "I was a real homeboy, and I didn't like to get away from Mom and Dad too long at a time, so it was a really good point in my life. I was forced to grow up a little bit and cut the apron springs.

"Going to South Carolina was good for me. Growing up as I had in my environment—with my parents being Christians, my brothers being Christians—we had a reputation. We were The Price Family, singing in church with our quartet. Back home, it was almost easier for me to take a stand as a Christian than not to.

"So I think the first real test of my faith was when I went off to school at South Carolina. For the first time in my life it was just me, Brent Price, out there in South Carolina. They didn't know who I was or how I was supposed to be. And of course on a brand new campus, you want to be accepted. It was the first time I came to a point in my life where I had to say, 'Do I really believe because I really believe, or is it because it's what my parents want me to do?'

"In that first year, it came through so strong that it was a real decision that I had made when I was nine. I found out really quick where my strength really lies, and that is in Christ. That was a really good turning point in my life."

The struggles that Price faced on the basketball court, though, caused Brent to question his recruiting decision. In fact, he says, "after I had been there for a couple of years, I didn't feel like it was leading me in the path that I was wanting to go. There were some problems within the basketball program that were not being handled well with the coaches and deeper into the program than that. And I didn't see the basketball team going anywhere. I knew that if they didn't go anywhere I wasn't going to be seen or have as much of an opportunity, so I made a tough decision after my second year at South Carolina. It probably was the toughest decision of my life, because I was kind of taking a step of faith in going to Oklahoma. They had a very talented team at that time, and I wasn't sure how I was going to fit in or if I was going to earn the playing time that I needed. I prayed about it and I felt like that was the thing to do. I did it, and it has paid off very well for me."

One of the advantages of transferring is something that to the player involved, it probably seems to be a detour. Price had to sit out an entire season at Oklahoma, as NCAA rules mandate. His first year there, he practiced with the team but could not play. This, in effect, gave him another year of maturity as he prepared for his last two seasons with the Sooners.

"My playing time increased and it was just a more fun style of basketball for me. We got to get up and down the court. I could enjoy myself and display some of the things I could do."

One of the things Brent Price proved he could do at Oklahoma was to light up the scoreboard. Especially in a contest with Loyola Marymount during his junior year. It was December 15, and it was no secret that this game would be a modern version of the OK Corral—a real shootout. Loyola Marymount finished second in the nation in scoring throughout the year, averaging 103 points. Oklahoma wasn't far behind, scoring 96 points a game on average.

For a shooter such as Price, it was a game made in basketball heaven. And Price was angelic. "I had 56 points that game. I was so tired after the first half, just getting up and down the court. I had 11 three-pointers. I was in a rhythm and everything seemed to fall. I remember my tenth three-pointer was from the corner. It hit off the backboard and went in. You know you're having a good night when that goes."

That performance put Price in the books with the third highest single-game point total for the season—right in front of Shaquille O'Neal's 53-point performance three days later against Arkansas State and Kenny Anderson's 50-point outburst against the same Loyola team. It was definitely a history-making effort.

By the time Price had finished his tour of duty at Oklahoma, he had put enough points on the board, handed out enough assists, and rained down enough successful three-pointers to attract the attention of the NBA. In the 1992 draft, the Washington Bullets selected Price in the second round as the 32nd pick.

It was time to write the third chapter in the Price history book of the NBA. Chapter 1: Denny Price Coaches the Suns. Chapter 2: Mark Price Directs the Cavs' Attack. Chapter 3: Brent Price Joins the Bullets.

But first, an interruption in the history lesson for a big event on the social calendar: a wedding.

"Other than when I became a Christian, the most life-changing event in my life would have to be when I got married," says Price. It was the summer of 1992, and he was marrying Marcie, his high school sweetheart. They had dated "off and on for many years. When I came to the University of Oklahoma, we ended up at the same school together.

"Our marriage is the most life-changing event because it is no longer just Brent Price. Now it is Marcie and Brent. I can no longer just worry about myself and be selfish. It's a team, and it takes a lot of work and a lot of patience. It's really a big change in your life when you make that decision."

One reason Price found marriage to be so different was because of his background. "Whether you realize it our not, you pick up so many traits from your family, so many traits that are passed on to you. And our families were so different in many ways. It was important for us to put that all out in the open to begin with so we could be aware of that. We never had any girls in our family, and I had to learn to be more sensitive, and I'm still learning."

"The most important thing I can do as a husband," Price says, "is to be open and to be aware of her needs and our differences. Sometimes you've got make yourself sit down and listen to what she is needing."

And Marcie has had to learn something that was relatively unknown to her too. "She was a tennis player in high school," Brent explains. "She never knew that much about basketball. That's OK, because sometimes you want to come home and get away from it. When you've been doing something all day, you don't necessarily want to come home and discuss it all over again. But she is picking it up quite well."

Price had some picking up to do also as he took his game to the new level of the NBA. For instance, he had to learn how to come off the bench. "I think that was my biggest adjustment. I have never had to do that. When I was a freshman at South Carolina, I still played about 20 minutes a game. So it was the first time in my career that I might sit over there all game long and then they might call upon me to go in there for about 5 minutes. It was hard for me to get into any kind of flow of anything and produce when I had been sitting there for three quarters. I think I've learned to produce in the time I'm given."

One of those times when he did come through during that initial season was against the Celtics.

"Growing up, everyone watches the Boston Celtics. Playing in Boston Garden, it was later in the season, and I got in the second half. We had been behind the whole game, and I came in and sparked our team. I made a couple of nice drives, a couple of nice shots and then hit a three-pointer. We had been down by about 12 or 14, and this was in the fourth quarter. I played the whole fourth quarter. I think it would have been a highlight if we had won, but I think Dee Brown ended up hitting a last-second shot to beat us by one. But it was a great game and I got to be a part of a great comeback."

When a new player comes into the league, no matter what his past history, he is sure to go through a bit of testing by his opponents. In their way of thinking, history is bunk. In other words, they don't care if the new kid did score 56 points in college. He has to prove himself all over again.

"As soon as you get into the game," Price recalls about his first year around the league, "they're going to bring it at you. They are going to test you in the basketball sense, which is OK. When I got in the game against Kevin Johnson of Phoenix, for instance, they just spread the court, and it was like, 'K. J., take him.' You can just hear them thinking: *They've got this rookie point guard in there, and we're going to test him right off.* It's up to you to stand up to that challenge."

Another challenge for this player with a family history of basketball must have been to play against his brother Mark. But imagine how it must have been for Denny and Ann. While the boys knew what they wanted to do—help their respective teams win—Mom and Dad had to deal with torn allegiances. But as far as rooting rights go, the younger Price felt he had the advantage. "From what I gathered, they were wanting both of us to play well. But since Mark is so established in the league right now, they were really pulling for me when I was in the game to do really well." As skirmishes in history go, it was certainly not the Civil War, but that sounds like a pretty diplomatic stance for parents to take in the battle between the brothers.

Of course Brent and Mark Price are not the only NBA brothers who had to go head-to-head on the court. Horace and Harvey Grant have battled under the boards. The Van Arsdale brothers, Dick and Tom, were sometimes on opposite sides during their heyday of the seventies. Gerald and Dominique Wilkins have been perhaps the most visible. And Albert and Bernard King took sibling rivalry to new heights.

But no two NBA bros have had quite the history of basketball success from both parents for such a long time. As Brent Price learns the ropes of the league and as his opportunities increase, it just could be that he, like his older brother, will make some NBA history of his own. Which is a nice thought to contemplate for a guy whose idea of a good vacation is visiting Williamsburg and Washington, D.C., so he can be more familiar with his country's heritage.

Q & A WITH BRENT PRICE

Q: *In 1993 and 1994, your brother Mark won the NBA Three-Point Shootout at the NBA All-Star game. How would you compare your jumper with his?*

Brent: It's probably a little different from Mark's. I'm sure he's changed his over the years just like I have. But basically the fundamentals are the same because we've had the same shooting coach. You can see resemblances in our game and our shots because our father has worked with each of us individually on our shot and he still does. It's not a carbon copy but it has the same fundamentals.

Q: *It's an often volatile world out there on the court. What do you think the player's role is as far as self-control?*

Brent: I think you have to think about self-control. You have to continually practice it, and it will come naturally. Obviously there are things that happen in a game where emotions are so involved. It is so physical and situations arise, and you don't always handle them the way you should. That's why you have to train yourself to react the right way. A lot of it starts when you're younger.

No matter what anyone says, we are all role models out there on that court, and you can either be a good one or a bad one. There are so many young eyes out there watching. We have a huge responsibility to behave ourselves in the right manner.

Q: *During the long 82-game season, you aren't always able to attend church regularly. What do you do as the season progresses to keep yourself spiritually sharp?*

Brent: First of all, nothing can replace your own quiet time with the Lord. And it's very important for me. I don't feel like I'm ready to play a game if I haven't spent my time alone with God, because that's where I draw my strength.

I give Him all the glory. I feel like he has placed me here. It is through his strength. I mean, I'm a 6-footer. I'm small. I don't have all the abilities that a lot of guys have, but God has allowed me to get to this point and to this level, so I need that time.

The other thing that helps is the chapel service. Some of the teams have chapel services before the games, and that's always neat because you get to gather with other Christian players.

Q: *Because the game is so out in the open, fans can easily see the trash talk that goes on. What do you think of it?*
Brent: I don't particularly like it. I don't try to partake in that. I guess I was always taught, being a coach's kid, that you go out, play hard, keep your mouth shut, and if you're going to do some damage, do it on the court, not with your mouth. I'm kind of from that school of thinking, and I think some of the trash talk gets out of hand. I think it takes away from the beauty of the game, so I'm not a big fan of it.

Q: *In your basketball career, have you had any big disappointments?*
Brent: Of course, I've had my share of disappointments. As a high school or college player, I was never part of a team that won a big championship. There's some big disappointments in my basketball as far as my senior year. You always want to go far. My team got beat out in the first round of the NCAA tournament. There's definitely been some big disappointments, but you just look to the next thing. You can't dwell on things like that. You've got to keep working ahead.

Q: *What kinds of things do you and Marcie do to support others and to help other ministries?*

Brent: Other than a few special camps and things where we've sponsored kids, I haven't joined any charity thing yet. I believe firmly in giving my share to the church. There are tons of people who contact you, and you've got to pick and choose what you give to. As Christians, we are called to do our share. It's hard, because everyone has a good cause, and it's hard to discern which ones you have the most convictions about.

THE NBA ROAD

1992: Drafted in the second round by the Washington Bullets

THE BRENT PRICE FILE

Collegiate Record

Year	School	G	Pts.	Avg.	FGM	FGA	FG%	FT%	Asst.
87/88	So.Car	29	311	10.7	98	213	46.0	85.7	78
88/89	So.Car	30	432	14.4	144	294	49.0	84.4	128
89/90	Did not play; transferred to Oklahoma								
90/91	Okla.	35	613	17.5	178	428	41.6	83.8	192
91/92	Okla.	30	560	18.7	182	391	46.5	78.9	185
NCCA Totals		124	1916	15.5	602	1326	45.4	82.8	583

NBA Record

Year	Team	G	Pts.	Avg.	FGM	FGA	FG%	FT%	Asst.
92/93	Bullets	68	262	3.9	100	279	35.8	79.4	154
93/94	Bullets	65	141	6.2	141	326	43.3	78.2	213
NBA Totals		133	566	4.2	241	605	39.8	78.7	367

Mark Price
Paying the Price for Excellence

VITAL STATISTICS

Born February 15, 1964, in Bartlesville, Oklahoma
6 feet, 178 pounds
College: Georgia Tech University
Position: Guard
1993–94 Team: Cleveland Cavaliers

CAREER HIGHLIGHTS

- Selected to NBA All-Star team four times
- Won NBA Three-Point Shootout two consecutive years
- Named to All-NBA first team, 1993
- Led the NBA in free throw shooting percentage in 1992 and 1993

PREGAME WARMUP

Mark Price was on the verge of superstardom with the Cavaliers, and by all accounts the Cavs were one of several teams who could make life tough for the defending champion Chicago Bulls in the Eastern conference.

Price had put in three improving years with the Cavs, each year adding to his scoring average. He had provided the steadying leadership the Cavs needed. The team had accumulated a talented core of players in Brad Daugherty, Hot Rod Williams, Larry Nance, Danny Ferry, Craig Ehlo, and Price.

And now the doctor was telling him that his anterior cruciate ligament was damaged, that surgery was needed, and that it would be almost a year before he could play basketball again.

Mark Price

Mark Price sat and listened without hearing as Dr. John Bergfeld explained to him what was wrong with his knee. The Cavaliers' point guard heard nothing else once the doctor announced the dreaded prognosis: "You won't be playing any more this season."

To someone like Mark Price, you may as well sentence him to prison as to tell him that after only 16 games of a 82-game season he'll have to store the old uniform and watch from the stands.

It was December 1, 1990. The night before, while playing against the Atlanta Hawks in the Omni, Price had slammed into the scorer's table trying to retrieve a loose ball. "I think about all the times I've been knocked down, all the big guys who have ping-ponged me around, and it was a scorer's table that took me out."

Mark Price was on the verge of superstardom with the Cavaliers, one of several teams poised to make life tough for the defending champion Chicago Bulls in the Eastern Conference.

Price had put in three improving years with the Cavs, each year adding to his scoring average. He had provided the steadying leadership the Cavs needed. The team had accumulated a talented core of players in Brad Daugherty, Hot Rod Williams, Larry Nance, Danny Ferry, Craig Ehlo, and Price.

And now the doctor was telling him that his anterior cruciate ligament was damaged, that surgery was needed, and that it would be almost a year before he could play basketball again.

No one in the Price family, it seems, had ever gone that long without basketball. Not his father, Denny, who played and coached for thirty years; not his mother, Ann, who has probably seen more basketball games than Dick Vitale; and not Matt, who played small college hoops and now lives in Chattanooga. Certainly not his brother Brent, who also plays in the NBA.

Because of that basketball-saturated childhood, Mark Price was never far from a hoop. He and his family had followed Dad around the country as Denny coached at college and professional levels. And when Mark, Matt, and Brent were young, they took up the game for themselves.

And just like both Mom and Dad, the three boys were good at it (see Brent's story beginning on page 181). Mark recalls that "at a pretty early age, I felt I had some talent and ability in basketball. My only problem was that I wasn't very big. My biggest growth spurt was from eighth grade to ninth grade. I was about 5 feet 4 in the eighth grade, and I went up to about 5 feet 10 in the ninth grade. That was pretty much it. Another couple of inches or so. As a senior in high school, I was maybe 5 feet 11, 150 pounds. I wasn't real big."

He still isn't. At 6 feet, he could pass for a member of the public relations department instead of one of the most popular players that the P. R. department has to protect from pesky writers.

Not being big has never stopped Price from playing and excelling at basketball, though. From junior high on, he says, "I was always one of the better players in my age group growing up. I enjoyed playing ball and looked at it as an opportunity to get my college education paid for if I could get a scholarship. I really worked hard toward doing that."

He had an unusual high school team from which to shoot for a college scholarship. A "storied team," Mark calls it, with the tallest player, the center, being only 6 feet 2. They reached the state championship game before losing. Along the way they faced teams with players up to 6 feet 9. For his efforts Mark was recognized as All-State that year. "In the preseason we had been picked to finish last in our conference, so it was kind of a fun year," Mark recalls.

Georgia Tech soon had Mark Price's name on a letter of intent to attend the Atlanta school. Had the Georgia Tech recruiter failed to win Mark's signature, he would have been at least in the running for some kind of travel trophy. Tech scout George Felton took seventeen trips to Enid, Oklahoma, to see Price play while he was in high school. In addition, Coach Bobby Cremins received his own personal Price Family serenade on one of his recruiting swings through Oklahoma. The Price Family Singers, consisting of Dad and the three boys, accompanied by Mom on the piano, gave this out-of-state guest the same attention as hundreds received in churches throughout Oklahoma.

Cremins got his man and with it a chance to turn around a basketball program that was in disarray. It didn't hurt that Cremins also brought John Salley and Bruce Dalrymple to town to team up with Price.

Not that John Salley was terribly impressed with the six-footer from Oklahoma when they first met. Recalling their first meeting, Salley, who stands just under 7 feet tall, says he thought to himself, *This little dude's gonna be shooting it 20 times a game?*

Well, not quite. Price did pump his jumper almost 14 times every game throughout his four years at Georgia Tech, resulting in 2,193 points—which is actually over 600 points more than Salley scored. But together they helped transform the Yellow Jackets.

"I think it was a storybook four years," Price says. "I went there pretty unsung to a program that was pretty bad at the time. Matter of fact, we were last in the ACC my freshman year. Two years later we won the ACC championship, so a lot of things happened real fast at Tech."

One of the intriguing things that happened during Price's stay at Georgia Tech has to do with the three-point shot. During his first year at Tech, the Atlantic Coast Conference experimented with the three-point line. It was a new concept in college basketball, and it had not yet been instituted on the national level. Therefore, some leagues gave it a trial run.

Mark Price had never had the advantage of the trey line before, but he certainly was not shy about using it. Perhaps it had to do with his style in high school. While at Enid, he explains, "I scored a lot. Teams start playing you harder. You had to step out farther and farther to get shots."

So, when he arrived in Atlanta, he discovered to his delight that successful faraway shots now were worth three points each. As a freshman, Price was 73 for 166 from beyond the arc, helping him to lead the league in scoring with an average of 20.3 points a game.

Now here's where the intrigue comes in. He never shot another three-pointer in college. The ACC dropped the bonus opportunity—until Price graduated. Price is not sure the opposing coaches didn't force the shot out of existence just because of him. "I'm sure it had something to do with it," he says.

The three-point line was no small factor in Price achieving what he still calls his "one claim to fame." Because of his shooting accuracy from "way downtown," he beat out a sophomore from North Carolina in the ACC scoring race. Kid from Wilmington named Michael. Jordan's 20.0 points per game average was just slightly below Price's 20.3.

The kid from Enid fell in love with Georgia Tech, the team, and the coach. And he remains a friend of the college. "I'm still real close with Coach Cremins. I still keep up with Tech real close. It was just a special time. I feel like I got to be a part of turning a program around. When I see that they are ranked in the preseason Top Ten or when they go to the NCAA tournament, I still feel like one of the guys who got that going."

Another thing he got going while at Tech was a relationship that resulted in marriage.

He was a junior. She was a freshman. On their first date, Mark and Laura went out for dinner after a basketball game.

On their second date, Price popped the question.

Not *that* question. He didn't ask her to marry him; he asked Laura if she was a Christian.

She confesses now that although she thought she was, she really wasn't. And that bothered Mark. Especially when he began to care for Laura "more than just as a friend," as she puts it. In fact, Price knew that for him it would not be good to let the relationship grow if Laura did not share his faith in Jesus Christ. So he was very close to telling her, "I can't see you anymore."

But Laura knew that she needed to make a change in her life, with or without Mark Price. Soon she had put her faith in Jesus. "When I told him I had accepted Christ," Laura remembers, "our relationship took off."

They were married after Mark started his career in the NBA.

Today the Prices have two children, Caroline and Brittany. Their daddy is a traveling man, for sure, but he tries to keep them close, even when he is far away. "I talk to my family every day," Price says. "I usually call them during the day or after the game. I try to keep in touch every day to let my little girls hear their daddy's voice."

Just as he worked hard to rehabilitate his knee and just as he works hard to keep his three-point shot sharp, Mark pays the price to keep his family life strong.

"I'd like to think I'm a good husband. You might get a different answer from Laura, I don't know. The thing that I give Laura more than anything else is just stability and trust in knowing that I'm there and she can trust me, and that I'm the spiritual leader in our family. I think the stability of knowing I'm always going to be there is probably one of the things I bring to the marriage."

And as for Laura, Mark knows how vital her role is in his life. "She's something special. It takes a special person to be married to a professional athlete, simply from the fact that she has to shoulder a lot of responsibility when I'm gone. She has to take care of things I might do, as far as discipline and things of that nature with the kids. She just keeps everything going."

Which is what Mark Price is paid to do for the Cavs. As the spark-plug point guard, he not only runs the show, but he also provides a big chunk of the offense. Yet he doesn't fret about the scoring part of the game if it doesn't come. He knows that his primary job is to get the ball in to Larry Nance and Brad Daugherty and let them go to work.

In fact, he is so important to Daugherty that Daugherty has said, only half-jesting, "When Mark Price retires, I retire."

For a player who has dished out more than 3,000 assists, that is an affirmation that he is doing what he should to help the team. "I'd be doing 20 assists a game and no points if I could do that. I have a lot of responsibilities—not only to look for my shot, but also to make sure everybody else gets theirs."

One way an unselfish floor leader like Price can help the team is by scoring every time he is given a free opportunity to do so. That means hitting free throws. Which is exactly what Mark Price does better than anyone who has ever played the game.

During the 1992–93 season, Price led the league in free throw percentage, hitting 289 out of 305 shots, a remarkable 94.8 percent. It was the second-best mark in NBA history for a single season, narrowly missing the 95.8 percent of Calvin Murphy. Think about it. Out of 305 tosses, he missed only 16 free throws all year! In addition, he entered the 1994–95 season with a career percentage of 90.5, which is the highest of any player in the history of the NBA.

On the defensive end of things, Price has not always been called on to guard the other team's top guard, but when he does, he surprises people. "His quickness is a shock" is how Nets coach Chuck Daly puts it. And former teammate and close friend Craig Ehlo says, "You know, he *looks* slow."

TV analyst and former NBA player Doug Collins calls him the "heart and soul" of the Cavs. "He's quick. It's a herky-jerky quickness."

Whatever it is, it's enough.

And whatever drives Price, it was enough to help him come back strong in the 1992–93 season after having that knee injury that could have ended his career. In fact, Price came back to be the first NBA player ever to recover from anterior cruciate ligament surgery so well that he made the All-Star team. The irony of that fact cannot be lost on a man who had told reporters before he tested his repaired knee that they should not "expect me to be an All-Star."

His comeback is a testament to his value to the Cavaliers. It was early in the season, and Cleveland had a paltry 1-4 record. And in the three seasons before his comeback year began, the Cavaliers had these stats to consider: With Mark Price, 54-40; without Mark Price, 27-54.

The Cavs were playing the Milwaukee Bucks at home, and when the announcer introduced Price, the fans gave him a standing ovation. Price answered by hitting his first three shots. And, of course, the Cavs won.

As the season progressed and he returned to form, he picked up where he had left off. In one game, he scored 39 points. At the free throw line, he made 77 straight tries. He led the team and was tenth in the league in assists with 602. He finished fifth in the league in three-point field goals. Commenting on his star guard's return, Cavalier General Manager Wayne Embry said, "Mark was perfectly suited to come back from that injury because of his dedication to basketball and his faith in God."

It was an amazing comeback. For eleven months Price was without basketball. What took him past the doubts, the pain, and the occasional boredom of his recovery?

It was a combination of music and his faith. During the rehabilitation time, he teamed up with George Payne and Hal Wright to put together their first album, a contemporary Christian music recording called *Stand Steadfast*. "It kept me sane and busy," Price says about the effort. It was a fulfillment of a longtime dream, and only because of the injury did he have time to put it together.

Price tackled the project with the same intensity he would have been using to go after loose balls if he hadn't been hurt. His wife, Laura, says, "Mark went at the album like he did everything else. He was a perfectionist. He kept the guys in the studio until one in the morning."

That Price's album would consist of Christian music is a credit to his entire family. But it would never have happened without a major decision he made when he was seventeen years old.

Price had grown up in a house full of people who believed in Jesus Christ, and he appreciated what that meant to him. In fact, with real admiration he quickly acknowledges his dad's high standards and ideals, standards that were based on the Bible. "I think my dad is probably the biggest influence on my life," Price says. "Just watching him and the way he represented himself as a Christian through good times and bad times, he left the biggest impression on me as far as his integrity and the things that he stood for."

Yet when Price was seventeen, just after his junior year of high school, he came to a startling realization about himself. Although he had traveled around Oklahoma singing about Jesus Christ, he had never really bought into what he was singing about. He was too caught up in his pursuit of hoops excellence.

"I grew up with my parents taking us to church and all that," he says as he begins to explain his somewhat late decision for Jesus. "But for seventeen years my favorite thing in life was basketball. I guess you could say that it was my god at that time in my life. I saw basketball as the thing that was going to make me happy. If I could be good at it, I'd get a college education.

"Then when I began having some success in basketball, I began to realize that winning basketball games wasn't going to fulfill my life and make me happy. So I really began to seek out Jesus and the Christ that I had heard about and read about so often growing up in church.

"I think so many kids today are similar to my situation. Kids who grow up in a church, where they hear everything so much that they kind of take everything for granted. I was in a situation where I knew my parents were Christians and we went to church. We were good people, and I felt that all that stuff counted. Finally I realized that every person individually is responsible for his or her relationship with Christ. What your parents believe doesn't count for you. I realized that I had to put my faith and trust in Christ."

Finally Mark Price made the decision that would change his life and would later sustain him through those eleven months of rehabilitation for damaged knee ligaments. One night at a youth revival he walked down an aisle at church to accept Jesus as his Savior.

The process had started earlier, though. "This was something that had been going on in my mind for six months to a year. I was really dealing with it in my mind and heart, and trying to figure out where I stood with God."

His faith in God and his love of music brought him through a year of recovery, and his phenomenal year of recovery culminated in 1992 with his being selected to the NBA All-Star team. The entire All-Star weekend in Salt Lake City was exciting. First came the Long Distance Shootout. It was the third time Price had gone for the top spot in this battle of long-range shooters. And this time was the charm as he bested Portland's Terry Porter for the title.

"I was much more relaxed than I have been in years before," Price commented after his display of downtown jumpers was over. "After being knocked out in the first round twice, I really didn't have high expectations coming in. I just tried to go out and relax, and I hit a couple of shots early. Any time you do that, it helps a lot. You should take what I did that week and put it in a bottle."

Then the next day Price showed that he could shoot the long "J" in game situations by nailing six 3-pointers during the All-Star game, an NBA record. "To shoot it like that in a game probably means more to me than winning the shootout Saturday night," Price said after the game.

Then in 1994 he won the shootout again, this time narrowly missing the record for total points.

For a while at least, Mark Price was the King of Threes. And sometimes, when you're just 6 feet tall among the tall, tall Sequoias of the NBA, it is nice to know that you can shoot over the trees with the threes.

After years of developing his long-range bomb, Mark feels that the other teams sometimes pay the price when he drops one of his treys on them. "I think more than any other shot, the 3-pointer can really drill a team. If you're up by a point at the end of a game and you come down and hit a three, all of a sudden the game's out of reach. It's great, especially for a guy like me who can't go in there and excite the crowd with a dunk."

When the Cavs' All-Star guard won the three-point shootout in 1993, it was clear to all that Mark Price, who had been so disturbed by the words of his doctor just thirteen months earlier, had not only come all the way back, but he had even taken his game to a new level.

However, all was not to go as well during the playoffs. As has happened so many times in recent years, the Cavs and the Bulls were duking it out for in semifinals of the Eastern conference playoffs. Suddenly, a rift seemed to be developing on the Cavs. Coach Wilkens had lifted Price from one of the playoff games with almost 8 minutes left, and he had not returned. The Chicago press, which was reporting on the Cavs-Bulls series, seemed to be suggesting that there was a problem between point guard and coach.

Denny Price was aware of the seeming difficulty, but he knew his son would not use it to cause problems. "Mark is not going to get in the controversy," he said. "He has strong feelings about Coach Wilkens. They have a good relationship. I give Mark credit for having the wisdom to know what to do and how to handle it. He has no answers for what Coach Wilkens did, but this is

Coach Wilkens's team. Mark respects his authority. He respects him as a coach and as a person."

Of course the Cavs would fall to the Bulls in the playoffs, not because of any split between Price and Wilkens but more because of a man named Michael Jordan. Sadly, this defeat spelled the end of the player/coach relationship between Wilkens and Price. Sensing that someone had to go, the Cavs' management fired their Hall of Fame coach.

Later, rumors would fly that he wanted Mark Price to join him in Atlanta when he took the Hawks' coaching job, and Price has a fondness for Atlanta because of his days at Georgia Tech, but nothing ever materialized.

What has materialized for Mark Price over the past eight years has been an NBA career that many people thought would never happen. Even his entrance into the league was unheralded, chosen as he was in the second round by the Mavericks in 1986 and then shuffled off to Cleveland in exchange for a second-round draft choice and cash.

His rookie year was nothing to write home to Enid about as he shot barely 40 percent from the floor as a backup to John Bagley. In the middle of the year he had to have an appendectomy. He averaged just 7 points a game. It looked as if after all those years of being the best wherever he played, he had climbed beyond the level of his competence.

To show their lack of faith in Price, the Cavs drafted a sharpshooting guard out of the University of California: Kevin Johnson.

By the end of training camp, the kid from California knew he was no match for the kid from Oklahoma. Still today K. J. calls Mark Price one of the toughest players he has to guard.

Year by year Price got better and better. Soon it was clear that for the Cavs to win, he had to be their leader. Injuries couldn't slow him down. Controversies couldn't dampen his enthusiasm. Disastrous playoff losses couldn't defeat his resolve.

Mark Price has paid the price of excellence since he was a little kid. And now everyone who watches the NBA knows that he is getting the rewards of his work.

Q & A WITH MARK PRICE

Q: *What do you think you learned from your dad as you watched him coach and as he instructed you?*
Mark: He taught us the basic fundamentals of shooting, things like that, but he wasn't one who pressured us to go out and practice. He felt that if that was something we wanted to do, then it was up to us to work at it. He was always there if we needed help or wanted advice, but he never forced us or pushed us into playing.

Q: *How will you instruct your own children about sports?*
Mark: You hear stories about parents driving their kids away from something because they push them too hard. I just want my kids to be happy. If they want to do something, I'll be there to support them, but I'm not going to push them to do something that I want them to do.

Q: *What is your role in maintaining self-control as a good example to young people in the volatile NBA?*
Mark: You have to first of all realize that in our own strength, we are really not capable of doing a whole lot. I have the Holy Spirit within me to help me in those situations. At the same time, we're all human beings. In the heat of the battle, sometimes you don't always do the right thing.

For a while I dealt with the fact that "Oh, no. I really blew it" by the way I acted. But as I began to pray about that and seek God out, I began to realize that God doesn't expect us to be perfect, and we're not going to be until we get to heaven one day. We're going to make mistakes. I try to use that. How I handle making those mistakes I think sometimes has more of an impact than just people thinking, "This guy's perfect." I think it is how we deal with failures and how we deal with mistakes that gives God the glory, because people can see that they've made the same mistake as well. How I've handled that differently might bring glory to God.

Q: *Craig Ehlo says you were instrumental in his salvation and that you were neighbors and friends when he was with the Cavs. How would you describe that relationship?*

Mark: Craig was my best friend on the team in Cleveland. We had gotten close over the years, especially since Craig came to know Christ. I had a chance when he came to Cleveland to share with him, and he was open and he put his faith in Christ. You know, Craig is a good basketball player, from that standpoint, but more as a friend and brother in Christ.

Q: *What do you do while on the road to keep yourself from temptation and to keep yourself true to Laura?*

Mark: I think temptations are out there for everybody. I might be in a profession where they are a little more prevalent at times. First of all, I try to keep my relationship with God close. If I'm spending time with God, I'll be able to pick up on those things a lot quicker. At the same time, you keep yourself out of situations that could get you into trouble. The old adage is, "You play with fire, you're going to get burned." I just try to remember that.

Q: *Who is your biggest challenge to guard?*

Mark: There are a lot of great point guards in the league from Isiah Thomas to Kevin Johnson to Tim Hardaway. It seems like they get better every year and faster. I don't know if they're getting faster or I'm getting older.

Q: *What bothers you the most about being an NBA player? What do you wish you could do without and still have the career you have had?*

Mark: The travel. Being away from my family. People tend to say, "Well, you get three months off. You can spend all the time you want." But it's still not the same as coming home every day and seeing your family. I know a lot of business people travel a lot, but it's just a very stressful life. Everything hinges on wins and losses. There's the pressure of being written about. Your life being a public forum in the newspaper every day makes it real tough. Yeah, it looks a lot more glamorous than it really is.

Q: *Most pro athletes today have certain charities and help organizations that they have an interest in. Which groups like that do you enjoy helping?*

Mark: I'm not the kind of person who likes to tell what I give to. We try to put most of our living in ministry-oriented charities. Nothing against other charities, but we just feel led to give to people who are furthering the gospel and doing things that way. We help out with churches and right-to-life things.

THE NBA ROAD

1986:   Selected by Dallas in second round (25th pick) of NBA draft

June 17, 1986:   Draft rights traded by Mavericks to Cleveland for 1989 second-round pick and cash.

THE MARK PRICE FILE

Collegiate Record

Year	School	G	Pts.	Avg.	FGM	FGA	FG%	FT%	Asst.
82/83	Ga. Tech	28	568	20.3	201	462	43.5	87.7	91
83/84	Ga. Tech	29	451	15.6	191	375	50.9	82.4	121
84/85	Ga. Tech	35	583	16.7	223	462	48.3	84.0	150
85/86	Ga. Tech	34	590	17.4	233	441	52.8	85.5	148
NCAA Totals		**126**	**2193**	**17.4**	**848**	**1740**	**48.7**	**85.0**	**510**

NBA Record (Regular Season)

Year	Team	G	Pts.	Avg.	FGM	FGA	FG%	FT%	Asst.
86/87	Cavaliers	67	464	6.9	173	424	40.8	83.3	202
87/88	Cavaliers	80	1279	16.0	493	974	50.6	87.7	480
88/89	Cavaliers	75	1414	18.9	529	1006	52.6	90.1	631
89/90	Cavaliers	73	1430	19.6	489	1066	45.9	88.8	666
90/91	Cavaliers	16	271	16.9	97	195	49.7	95.2	166
91/92	Cavaliers	72	1247	17.3	438	897	48.8	94.7	535
92/93	Cavaliers	75	1365	18.2	477	986	48.4	94.8	602
93/94	Cavaliers	76	1316	17.3	480	1005	47.8	88.8	589
NBA Totals		**534**	**8786**	**16.5**	**3176**	**6553**	**48.5**	**90.5**	**3871**

David Robinson
It All Adds up to Greatness

VITAL STATISTICS

Born August 6, 1965 in Key West, Florida
7 feet 1, 235 pounds
College: the U.S. Naval Academy
Position: Center
1993–94 Team: San Antonio Spurs

CAREER HIGHLIGHTS

- Selected to NBA All-Star team five times
- Led NBA in scoring in 1994 with 29.8 point average
- Named NBA Rookie of the Year in 1990
- Named NBA Defensive Player of the Year in 1992
- Played on two U.S. Olympic teams
- Chosen College Player of the Year in 1987
- Selected College All-American twice (1986, 1987)

PREGAME WARMUP

Although the national championship eluded Navy's grasp, something of more far-reaching magnitude happened: The David Robinson legend was born. The nation stood in admiration of a player who had come so far so fast yet refused to let fame turn his head. Words like *commitment* and *excellence* and *loyalty* were all hauled out of mothballs as sportswriters tried to describe this young man who had decided to stick to his promise to complete his term at the Naval Academy rather than transfer.

It was a foregone conclusion after his sophomore year that his future seemed more likely to include pro basketball than it would commanding a submarine, so many suggested that he should bail out. What made the prospect of leaving school even more appealing was the fact that if Robinson achieved his degree, he would be obligated to give the Navy a five-year hitch.

Naval commitment or no naval commitment, the San Antonio Spurs wasted no time in drafting Robinson first in the 1987 draft. They knew that it was possible that he would not be available to them for several years, but they took the plunge.

They didn't have to wait as long as they might have had to. After Robinson graduated, the Navy reduced his active service requirement to two years, so he was able to start his pro career in 1989. All he did during his first year was to be named the Rookie of the Year. He appeared in all 82 games, averaged 24.3 points a game, and was the only rookie in the All-Star game. Three times he was named the NBA Player of the Week, and he was named the NBA Rookie of the Month every month of the season.

David Robinson

What is it about a person that causes us to consider him great? The measure of greatness will differ from profession to profession, of course. Different characteristics are needed to be a great leader, a great father, an outstanding carpenter, or superb athlete. In the relatively short history of the United States, for instance, we wonder which of our leaders were indeed great. We name a few. George Washington for his courage in the face of great odds during the revolution and for his foresight as President. Abe Lincoln for his wisdom during a civil conflict that tore the country apart. Martin Luther King, Jr., for his resolve and dedication to the cause of equality for all.

In sports we look for greatness in characteristics that help the athlete push the game to a higher level. What characteristics do we look for in basketball? Determination, for one. Pete Maravich was great for his singlehanded determination to recreate the guard position, as was Bob Cousy before him. Innovation, for another. Wilt Chamberlain, Bill Russell, and Kareem Abdul-Jabbar redefined the center position with their versatile ways to score and defend against opposing players. Add speed and leaping ability. Thus David Thompson in the seventies, Magic Johnson in the eighties, and Michael Jordan in the nineties all demonstrated a greatness that took the game to higher and higher levels.

But there's another part of greatness for athletes that comes from something other than athleticism. Some of the most gifted athletes don't have it. Their arsenal includes incredible skills that lead to greatness in the contest, but there is something flawed about their character. They have respect within the lines of the basketball court, but not outside them. Without the characteristic called character, they fail as role models and fall short of true greatness.

Potential greatness in some sports stars is diminished by stories of excess. There's the millionaire athlete who blows it all on extravagant living; the promiscuous athlete who disgusts us with his stories of sexual conquest, and the obsessed athlete who ruins his reputation with indiscriminate gambling.

Rare is the athlete who possesses both the athletic greatness and the personal greatness—the one who earns our respect on the field of play and our admiration off it.

David Robinson is one such athlete.

The word *athlete* seems too limited a word to describe a person of Robinson's vast abilities. Indeed basketball is almost an afterthought to him, a pursuit that he did not begin until his senior year of high school, and then almost reluctantly.

As for the idea that he would today be a perennial NBA All-Star, an All-Defensive first team, an All-Everything, he may as well have wished he could fly one of those Navy jet fighters that he can't even squeeze his frame into. "I had never thought about it," he says about dreaming as a high school player of being part of the NBA.

It is obvious today that his marvelous athleticism is one reason he was able to go from a nonplayer to College Player of the Year in just four years. For even if he did not play organized basketball until his last year at Osbourn Park High in Manassas, Virginia, he was not new at sports. "I played everything," he says about his boyhood sports activities. "I was just an athlete. I think that one of the things that really helped me since growing to be so tall was the fact that I can run and jump and do all those things, because I've always been an athlete."

In high school he loved playing baseball as much as basketball, and he still calls baseball "my favorite sport. I played that my senior year in high school and it's always been my favorite." Yet when he kept growing and growing, he eventually faced the inevitable. He was destined to play basketball. "You get to be 6 feet 7," he says, "and you just have to start playing basketball. You don't really have a choice."

Here's how it happened. Robinson's dad Ambrose, a Navy man, had settled the family in the Virginia Beach area, where David was attending high school. Yet before his senior year, Ambrose's hitch in the Navy ended with his retirement, and the family decided to move to northern Virginia. Instead of staying behind and finishing high school at Green Run in Virginia Beach, David chose to go with the family.

Although he had played only pickup ball before enrolling at Osbourn Park, he was able to step in immediately and play when the starting center sprained his ankle just before the first game. That's also when Robinson began to grow physically. "I grew about three inches a year for about four years."

As athletic as he was, the sprouting center attracted very little recruiting attention. "I got some interest from college scouts," he recalls, "but not anything major. There wasn't an overwhelming outpouring of scholarships. There were a few local offers and Division II schools and a couple of other schools were showing some late interest, because I was a late bloomer."

All this general disinterest in David Robinson had little effect on the young man. You get the idea that if nobody would have come around knocking, seeing if he could play ball for them, he wouldn't have cared. It's part of the David Robinson persona. Here he is doing something that many people would give anything to do, and it almost seems as if he would have been just as happy if it had never happened.

After all, it's not as if it was basketball or nothing. In his case, it's basketball or almost anything.

Perhaps he could have taken his precociousness in math and become a professor at MIT. After all, he was attending classes for the gifted in the first grade, and he was taking advanced college computer courses when he was fourteen. When he took his college board test, he scored 1,320 out of 1,600. To give that some perspective, an incoming freshman has to get a 700 to play sports.

"I got a chance to get exposed to a lot of things in high school. I had some great opportunities. I was in the gifted program in junior high, so I got to go to other schools and learn new things. That was fun and that always got me going. When I went to high school, I took accelerated math courses. It came so easily to me, that's why I majored in math once I went to Navy."

So recruiting offers or no recruiting offers, it was off to the Naval Academy for Robinson. "I had already pretty much decided that I wanted to go to the Naval Academy. The recruiters complicated that a little bit, but not very much. I really liked basketball, but I was pretty focused on going to the Naval Academy because I wanted the discipline and the education."

And he wanted to please his mom. It seems that despite having to endure the life of a Navy wife while her husband served, Freda Robinson was gung ho for her firstborn son to go to the academy. The assumption might be that Dad would be pushing hard for his son to follow in his bootsteps. Not so, says David. "It was actually the opposite. My mother encouraged me to go to the Naval Academy because it was a great school and for the discipline. But my father was in the Navy and he didn't know how much I would enjoy it. It had been pretty good for him, but he didn't think I should do it because of the Navy commitment afterward. He wanted me to play pro basketball, and at the time, I thought it was ridiculous."

Of course, no one knew that David would grow seven more inches while at the Academy. No one knew that he would accelerate from averaging 7 points a game in his freshman year at Navy to averaging 25 points a game during his final three years. No one knew that he would become an elegant, powerful force in college basketball. So it was at Annapolis, Maryland, that David Robinson would begin his college career in obscurity and end it in the glare of fame. And in between he gave the Naval Academy its best public relations opportunity since 1946 Academy graduate Jimmy Carter was elected President.

But first he had to learn how to play the game. "It didn't come naturally to me," he says. "I didn't have the moves. Basket-

ball was more work than fun. I just wanted to play so I could get my letter."

Surprise! On the way to getting a letter, he suddenly became a superstar. He got the letter after his mediocre first year. By the time he graduated, he was the best college basketball player in America.

Once he caught on to the game, he turned an average basketball program into a media darling. Bedecked in braces and carrying his growing frame with the majesty befitting any service academy student, Robinson barnstormed America and became its newest hoops hero.

His first foray into stardom came early in the 1984 season. Playing in a December tournament in Carbondale, Illinois, Robinson scored 68 points in two games against Southern Illinois and Western Illinois.

The really big show began for Navy, though, a little over a year later when the Midshipmen surprised Syracuse 97-85 in the second round of the 1986 NCAA tourney. Now basketball fans across America could see for themselves the special nature of this mountainous Middie.

That tournament not only began to shine the spotlight on Robinson, but it also provided what he calls his college highlight. Beginning the tournament as the nation's 17th-ranked team, the Midshipmen first defeated Tulsa by 19 points, 87-68. Then the Academy stood its ground against the 9th-ranked Orangemen of Syracuse on their home court as Robinson scored 35 points, grabbed 11 rebounds, and blocked 7 shots. Next, it was on to the semis and the round of 16, where Navy nipped a surprising Cleveland State, 71-70.

The end came, though, in the regional finals as No. 1 Duke, behind Tommy Ammaker and Johnny Dawkins, beat Navy 71-50. Although the national championship eluded Navy's grasp, something of more far-reaching magnitude happened: The David Robinson legend was born. The nation stood in admiration of a player who had come so far so fast yet refused to let fame turn his head. Words like *commitment* and *excellence* and *loyalty* were all hauled out of mothballs as sportswriters tried to describe this young man who had decided to stick to his promise to complete his term at the Naval Academy rather than transfer.

It was a foregone conclusion after his sophomore year that his future seemed more likely to include pro basketball than it would commanding a submarine, so many suggested that he should bail out. What made the prospect of leaving school even more appealing was the fact that if Robinson achieved his degree, he would be obligated to give the Navy a five-year hitch. And that would mean foregoing that suddenly probable NBA career.

But remember, this was not a young man with just two options. In fact, he had even told his dad, "Basketball is just something else to do. I'm going to be a success at whatever I choose." His list to choose from included his skills and interests in music (he can play the classics on the piano), electronics (he put together a large-screen TV from a kit as a teenager), computers (math major), and literature.

However, when his monstrous senior year was over and he had been named College Player of the Year, he had carved out a path that would almost force him to include basketball, even if he had to wait. For example, he became the first player in NCAA Division I history to finish with more than 2,500 points and 1,300 rebounds while shooting more than 60 percent from the field. Naval commitment or no naval commitment, the San Antonio Spurs wasted no time in drafting Robinson first in the 1987 draft. They knew that it was possible that he would not be available to them for several years, but they took the plunge.

They didn't have to wait as long as they might have had to. After Robinson graduated, the Navy reduced his active service requirement to two years, so he was able to start his pro career in 1989. All he did during his first year was to be named the Rookie of the Year. He appeared in all 82 games, averaged 24.3 points a game, and was the only rookie in the All-Star game. Three times he was named the NBA Player of the Week, and he was named the NBA Rookie of the Month every month of the season.

It would be a pattern of success that each year would seem to repeat itself and grow even more impressive. Statistically and in every other way that he contributed to the success of the Spurs, each year seemed to build on the last. His stats grew larger and his legend grew greater as each year new comparisons would be made between him and his fellow stars. One basketball expert, Cotton Fitzsimmons of the Phoenix Suns, went so far as to say, "He's the greatest impact player the league has seen since Kareem Abdul-Jabbar." What's more, Fitzsimmons felt that Robinson was a more imposing player than people like Michael Jordan, Magic Johnson, and Larry Bird.

Part of the greatness of a person like David Robinson is that he somehow does not fit into any mold. Even in matters that go beyond basketball and touch the heart, Robinson is somehow different. While many athletes of his magnitude seem uneasy with themselves and unsettled spiritually, Robinson has always generated a feeling that he had no deep-rooted need to search for God. In other words, he always seemed to be at peace.

Yet, his honest appraisal of himself during the second year of his NBA career revealed a weakness that he knew he had to change. "When I got into the NBA, I always thought of myself as a Christian. I always thought of myself as a pretty good guy, mostly because I didn't like to go out and do a lot of different things,"

Robinson says of a time when he sensed the need for a spiritual awakening. He had grown up in a Christian family and his mother required the children go to church. But the pressures of pro basketball were beginning to wear on David.

"The pressure just increased. There were more opportunities—things out there, the money and everything else. It was just there in front of me. A lot of things I hadn't faced before. You always think you're going to handle those things really well, but it doesn't happen that way in real life. Those challenges will always overwhelm you unless you are really grounded in Christ. And I wasn't.

"So in 1991 a minister from Austin, Greg Ball from a group called Champions for Christ, came to my house and talked to me about it."

In reality, it wasn't the first time a minister had sat down with Robinson to talk about spiritual things with him. In 1986, David had been a member of a United States basketball team that traveled to Spain to play in the world basketball championship. Robinson had led his fellow Americans to surprising victories over Yugoslavia and the USSR to help the U.S. win the gold medal. In the process, Robinson had manhandled the legendary Soviet player, Arvidas Sabonis, to help the Americans win and to make NBA teams salivate just a bit more as they waited out Robinson's naval career.

As the team was flying home from that tournament, also on board the plane was a group of evangelists who had been at a meeting. "One of them came up to me and was talking to me about Jesus," Robinson recalls. "He said, 'Do you want to pray, because you need Jesus.' And I said, 'Sure, I guess.' So I prayed with him, but I didn't really understand what he was talking about. It sounded pretty good, I guess. But it wasn't a heart commitment. Nothing at all changed in my life.

"That always stuck in the back of my mind. I knew there had to be something more to this stuff than what I was experiencing. I always questioned it and thought, *Maybe I should read and study the Bible more.*"

When Robinson joined the Spurs, team chaplain Joe Sahl spent time with the rookie and gave him some Bible study materials. The player didn't read the materials in depth, "but it was al-ways in the back of my mind," David recalls.

"Then in June of 1991, when Greg Ball came over to my house to talk with me, he just asked a couple of simple questions. He asked, 'Do you love God?' and I said, 'Yes, I guess.' It would be kind of stupid to say I didn't."

"How much time do you spend praying and talking to Him? How much time do you spend worshiping Him and reading the Word?"

"Hey, I think I've got a Bible around here somewhere. I don't really read it much, but I've got one." David felt defensive.

"Well, for the people that you love, you really make time for them," Greg said. "You want to get to know them and you have a heart for them."

For David, it was a revelation. "He just showed me I didn't really have a heart toward God. He really convicted me that day, and that day I made a commitment to the Lord."

David wound up praying: "Lord, I just want to learn every-thing I can about you. I want to just give everything I have to you because you have really blessed me."

As David recalls, "God had given me everything that I could think of. And I never even had given Him any appreciation for it. So from that day forth, I just said, 'This is it. Everything I give back to you.' And he blessed me a hundred times. He just began to open up my eyes and began to teach me."

As a result of that change in David's life, combined with his January 1992 marriage to Valerie Hoggatt, the interests in his life have taken on a bit of a new look in the past few years. Oh, he still loves the numbers of math and he stills takes a keyboard with him on road trips, but when basketball is not occupying his time, he is happiest either reading his Bible or spending time with Va-lerie and their son, David, Jr.

David and Valerie met during his Navy days between Annap-olis and San Antonio when a reporter-friend introduced the two of them. They dated for several years before getting married. With teammates Avery Johnson, Sean Elliott, and Terry Cummings serving as groomsmen, David and Valerie said their vows at Tried Stone Baptist Church in San Antonio.

A year later, David Maurice Robinson, Jr., entered the world to add another new dimension to his daddy's life. Daddy Robinson cannot say enough good things about his little family.

"My wife is the most important person I have down here on this earth," says David. "I feel a great responsibility to God to take care of her and nurture her and bring her along in the Word and to make sure she grows. So our relationship is first and foremost.

"My relationship with my little fellow is an amazing relationship," says Robinson. "Anybody who ever has kids knows. He's the greatest. Just like any parent, I'm concerned about what he's going to have to face. I do a lot of praying about them. This is my heart and soul. As much as I love basketball, it has to come behind my taking care of home. I take care of home first, and then this [the NBA career] is my second deal.

"Right now especially, I feel that the Lord is telling me that it is so important in the first few years that I get a good base to develop the relationship with my son so it gets to the point where it can stand anything. The challenges will definitely come. There's a lot of pressure. You've got to give the enemy a lot of credit. He's really good at what he does. He sneaks in that back door when you're not looking. So I think right now is a time when we are focusing on some things that we can possibly get hit."

Besides taking care of little David, Valerie and her pro star husband are also interested in helping the less fortunate. "We want to be able to reach out to others more actively," says David. With that in mind, the Robinsons have started the David Robinson Foundation, a Christian mission that is designed to support programs that address the physical and spiritual needs of the family.

In addition to that commitment to others, David enjoys Christian ministry outreaches such as the one he and a couple of his teammates put together in 1993 in San Antonio. "Avery Johnson, David Wood, and I would spend all of our Bible study time praying and fellowshiping. And it just got on our hearts to bless San Antonio because they support us so much. We wanted to give them something back."

What they gave was "Jammin' Against the Darkness," a two-day program at San Antonio's HemisFair Arena. The three players spoke, as did Wood's friend, a minister from Portland, who ended his message with an invitation for people to come forward.

"We had a lot of people get saved. The best thing about it was that the Lord put it all together. It went from kind of just a concept. At first we were not all that excited about it. We didn't know what we could put together. But it became the biggest crusade ever in San Antonio. It was fun. We had over 11,000 people each night and the best part about it was that so many men of God, real strong men came together. The fellowship and the prayer together was just unbelievable. We all grew so much.

"God put together very different people," Robinson says of the three amigos who spearheaded the "Jammin'" event. "David, Avery, and myself are all very different. Even as Christians, although we are all committed, we are all very different. Avery is like a little warrior, like a little fighter. I'm kind of the intellectual, the teacher. And David is the evangelist. He's the bold one. He's the adventuresome one. He just likes to go out and talk to people. It was great to have us all on the same team, because everybody on the team doesn't really relate to the same kind of guy. It was a great way to meet the challenge."

The three amigos were forced to part ways after the 1993–94 season, though, with Johnson moving to Golden State and Wood going with Sean Elliott to Detroit.

No longer surrounded by such a clear support system, although other believers such as Terry Cummings were still with the Spurs, it could have been a bit tougher for Robinson as he headed into the 1993–94 season. Robinson acknowledged the difference. During that season, he said, "The Lord's really challenging me to step up and be more of a leader than I've ever had to be before."

Taking on that spiritual challenge certainly had no ill effects on his game. Beginning with the inaugural game in the Spurs' new home, the Alamodome, David served notice that he was ready and willing to wear the mantle of retired annual MVP Michael Jordan. As 32,523 fans filled the Alamodome to establish an opening-night record, David led the Spurs past the Golden State Warriors 91-85. He poured in 32 points, grabbed 8 rebounds, and blocked 4 shots. It was just the beginning of a remarkable year, in which he captured the league's scoring title, averaging 29.8 points per game.

His auspicious beginning would mark a year that could have been labeled the return of the big man. With Robinson roaming the middle for the Spurs and Shaquille O'Neal of the Magic, Patrick Ewing of the Knicks and Hakeem Olajuwon all playing All-Star caliber basketball, the battle for the top rung of the basketball ladder seemed to be a battle of the big guys. Indeed after the first month of the season, the best offensive performances were 44 points by Ewing, 43 by Robinson, and 42 and 41 by O'Neal.

Robinson, however, saved his best for last. On the final night of the regular season, he poured in 71 points to become only the fourth player in NBA history to score 70 or more points in a game. Earlier in the season, he had received the Player of the Week award three times in a one-month period.

With his heroics in the final season game, David won the 1994 NBA scoring title over rival center Shaquille O'Neal; later David was named runner-up to Hakeem Olajuwon as the 1994 Most Valuable Player. One of the reasons Robinson had been able to concentrate on his scoring was the Spurs' acquisition during the off-season of Detroit "space cadet" Dennis Rodman. No matter what color hair Rodman wore to the arena on any given night, he also was there to control the boards. "He's been tremendous," Robinson said of his tattooed teammate during the 1993–94 season. "I know that night in and night out I don't have to do everything. I don't always agree with what Dennis does and what Dennis says, but he knows how to win. He may not always do things that are pleasing to the Lord, but he's honest and he's straightforward." And he gets all those rebounds—enough of them in 1994 to win the rebounding title for the third straight season.

It is part of the mystique of David Robinson that he can so calmly and diplomatically accept a teammate so different from himself. Where Robinson is a family man, Rodman is divorced. Where Robinson prefers treating officials with respect, Rodman thrives on confrontation. Where Robinson always appears in public in classy menswear, Rodman prefers blue hair and disheveled clothes. But perhaps Robinson has pinpointed the common ground when he agrees that his rebounding buddy is really a soft person at heart.

Softness is perhaps the only rap David Robinson has heard about his own game. One critic has even gone on record to say that Robinson is too soft to win the NBA championship. Yet if the 1993–94 season did anything, it disproved that theory about David Robinson. Sure he is a tender man who loves his family and appreciates his parents. Sure he is not given to harsh words of criticism for opponents. Sure he is a committed Bible reader and a strong Christian.

But in his head-to-head battles with the toughest, strongest, meanest centers the NBA has to offer, David Robinson has shown over and over that he doesn't have to be nasty to be effective. It's a marvelous combination: strength of character, resolve of spirit, peace of heart, and the inner drive to win.

The numbers on the court continue to prove that David Robinson is a great athlete. And his personal traits continue to impress people throughout the sports world that he is a great person. Put it together, and it all adds up to greatness.

Q & A WITH DAVID ROBINSON

Q: *How would you describe your family background as you grew up in a Navy family?*
David: I had an older sister. She's 2½ years older than me. And my younger brother came along in 1971. We were very middle class. We made ends meet. We weren't especially prosperous. We weren't real poor. We did OK. We got a chance to go to good schools. We just basically had pretty average growing-up years. We were fortunate, once we got to the Virginia Beach, Norfolk area, my dad kind of went back and forth between a couple of ships there and we didn't have to move around. We were there for about ten years.

Q: *Compare your two Olympic experiences. First you played with the 1988 team that won a bronze medal and then you went with the Dream Team to Barcelona in 1992.*

David: There's a big difference between those two teams. In 1988 we had a lot of talent, but it wasn't nearly the same type of experience as with the 1992 team. Then we had more seasoned players, so it was a much more relaxed atmosphere—a much more professional type of atmosphere. There was a great level of respect for each other. In 1988, I don't think that level of respect was there. It was more of a competitive, ego type of thing.

Q: *Today your parents are in charge of The Robinson Group, which runs the business end of things. Is this something you have done as a thank you to them?*
David: They were always there for me. They obviously haven't been perfect, but they have loved me. They really have been there any time and every time I needed them. It's hard work and it's a selfless job, and I saw all the things that they went through just to try to give us opportunities, and I've always just really appreciated that. I know there's no way I could repay them for what they've done. When I came into the league, my parents were working and I wanted them to have flexible hours, so I gave them the opportunity to have their own business. It isn't my thing, it's their thing, but they help me with my scheduling. They do a lot of double-checking of things in the financial realm.

Q: *How do you handle the media hype that surrounds you and your opponents, especially the young guys like Shaquille O'Neal?*
David: I don't pay much attention to the media's hype. They love you one day and then the next day they're gonna find a reason not to like you. But you know, those young fellows are good, really good! I get up for all of them and I've been pretty fortunate so far. I like the fact that they get a lot of attention. I think it just makes the game so much better. It keeps people's interest, especially when you lose guys like Michael Jordan and Magic Johnson and Larry Bird. So to have these new guys coming in is tremendous.

THE NBA ROAD

1987:	Selected by the San Antonio Spurs (first pick of first round)
1987–89:	Served in the military (U.S. Navy)
1989:	Reports to San Antonio and a pro basketball career

THE ROBINSON FILE

Collegiate Record

Year	School	G	Pts.	Avg.	FGM	FGA	FG%	FT%	Reb.
83/84	Navy	28	214	7.6	86	138	62.3	57.5	111
84/85	Navy	32	756	23.6	302	469	64.4	62.6	370
85/86	Navy	35	796	22.7	294	484	60.7	62.8	455
86/87	Navy	32	903	28.2	350	592	59.1	63.7	378
NCAA Totals		127	2669	21.0	1032	1683	63.1	62.7	1314

NBA Record

Year	Team	G	Pts.	Avg.	FGM	FGA	FG%	FT%	Reb.
89/90	Spurs	82	1993	24.3	690	1300	53.1	73.2	983
90/91	Spurs	82	2101	25.6	754	1366	55.2	76.2	1063
91/92	Spurs	68	1578	23.2	592	1074	55.1	70.1	829
92/93	Spurs	82	1916	23.4	676	1348	50.1	73.2	956
93/94	Spurs	80	2383	29.8	840	1658	50.7	74.9	855
NBA Totals		394	9971	25.3	3552	6746	52.6	73.8	4686

David Thompson
Rescued at Last

VITAL STATISTICS

Born: 1954 in North Carolina
6 feet 4, 195 pounds
College: North Carolina State
Position: Guard/Forward
Retired: 1984

CAREER HIGHLIGHTS

- Selected first-team NBA All-Star two times
- Named NBA All-Star Most Valuable Player in 1979
- Scored 73 points on April 9, 1978 against Detroit Pistons
- Selected ABA Rookie of the Year in 1976
- Named ABA All-Star Most Valuable Player in 1976
- Named to All-American First Team three years (1973–75)
- College Player of the Year in 1975
- Played on NCAA championship team (1974)

PREGAME WARMUP

One of the greatest basketball players of all time, David Thompson is not listed on the pages of honor at the back of the *NBA Register.*

Thompson was, without a doubt, one of the best basketball players ever to come out of college. Yet he was stopped short of joining the elite of professional hoops by his own undoing. He let drugs and drink do what no defense could do—ruin his reputation, run him out of the league, and destroy what could have been one of the greatest basketball careers the NBA had ever seen.

Known as Skywalker because of his otherworldly ability to leap above the fray, David Thompson needed hang-time figures to adequately describe his soaring slam dunks. He was so gifted athletically that he could get the bottom of his sneakers 42 inches off the ground from a standstill. You can look it up, because it is recorded in the *Guinness Book of World Records.* Yet he won't be found in the NBA listing because of a career that fizzled due to alcohol, cocaine, and a severe knee injury after he was pushed down steps at a nightclub. He would be rescued at last a few years later when he accepted Jesus as His deliverer.

David Thompson

A list entitled "All-Time Great Players" highlights the back of the *NBA Register*. Included in that selection of player biographies and statistical records are such players as Kareem Abdul-Jabbar, Rick Barry, Elgin Baylor, Dave Bing, Larry Bird, Wilt Chamberlain, Bob Cousy, and Julius Erving. It's a veritable alphabetical listing of the greatest former players in NBA history.

One of the greatest basketball players of all time, though, is not listed on these pages of honor. His name is David Thompson, and he was, without a doubt, one of the best basketball players ever to come out of college. Yet he was stopped short of joining the elite of professional hoops by his own undoing.

Thompson let drugs and drink do what no defense could do—ruin his reputation, run him out of the league, and destroy what could have been one of the greatest basketball careers the NBA had ever seen.

Known as Skywalker because of his otherworldly ability to leap above the fray, David Thompson needed hang-time figures to adequately describe his soaring slam dunks. He was so gifted athletically that he could get the bottom of his sneakers 42 inches off the ground from a standstill. You can look it up, because it was recorded in the *Guinness Book of World Records*. Yet he won't be found in the NBA listing because of a career that fizzled due to alcohol, cocaine, and a severe knee injury after he was pushed down some steps at a nightclub. He would be rescued at last a few years later when he accepted Jesus as His deliverer.

David Thompson could dunk a basketball as an eighth-grader —when he was 5 feet 8. He grew into the top player in the state of North Carolina. But coming from the small town of Shelby, he says, "it took a long time for people to notice me." After they did, though, the recruiters came in droves.

David was the youngest of eleven children in a family where church attendance was important. "I was raised in a Christian home," he says, "My father was deacon at Maple Springs Baptist Church. At the age of five, I sang in the church choir."

The family was not well off by any means. David's dad was a school custodian, and the family lived on a poorly maintained dirt road.

He may have pleased his parents by singing in the church choir, but basketball was his real love, and he wanted to play pro ball. "I wanted to do everything right," he says about the recruiting war that surrounded him. "I wanted to go to a situation that would be best for me. I knew that to play pro, I would have to go to a good major college, a place where I could showcase my skills. That's why I chose North Carolina State. They had some good young guys like Tommy Burleson and Monte Towe, and I figured that with teammates like that we would have a good chance to win the national championship."

By the time he enrolled at N. C. State, he had grown from that 5-feet-8 junior high leaper into a 6-feet-4 phenomenon. Soon the whole country was agog as he soared his way onto the major college scene. It looked like nothing but perennial power UCLA could stand in his way of fulfilling that championship wish. But then an unlikely roadblock stopped the dream: the NCAA.

It seems that N. C. State had broken some rules on the way to recruiting David, so his team had to sit out of the NCAA tournament after his sophomore year. It wasn't like they gave him a Corvette or something. It all boiled down to two things: David had been allowed to stay in a dorm room before he enrolled at the school and he had played in a pickup game with an N. C. State assistant coach. For that, the Wolfpack in 1973 had a first-team

All-American, an undefeated record at 27-0, and no place to go after the season.

After the probation year, David and his teammates took aim at UCLA. The Bruins, who had won back-to-back national titles in 1964 and 1965, took only a year off before winning seven straight championships, from 1967 through 1973. *Dynasty* was the word being used, and N.C. State players knew it would not be an easy task to unseat Coach John Wooden, All-American Bill Walton, and the UCLA tradition. The regular season ended with North Carolina rated number 1 at 26-1, while UCLA was number 2 at 24-2. Since David Thompson began playing varsity for the Wolfpack, they were 53-1.

But now the NCAA tournament playoffs would determine the true champion. Early in the season, the two teams had met in a tuneup for the big showdown that would surely come in March. In that game, two streaks were on the line. UCLA had won 78 straight and the Wolfpack had won 30 in a row. Something would have to give. The Wolfpack blinked bigtime, as UCLA chased away the wolves, 84-66. The nation's top-ranking teams played in supposedly neutral St. Louis, yet more than 4,000 N. C. State fans traveled to the arena. Even so, the Wolfpack became the Bruins' 79th straight victim. It was David Thompson's first loss as a varsity collegian.

The rematch did come, but David almost missed it. Playing in the Eastern Regional against Pittsburgh, Thompson's high-flying act came tumbling to a frightening halt. It was one of those ironic times when an athlete's superb ability nearly backfired on him. In this case, the combination of that world record vertical leap and the adrenaline rush of trying to earn a shot at UCLA looked for all the world like it would destroy David Thompson.

Thompson had it in mind to block a Pitt player's shot. The player cocked and got ready to fire, and Thompson went airborne. During his descent, though, David clipped Phil Spence of the Wolfpack, standing on the runway. Thompson was sent spinning out of control. The head of this marvelous athlete crashed loudly onto the floor.

Fans and players alike sat in hushed silence as David lay sprawled on the hardwood. Fears of a broken neck and paralysis raced through the crowd. Coach Norm Sloan, who just seconds ago was coaching his heart out trying to get his team to Greensboro for the Finals, was devastated. He told reporters later, "I wished I wasn't even associated with this team or this game."

Anyone who watched the scene remembers the horror of it. In later years sports fans have seen similar scenes in which baseball power hitters take a fastball to the face or quarterbacks get their knees rearranged by marauding linemen. After ten minutes of working on David, the medical corps that was attending him wheeled him away.

As the game wore on and the Wolfpack waited, word began to return about their fallen mate. First came news that he would be OK and that the X rays were negative. Then came David Thompson himself, his head wrapped in a bandage. He could only watch, but the Wolfpack didn't need him. They won 100-72.

By rematch time at the Final Four, Thompson was well enough to hold Keith Wilkes of UCLA to 5 of 17 scoring while racking up 28 points of his own, including a jumpshot that put the Wolfpack ahead 76-75, a lead they would not relinquish. N. C. State went on to win 80-77. Two days later they polished off Marquette to earn the national championship.

It was the only time the Wolfpack would have a chance at the title while Thompson was at N. C. State. In his senior year, the team went 22-6 but failed to earn a trip to the tournament. Despite that, David was named Player of the Year in most polls and was drafted first by both the NBA and the ABA on their draft days. He signed with the Denver Nuggets and helped the ABA celebrate what would be its final season; he then stayed with Denver as it joined the NBA. The Nuggets rewarded their top draft choice with a five-year contract worth $2.5 million, the richest contract ever given a rookie.

David had several highlights during his rookie season, including being selected to the ABA All-Star team and winning the Rookie of the Year award. But his biggest thrill was competing against Julius Erving in the ABA All-Star game slam-dunk competition. Although he lost to the Doctor, David had a chance to unveil his incredible vertical leap and his Skywalker act.

Before the next season, the NBA absorbed the top teams in the ABA, and Thompson was no longer a part of a league that some people looked on as second-rate. He would now display his artistry in the only game in town. And he did not disappoint. In his first five years of pro basketball, he never averaged less than 25 points a game.

The switch from the ABA to the NBA left David Thompson and his teammates unawed. After the first week of the season, the Nuggets were the only unbeaten team in the league. Included in that first week was a 93-85 victory over the Bulls in which Thompson scored 36 points.

Besides finding out that their team could play in the NBA, the Nuggets were finding out that Thompson could play guard. With Dan Issel, Bobby Jones, and Gus Gerard forming a strong front line, Thompson teamed up with point guard Ted McClain. David said the new position helped him to "be more alert and see things better."

What All-Star guard Earl Monroe saw of Thompson impressed him. "My, my, " said the Pearl of the Skywalker. "It would be hard for this young man to look bad."

David looked especially good on April 9, 1978. He and George "The Iceman" Gervin of the Spurs were locked in a battle for the scoring leadership. During the final game of the regular season, David knew he would need a remarkable performance to overtake Gervin. Playing against the Detroit Pistons, Thompson went wild, hitting 28 field goals and 17 free throws to tally 73 points. By halftime he had 53 points. This gave the Nuggets' high-flying scorer the third best single-game effort in NBA history behind Wilt Chamberlain's 100- and 79-point performances.

In the end, it was not quite enough. Although Thompson and Gervin both averaged 27.2 points per game, Gervin won the title on the strength of his 2,232 points. Thompson, who played in two fewer games, scored 2,172 points.

During his first few years in the league he seldom looked bad on the court; but all was not well with David Thompson. Drugs and alcohol were slowly stealing his game. The seeds of destruction had actually been planted during his college days.

David had been brought up in a Christian home and was taught about the dangers of the wrong kind of lifestyle; yet he still got mixed up with the wrong people. "Being on my own at N. C. State and not being around a good strong Christian influence, I joined the crowd. I gave in to the peer group pressure and I started drinking. During college orientation weekend, there are a lot of parties and beer blasts and other social functions where there is drinking.

"My parents didn't know very much about my drinking. I hid it from them. Every time I would come home, I wouldn't drink around my parents. I did everything in private. And I was in denial —that's one of the main symptoms of an alcoholic or drug addict. I kept my drinking problem from them for a long time, so they were unaware of it. My parents supported me 100 percent, and they were at a lot of the games, but I was able to hide my personal life from them."

The drinking that began in what he thought was an innocent way in college, though, became a monstrous problem once he hit the pros, as his craving changed over to drugs. It got so big that he eventually couldn't hide it from anyone.

"I first experimented with drugs late in my rookie season in the ABA," David recalls. "I mentioned to a teammate that I was really feeling rundown. He said he could help me, and he brought out a bottle with some white stuff in it. It was cocaine. I was a little bit apprehensive about using very much. But during the next year, at most of the parties I attended, cocaine was readily available. And most of my teammates had their own supply, so it was pretty easy to get cocaine at that time.

"My usage got greater and greater as my playing career progressed and my drinking habit got bigger," he says. "By 1981, I was still making All-Star teams and still scoring big, but cocaine was taking over my body. There were rumors out there that I had a drug problem, but like with my parents, I was able to hide my problem pretty well. And I was in denial, big-time, at that time."

David Thompson, splendid athlete, eventually became David Thompson, carpetbagger. He was earning the money, but he couldn't play the way he and the whole country knew he could. "I was getting sick and getting colds a lot. I started missing practices and even games. I had a lot of excuses, but the real reason was cocaine and the bottle."

After going to Seattle in a trade, David went into drug rehab and appeared to have the problem licked. Then on a road trip to New York, David and some friends attended Studio 54, a downtown nightclub. While there, David was pushed down some steps, and he suffered a knee injury that ended his career.

With the marvelous career over, Thompson faced his frustrations of failed expectations by going back to the bottle and the cocaine. "At that point, I didn't know what to do with myself, because I no longer had basketball. A lot of my self-worth and self-esteem came through my performance as a basketball player. Without basketball I was in a lot of pain and a lot of suffering. My only way of knowing how to deal with pain and suffering was to go back to what gave me that instant gratification.

"I continued to use drugs and alcohol for a couple of more years. Finally, in 1986, I had to enroll myself into a treatment center again—this time not to save my career or to save my relationship with my wife and kids, which was the reason I went in for the first time—but this time to save my life.

"Things went well through the treatment, but after I got out I was approached by the Internal Revenue Service because of some bad investments I had made. The IRS came and took my million-dollar dream home in Denver, they took my four-level condominium in Seattle, my Rolls-Royce, my Porsche, and my Mercedes. With all of this happening, I wasn't strong enough, and so I relapsed again.

"About thirty days later, I was involved in an altercation with my wife. She called the police. I was placed on six months probation and the conditions of the probation were for me to stay clean and sober, to go to counseling once a week, and to attend AA [Alcoholics Anonymous] five days a week. I violated probation, and they put me in jail for four months."

Here he was, the man who in 1975 had received the highest contract ever given to a rookie athlete, the man who had been an All-Star MVP, the man who had won the national championship, the man who had scored 73 points in one NBA game—in jail. He had nothing left. No career. No money. No family. Nothing but those walls and those bars on the door. The sports world had left him behind.

But some people remembered him. While Thompson sat four months in that Seattle jail, pastors from the area began to visit him. And during the times when Thompson sat alone with his memories, he came face-to-face with what substance abuse had done to him. It had ruined him.

"I was at the bottom," David recalls. "It couldn't get any lower than that. But I was very fortunate that I had people who cared about me. While I was in jail in the Seattle area, local ministers came in and we fellowshiped, read the Bible, and that's when I accepted Jesus Christ as my personal Savior. That's when my life started to turn around.

"Accepting Jesus Christ as my personal Savior healed me. It got me off drugs and away from alcohol, and it got my life and my family back together."

No longer does David Thompson have to live with the devastating effects of drugs and booze. He has turned his tremendous energy and his restored good name to good purposes. And he is back in the NBA, this time helping youth avoid his mistakes. He is youth program coordinator with the Charlotte Hornets. He visits schools and other youth gatherings to talk about staying in school and staying away from drugs and alcohol.

"I include a lot of my own personal testimony. I am also involved in Junior Hornet League and Hornet pregame clinics, where we teach basketball and promote education and drug-free living." In addition, Thompson is a member of a speakers' bureau called Unlimited Success. He and other retired athletes, such as Bobby Richardson and Bobby Jones, travel around the country sharing their stories and the gospel of Jesus Christ.

So, what does this former skywalker tell the people who come to hear him? "You have to be strong enough to make the right choices. A lot of your successes and happiness in life depends on making the right choices, and I know through my experiences that drugs and alcohol aren't the way. What you should try to do is hang with the winners—people who look to do something successful and good with their lives—and not hang around with people who are involved in drugs and alcohol, because that's a dead-end street."

Many former pro athletes who sink into some kind of post-career problem cannot ever get past the bitterness of lost dreams. They continue to blame someone else for their problems, and they fail to see that there is an answer to them. Not so with David Thompson.

"Since that time in Seattle, so many good and positive things have happened in my life," David says. "My compulsion to use drugs and alcohol has been removed. I've been clean and sober now for several years, and that in itself is a miracle. When you have a problem with drugs and alcohol, it has a tendency to break up your family. I was separated from my wife and kids for a long period of time, but the Lord has put my family back together. I owe that to my relationship with Jesus Christ.

"When I was going through my problems, I knew what direction I needed to go, but I was filled with guilt, a lot of denial, and a lot of negative feelings. When those pastors read about my being in jail, they came over a couple of times a week, and we prayed and read the Bible. I felt something different in my life. It felt like a void had always been there, but when we prayed and read the Bible, I felt something warm, something growing inside of me.

"I've learned that the Lord Jesus Christ should always be your Number 1 priority. I don't have the wealth and fame I once had, but in a lot of ways my life is far richer than it has ever been because I've got Christ in my life.

"You can have all the wealth and fame in your life, and still be out there like a lost soul with no direction like I was. Now my life is great. And I owe that all to my relationship with Christ."

Coming out of college, it seemed improbable that David Thompson would not gain acceptance as one of the greats of pro basketball, and in some ways he did. Yet through the trials that he suffered at the end of his career, he discovered something far greater than inclusion in some list of retired athletes. He found out how to get his name listed among the redeemed. For David Thompson has been rescued from much more than the ill effects of drugs; he has been rescued from the penalty of sin. For this skywalker, it's a great new way to fly.

THE NBA ROAD

1975: Drafted Number 1 by both ABA (Denver) and NBA (Atlanta). Signed with the Denver Nuggets of the ABA.

1976: Denver becomes part of the NBA

1982: Traded to Seattle Supersonics

THE THOMPSON FILE

Collegiate Record

Year	School	G	Pts.	Avg.	FGM	FGA	FG%	FT%	Reb.
71-72	NC State	27	666	24.7	267	469	56.9	82.5	220
72-73	NC State	31	805	26.0	325	594	54.7	74.5	245
73-74	NC State	28	838	29.9	347	635	54.6	73.1	229
NCAA Totals		**86**	**2309**	**26.8**	**939**	**1698**	**55.3**	**76.3**	**694**

ABA (Regular Season)

Year	Team	G	Pts.	Avg.	FGM	FGA	FG%	FT%	Reb.
75-76	Nuggets	83	2158	26.0	807	1567	51.5	79.4	525

NBA (Regular Season)

Year	Team	G	Pts.	Avg.	FGM	FGA	FG%	FT%	Reb.
76-77	Nuggets	82	2125	25.9	824	1626	50.7	76.5	334
77-78	Nuggets	80	2172	27.2	826	1584	52.1	77.8	390
78-79	Nuggets	76	1825	24.0	693	1353	51.2	75.3	274
79-80	Nuggets	39	839	21.5	289	617	46.8	75.8	174
80-81	Nuggets	77	1967	25.5	734	1451	50.5	78.9	287
81-82	Nuggets	61	906	14.9	313	644	48.6	81.4	148
82-83	Supersonics	80	1600	20.0	660	1384	47.6	75.1	205
83-84	Supersonics	19	240	12.6	89	165	53.9	84.9	44
NBA Totals		**514**	**11674**	**22.7**	**4428**	**8824**	**50.2**	**77.3**	**1856**

Buck Williams
Order on the Court

VITAL STATISTICS

Born March 8, 1960, in Rocky Mount, North Carolina
6 feet 8, 225 pounds
College: University of Maryland
Position: Forward
1993–94 Team: Portland Trail Blazers

CAREER HIGHLIGHTS

- Selected NBA Rookie of the Year in 1982
- Named to NBA All-Defensive first team in 1990, 1991
- Became only the 20th player in NBA history to have more than 10,000 points and 10,000 rebounds
- Led NBA in field goal percentage in 1991 (60.2) and 1992 (60.4)
- Holds New Jersey Nets records for games played, total minutes, total points, field goals made and attempted, free throws made and attempted, and rebounds

PREGAME WARMUP

What would have happened if the other sport that Buck Williams attempted in the eighth grade had panned out? "I tried football in eighth grade," Williams says. "But I never got dirty. Coach Henderson was one of the football coaches, and I'm not sure, but to this day I still think he discouraged the football coach from playing me. He was afraid I'd get hurt. He had other ideas for me. So I played junior high football, but I only played maybe twice the whole year. I could have mixed it up on the line there, I think, but I never got a chance to do it."

If he could have mixed it up on the line like he has mixed it up for the Portland Trail Blazers and the New Jersey Nets, it sure would have been fun. But then again football may have been too chaotic for a man of order like Williams.

Buck Williams

In Buck Williams's world, fair play and justice are not just nice-sounding words that describe what a referee is supposed to bring to a basketball game. He has sought them in all areas of life. And when he does not see people getting a fair shake in life, he's not happy.

Buck has seen injustice occur in his own family, so he knows firsthand what it can do. As a student of his family's history, he discovered, for instance, some rather unscrupulous dealings.

It all started when he heard some rumors that in his family's past some relatives had "taken some land that the family owned and not done right by it," as he says. He decided to research the story and found, sadly, that it was true.

"My grandfather owned some land in Sussex County, Virginia, and when he died, I guess he had to pay some taxes on it," Buck explains. "But the family didn't have the money to pay it. So most of the family members wanted to collect money from each other to pay off the taxes for the land. However, some other family members decided that 'Hey, we have the money, but we're not going to pay it. We're going to take it through foreclosure.' Then they bought the land back for themselves and later sold it. So my family lost that land because the other family members sold it."

But the worst injustices that happened to Williams's family were brought on by outside sources. Williams discovered those difficulties when he extended his genealogical search of his mother's family back to 1795. His own search for his roots led him to better understand the plight of African-Americans during the era before the Civil War, as well as a new understanding of the atrocities that have been visited upon other people groups in recent history.

Long before the film *Schindler's List* made people aware again of the tragedy of the Jewish people in World War II, Williams was thinking about their dilemma. He says his genealogical search of his family changed his perspective. "It really gave more meaning to the Holocaust and what the Jews went through during their plight with Germany, and it gave us more light on how these kinds of things happen. They all happen with a thought—maybe some kind of weird thought. And then that person gets some support. It also made me see just how meaningless certain people's lives are, or how meaningless other people think they are."

After finding what he did, it is easier now for Buck Williams to have compassion for the difficulties of people today who seem to be cast aside by society. As one whose family was at one time easily viewed as disposable but who has now become rich and famous, he is not about to ignore the struggles of the less fortunate.

"Look at our judicial system," Williams argues, "and I honestly feel that certain people's lives are not valued. If you go through court and you don't have the representation that someone else may have, you could go to jail. If you don't have the money or the means or the name that other people have, you could easily be misrepresented, and you could be innocent and go to jail. I think there are just so many unjust situations in our society, and I think we need to try to strike a balance and stay true to our commitments that we made years ago through the Constitution."

This man who can see so clearly that there needs to be order in the courts has gotten to his position as a kind of spokesman for the downtrodden because of his own order on the court. And because his life off the court is in order.

He showed his order on the court following three highly promising seasons at New Jersey. During his first two years with the Nets (1981–83), the team lifted themselves from a losing season to winning records of 44-38 and 49-33. They had doubled their number of team victories in only two years. After a third year in the playoffs and 45 wins, the Nets spiraled downward, however. Consider the Nets' win-loss records from 1986–89:

1985–86	39-43
1986–87	24-58
1987–88	19-63
1988–89	26-56

Yet Buck Williams kept at the task. As far as he was concerned, his job was to maintain order on the court, even if the order included only him. Looking back on the way Williams played while with New Jersey, Coach Rick Adelman said of him, "He was on a team that at the end of the year was going nowhere, and he played like it was the first of the year."

In 1985–86 he was the only Net to play in all 82 games; he scored more than 20 points 22 times, and finished third in the league in rebounds, averaging 12 per game. In 1986–87, he again was the only Meadowlands occupant to play in every game, and he led the league in defensive rebounds (701). In the horrific campaign that followed, Williams overcame his first serious injury in his career to be named to the All-Defensive Second Team, to average a career-high 18.3 points, and to generally carry what had become a bad team on his considerable shoulders. Then, finally, mercifully, on June 24, 1989, Buck Williams, who had given so much to New Jersey, was traded to a true contender, the Portland Trail Blazers, for Sam Bowie and a first-round draft choice.

So how does Williams look back on those years in the Meadowlands, especially the last few? The same way he looks at most anything in his life: in an orderly way, recognizing God's part in it. "It's kind of interesting," Williams begins as he tries to make sense out of what became a less than pleasant experience, "because I always tell people that the Bible says through trials and tribulations, we find character and hope. When I was going through the situation in Jersey, we were losing and the last couple of years were probably the low point in my career.

"People would ask me, 'Buck, how can you play so hard when you're not going to win any games?' I just said that through it all, I knew I was becoming a better person—I was building character."

"My spiritual life grew and people began to see that there was something different about Buck Williams." What kept him growing and enabled him to act in a noticeably good way was that he "kept close to my family, did a lot of praying, and stayed in the Bible. My relationship with God encouraged me."

Of course, we can look back now and see that Williams's career was enhanced when he was traded to the Blazers. But in 1988 and 1989 as he kept going out there night after night to face defeat, he could not see such a bright basketball future.

"I just had no idea that God had another plan for me," Williams says about those pre-trade days. "He redeemed me and took me out of one situation and put me into a situation that was probably the best thing that happened to my career.

"When I was traded I asked God, 'Why are you going to send me all the way out to Portland?' Well, he sent me out there to get my blessing. Sometimes God sends you places that maybe you feel are not in your best interests, but when it all turns out, it's probably the best thing that happened. Even through adversity it happens. It worked out well and I was able to get with a team with a lot of talent and a team that was committed to winning, and my career flourished. I have always been thankful and I feel blessed that God would redeem me like that.

"Through it all, it really made me a better person. It gave me more character. I think you wonder sometimes why a particular adversity is happening, and afterward you find yourself just much stronger. That's what happened to me through playing in New Jersey. I just became a much stronger Christian.

"That's how we grow. You know, we hate to have adversity, but it's part of it, it's part of life. It's how you handle adversity that makes a difference."

Where does such character—a character that allows Buck to maintain both on and off the court a consistency that avoids the highs and lows of life—come from? You don't have to look far to see the reasons for the sense of order in Williams's life. You could start with his family background in Rocky Mount, North Carolina, where he and his brothers and sisters grew up. "It was a lot of fun," he says now about those days. And then there were his parents, who he describes as his greatest role models.

"We are very close. I always tell people that I learned my work habits from my parents and they were very influential in my life. They helped shape and mold me into the person I am today."

You could move on to the first major influence of his remarkable basketball career: junior high coach Reggie Henderson. "I didn't start playing organized basketball until I was in eighth grade. Coach Henderson was instrumental in helping me get started. He coached me in junior high school. Later he got the job at the high school. So he coached me for my last two years. The first year he coached me, we had a decent team, but my senior year we won the state championship. It was quite a thrill to win a state championship." In addition, Williams was selected to the All-State basketball team after averaging 20 points and 20 rebounds a game during the state tournament.

"Everybody talks about having a mentor," Williams says. "Coach Henderson has been my mentor for a very long time and I owe a great deal of my success to him. We are best of friends. We talk on the phone, we get together whenever we can, and we have just a very good relationship." Obviously Reggie Henderson was part of the reason Buck Williams hopes for order and fairness —both on and off the court.

What would have happened, though, if the other sport Williams attempted in the eighth grade had panned out? "I tried football in eighth grade," Williams says, a hardy laugh punctuating the recollection. "But I never got dirty. Coach Henderson was one of the football coaches, and I'm not sure, but to this day I still think he discouraged the football coach from playing me. He was afraid I'd get hurt. He had other ideas for me. So I played junior high football, but I only played maybe twice the whole year. It didn't bother me much, but I was quite intrigued about the game of football and any experience would have been fun for me. I could have mixed it up on the line there I think, but I never got a chance to do it."

If he could have mixed it up on the line like he has mixed it up for the Portland Trail Blazers and the New Jersey Nets, it sure would have been fun. But then again football may have been too chaotic for a man of order like Williams.

Perhaps the greatest reason for Buck Williams' sense of order has nothing to do with family or basketball. It has to do with his faith.

"Christianity was always a part of my household. It was the belief we always grew up with. My mother always encouraged it and made sure I was always in church on Sunday."

Not that the results of her efforts always paid off in Buck being the kind of little angel she hoped he would be. "I can remember some days when my friend and I would sit in church for a while. Then we would look outside and see that it was sunny, so we would sneak outside. We'd go to the bakery down the street and spend the money that we should have been putting in the offering."

When Buck wasn't making clandestine trips to the bakery, though, what he was taught really did sink in. "Church helped me shape my morals and values. It was really sort of an extension of what I was being taught at home. When I found myself out in the world, I had a foundation to build on. I knew the sort of direction I had to be headed in."

But it is more than just church that guides Williams to be a respected citizen. "To have a personal relationship with Jesus Christ has been phenomenal in my life. I often wonder why I make some decisions. Well, it's not me making them, but God is really taking control in my life and sort of steering me in the right direction when it comes time to make decisions. I always tell people who are asking, 'Buck, how can you stay injury-free, and how do you make the decisions that you make' that it's not so much I'm making them, it's just that I'm leaning on God and praying that he can give me the kind of guidance I need."

One of the first major tests of this divine guidance system came when it was time to choose a college after Williams's stellar high school career. With much advice from others and prayer on the family's part, Buck chose the University of Maryland. For three years, he played for Coach Lefty Driesell. While at College Park, he piled up some impressive stats and honors as a Maryland Terrapin. He was the Atlantic Coast Conference Rookie of the Year in 1978–79 after leading the conference in rebounding. As a sophomore and as a junior he was second team All-ACC.

In 1980, Williams made the U.S. Olympic team. Long before the talk of dream team and the glory of recapturing the gold for the United States, this Olympic Games was marked by political posturing. At the time of Williams' selection to the team, U.S. President Jimmy Carter was concerned with what the Soviet Union was doing in Afghanistan.

Ironically, the young Williams, who stood so much for justice and treating people right, suffered because of the U.S. stand against the Russians' treatment of the Afghans. President Carter proclaimed a boycott against the Olympic Games, preventing the

U.S. teams from going to Moscow to participate in the athletic contests.

Yet as he looks back on that missed opportunity at world-wide recognition, Williams dwells on the good that came from his selection to the team, not the disappointment of not being able to compete.

"I think the best thing that happened to me was that I got an opportunity to play against some NBA players." The U. S. Olympic basketball team played a series of exhibition games against the NBA, and it was a chance for many college All-Americans to show their stuff against the big boys. Buck didn't know it at the time, but scouts and fans alike soon took notice that he could not only play with the NBA guys, but he belonged in their league.

He returned to Maryland as a junior to set a school record for field goal percentage by hitting 64.7 percent of his shots. He made 183 of 283 attempts from the field. For his college career, he finished with a 61.5 percent shooting mark.

If anything shows that Buck Williams concentrates while on the basketball court and knows how to maintain order amidst the chaos of fastbreak hoops, it is that shooting percentage. Even through his pro career, Williams has maintained one of the highest marks in the league. He obviously keeps his eye on the goal.

However, there was one time when he was at the University of Maryland that he got distracted during practice. Perhaps it was one too many Lefty Drissell stories or maybe the tedium of practice got to him, but his eyes strayed one day from the task at hand. Yet Buck Williams will be forever grateful for this uncharacteristic time when his mind and eyes wandered from hoops.

"I was practicing one day in Cole Field House," Williams begins as he confesses to his guilt. "Obviously I wasn't paying much attention to what was going on in practice, and I happened to look up. High above the floor, at the top of the coliseum in the catwalk, I happened to see this face looking down on our practice. I could just make out that there was a beautiful girl up there. I could see this long hair, and I could see that she was just a beautiful person. I kept looking up there. One of the other guys on the team saw the same beautiful girl I did. He sent somebody up to try to give her his telephone number. She said, 'I don't want it, I would really appreciate it if you would give Buck Williams my number.' So I got her phone number and we talked on the phone and it was sort of a chemistry between us. She was a down-to-earth person. We got together and went out and it's been history ever since." Her name was Mimi, and she would eventually become Mrs. Buck Williams.

Of course a beautiful wife was not the only thing Williams came away from the University of Maryland with. His hoops exploits earned him an opportunity to play in the NBA. Yet despite all of his high percentages and his rebounds during his first three years at Maryland, he did not think he was ready for the big time.

After a junior year in which the Terrapins won 21 games, ended up ranked 18th in the country, and lost a second-round game in the NCAA tournament to eventual champion Indiana, Williams was ready to return for his senior year at Maryland. He had experienced his college highlight in going to the second round of the playoffs, and he was ready to return. Until something he read changed his mind.

"It was sort of interesting," Buck says now. "I had no idea I was going to turn hardship and go to the NBA. At the last minute I happened to read an article in *The Washington Post* and Bob Ferry, who was the GM of the Bullets, stated in the paper that if underclassmen like Buck Williams would decide to leave college, they would probably go in the top five or ten picks.

"So that gave me an idea that I might be wanted. I got on the phone and called some people, and after we got some guarantees I decided to come out. It was the best decision, and with the conditions of my family, it was a way I could improve their condition and do some things I wanted to do for them. I missed my senior year of college and the social aspect of it, which you can never regain once you lose it. But later I went back and finished my degree, so it was a good decision."

He would need that degree in business administration, because the newspaper report was right. Williams was drafted in the first round as the third pick overall by the New Jersey Nets, and the NBA paychecks were soon to follow.

And so was a chance to meet the man who Buck Williams had followed closely as he was working his way up the basketball ladder: Julius Erving. "I think Dr. J was one of the classiest people who ever played the game," says the man who is noted for some class himself.

Their first meeting shows a lot about Williams and about the respect players had for Dr. J. He compares it to the feelings rookies had in the early nineties when they first met Michael Jordan. "Your mouth sort of drops open, and you're kind of in awe of this person—this icon." Erving had entered the New Jersey locker room after a game to visit with the Nets' trainer, a friend from his early pro playing days.

"He came over to our locker room, and I kind of glanced up and I saw him, and I thought, *No, No! I can't believe it!* My heart started beating fast, and my mouth fell open. What made it even that much more pleasing was that he came over and shook my hand. So that was the ultimate, to idolize someone and then to have that person know who I was and he wasn't standoffish. He was a real down-to-earth person, and that made it that much better."

What did not get better for Buck Williams as the years went by was how things went in New Jersey. His first year with the Nets was nothing if not promising, though. Besides a new forward in Williams, the Nets also had a new coach in Larry Brown, a high-scoring guard in Ray Williams, and a college teammate in Albert King.

Those newcomers, along with another former Terrapin Len Elmore and steady Otis Birdsong, lifted the Nets to a 44-38 record and a berth in the playoffs. There they dropped two straight games to the Bullets. For his trouble, Buck Williams was named the NBA Rookie of the Year, based on such highlights as finishing third in the league in rebounding, fourth in field-goal percentage, ringing up 52 double-doubles, and grabbing 10 rebounds in the All-Star game.

For 1982–83, the Nets added a huge obstacle in the middle: Darrell Dawkins. He clogged up the middle so badly that he led the league in personal fouls with 379 and in fouling out with 23. But he must have helped, for the Nets improved their mark to 49-

33. Buck Williams again led the way with his 58.8 percent shooting and 1,027 rebounds, which would be the most of his career.

The Nets' coach Larry Brown watched his amazing forward and knew he was observing someone special. "Buck Williams doesn't have a selfish bone in his body," he remarked. The good will between players and coach seemed to be mutual, based on the success the Nets were achieving.

Then came a shocker for the Nets players. Just before the season ended, Brown, who had applied for a college coaching position without the blessing of Nets' management, was ousted as the skipper of the Nets. Apparently disheartened by the turn of events, the Nets fell in two games to the Knicks and were again victims of an early playoff exit.

Two years, two playoff berths, four losses.

Stan Albeck took over and would lead the Nets to another winning season. And finally they had some success in the play-offs. In fact, they beat the mighty Philadelphia 76ers and their big guns, Julius Erving, Bobby Jones, Moses Malone, and Andrew Toney, in five games to advance to the Eastern Conference semifinals against the Bucks. In that series, however, Sidney Moncrief, Bob Lanier, Marques Johnson, and company were too much for the Nets, beating them in six of a best-of-seven series.

That was as good as it was going to get for the New Jersey Nets. Although the Nets finished 42-40 in 1984–85 behind Williams and his league-leading 3,182 minutes played during the regular season, they dropped all three playoff games to a Detroit team that was passing them on the way up the NBA ladder. For the next four years the Nets would have losing seasons, winning as few as 19 games in 1987–88.

No doubt Buck Williams appreciated his trade in June 1989 to the Portland Trail Blazers, and he showed his appreciation by helping his new team to a winning record. In 1988–89, Portland was 39-43. The next year with Williams, the Blazers went 59-23 and played in the NBA Finals against the Pistons. Granted, the improvement was not all the result of the newcomer from the East, but he played a key role. A look at his accomplishments reveals his value.

In both years, the Blazers averaged 114 points a game. But with Buck Williams shoring up the defense—he was named to the NBA's All-Defensive First Team and grabbed 800 rebounds, the most on the Blazers in eight years—the team carved more than 6 points off its points-against average. That was a major reason for the 20 extra victories.

Two years later, the Trail Blazers were again in the NBA championship series. This time it was the Chicago Bulls who broke their hearts, winning the series 4 games to 2.

It's said that fans don't remember the losers. And that might be true to a point. In the National Football League, the Dallas Cowboys get all the credit and the Buffalo Bills get the jokes. But it is important to remember how far a team must go just to be in the big dance.

For a player like Buck Williams, those two NBA Finals appearances have been bittersweet. Of course they are gratifying after so many years of excellence without team results in New Jersey. "Going to the finals those two years has been the highlight of my career," says Williams. "We had a chance to win a championship and unfortunately we didn't win it. But I can say I was there and had an opportunity, and I think every professional athlete just wants to have an opportunity to win a championship."

Just a chance. That's what Buck Williams thinks people should have. He got his chance in high school and came home with a state championship. His chance in college ended in a second-round loss. And his big chance in the NBA ended where so many other dreams have ended in recent years, at the feet of Michael Jordan.

Yet for Buck Williams, his concerns go deeper than his own interests and dreams. He would like to see every person treated in a way that gives him or her an opportunity to succeed. That in part explains an honor bestowed on Williams by sportswriter Sam Smith, the author of *The Jordan Rules*. In a column for the *Chicago Tribune* during the 1994 season, Smith named Buck Williams as one of his "five best players to have as teammates." The sportswriter called Williams the classic unselfish player, who "sets screens and rebounds" so his teammates can score. It is a fair measure of the man Buck Williams has become.

Whether on the court or off the court, treating people fairly seems to be the order of the day for Williams. "I want to touch someone's life. If I touch one person's life for good, then my own life will not be in vain."

Q & A WITH BUCK WILLIAMS

Q: *How do you maintain self-control in the heat of battle when you have to mix it up pretty hard under the boards?*
Buck: When you talk about the fruits of the Spirit, one of them is self-control. I try to have self-control, but it's very difficult at times, especially when you get some bad calls or the situations are not going your way. It's just part of trying to be Christlike, and that's pretty much what I try to do.

Q: *What is the key to success?*
Buck: If you're an athlete, you can't be afraid of hard work. Plus you need to be consistent. Consistent in life and consistent in your Christian walk. I think that whatever you do in life, if you're consistent at it, you're going to be pretty good.

Q: *What do you have in mind for your future when your career in the NBA comes to an end?*
Buck: I have a strong interest in becoming an entrepreneur. While in New Jersey I worked with a real estate company. And I've done some research into car dealerships to see what it takes to run one. Whatever I do in terms of a second career, I want it to be meaningful.

THE NBA ROAD

1981: Selected by New Jersey in first round (third pick) of NBA draft

June 24, 1989: Traded by New Jersey to Portland for Sam Bowie and a 1989 first-round draft pick

THE WILLIAMS FILE

Collegiate Record

Year	School	G	Pts.	Avg.	FGM	FGA	FG%	FT%	Reb.
78/79	Maryland	30	300	10.0	120	206	58.3	55.0	323
79/80	Maryland	24	371	15.5	143	236	60.6	66.4	242
80/81	Maryland	31	482	15.5	183	283	64.7	63.7	363
NCAA Totals		**85**	**1153**	**13.6**	**446**	**725**	**61.5**	**62.3**	**928**

NBA Record (Regular Season)

Year	Team	G	Pts.	Avg.	FGM	FGA	FG%	FT%	Reb.
81/82	Nets	82	1268	15.5	513	881	58.2	62.4	1005
82/83	Nets	82	1396	17.0	536	912	58.8	62.0	1027
83/84	Nets	81	1274	15.7	495	926	53.5	57.0	1000
84/85	Nets	82	1491	18.2	577	1089	53.0	62.5	1005
85/86	Nets	82	1301	15.9	500	956	52.3	67.6	986
86/87	Nets	82	1472	18.0	521	936	55.7	73.1	1023
87/88	Nets	70	1279	18.3	466	832	56.0	66.8	834
88/89	Nets	74	959	13.0	373	702	53.1	66.6	696
89/90	Blazers	82	1114	13.6	413	754	54.8	70.6	800
90/91	Blazers	80	933	11.7	358	595	60.2	70.5	751
91/92	Blazers	80	901	11.3	340	563	60.4	75.4	704
92/93	Blazers	82	678	8.3	270	528	51.1	64.5	690
93/94	Blazers	81	793	9.7	291	524	55.5	67.9	843
NBA Totals		**1040**	**14849**	**14.3**	**5653**	**10198**	**55.4**	**66.4**	**11364**

David Wood
Blue Collar Worker

VITAL STATISTICS

Born November 30, 1964 in Spokane, Washington
6 feet 9, 230 pounds
Colleges: Skagit Valley; University of Nevada-Reno
Position: Forward
1993–94 Team: Detroit Pistons

CAREER HIGHLIGHTS

- Had a career high of 26 points while with the Houston Rockets
- Played in all 82 games with the Rockets in 1990–91
- Shot 45 percent (22 of 49) from 3-point range in 1993–94

PREGAME WARMUP

You don't watch David Wood for the same reasons you watch Dominique Wilkins or Penny Hardaway. You'll not see him giving you highlight film dunks or in-your-face drives. What you see is a workman. A lunch-bucket toting, hard-hat wearing laborer with a union card that says "Work over your opponent tirelessly and hit the boards relentlessly and pick up the leftovers offensively."

You might see David Wood enter the job midway through the first quarter and punch out 5 minutes later. But when he is at work, this blue collar player takes no breaks. And he takes no prisoners.

David Wood

A few years ago, the Sara Lee company, makers of frozen cakes and other delectables, came up with a memorable slogan to advertise their goodies. Their ads claimed that "Nobody Doesn't Like Sara Lee." It was hard to argue with that slogan, for even if you worked for Little Debbie's, you would have to admit you can hardly dislike something that tasted that good.

With apologies to whoever came up with that advertising gem, let's try it with a little twist. Let's see what it would sound like as, "Nobody doesn't like David Wood."

Of course not everybody knows who David Wood is, so perhaps we should start there.

David Wood is a professional basketball player. He has played for the Chicago Bulls, the Houston Rockets, the San Antonio Spurs, and the Detroit Pistons. He almost played for the Sacramento Kings.

Indeed, as an NBA player, David Wood has friends in high places. No less a basketball icon than David Robinson counts him as a close friend.

As teammates in 1992–93 with the Spurs, Wood and Robinson developed a relationship based on their shared faith in Jesus Christ. A highlight of their year together was their outreach, along with the Spurs' Avery Johnson, to the San Antonio area that enabled more than 20,000 people to hear the gospel. Hundreds of attendees gave their lives to Jesus Christ during that outreach. (See page 124.)

To David Wood, that is what life is all about, for to know him at all and to talk to him for even the shortest time is to discover that he knows a secret that not many people who make it to the NBA discover. There is a deeper purpose for our being here, even for those who are basketball players.

As an NBA player, David Wood is one of those blue collar workers. He's rarely a starter. He averages in the single digits in points. In fact, his bio didn't even appear in the 1992–93 official *NBA Register*, even though he played that year for the Spurs.

But he gets the job done. Fully reliable, he puts in a hard night's work for his coaches and teammates.

You don't watch David Wood for the same reasons you watch Dominique Wilkins or Penny Hardaway. You'll not see him giving you highlight film dunks or in-your-face drives. What you see is a workman. A lunch-bucket toting, hard-hat wearing laborer with a union card that says work over your opponent tirelessly and hit the boards relentlessly and pick up the leftovers offensively.

You might see David Wood punch in midway through the first quarter and punch out five minutes later. But when he is at work, this blue collar player takes no breaks. And he takes no prisoners.

Typical of a David Wood performance was a game in late 1993 with Detroit when the Pistons were out west to play Portland. His various contributions included:

- a steal and a feed to Olden Polynice for a monster slam
- taking a vicious charge from a driving Clyde Drexler
- hitting a three-pointer on a shot that looks too smooth to be coming from a guy 6-feet-9 inches tall
- grabbing some rebounds
- bouncing hard off people and hustling at both ends of the court

Players with considerably better tools have come and gone in the NBA while David Wood was quietly carving out a spot in the league.

So one of the reasons Nobody Doesn't Like David Wood is that he's a blue-collar NBA player. While we can't all relate to Jordanesque acrobatics on the court or Shaqian strength, we can all relate to a guy who is not afraid to make it on hard work and heads-up play.

While many fans might need an introduction to Wood, one man who didn't forget him was Don Chaney. In 1990–91, Chaney was at the helm of the Houston Rockets. As Chaney led the Rockets to a 52-30 mark, he regularly tapped on the shoulder of a rookie out of the University of Reno named David Wood. The rookie became one of his mainstays. Wood played in every game for the Rockets that year, scoring 432 points and grabbing 246 rebounds.

When Chaney took over as head coach of the Detroit Pistons for the 1993–94 season, he made sure he got Wood. In the trade that sent Dennis Rodman to the Spurs for Sean Elliott, Wood came over to the Pistons as well. Chaney later said of his new forward, "David Wood always gives you 100 percent. He is a dependable player off the bench."

For a while during the 1993–94 season, though, Wood did more than come off the bench. In a move that was designed to try to shake up the Pistons, who were in the midst of a horrendous season, Chaney elevated Wood into a starting role. "We have to have a guy like Wood," Chaney said at the time. "A guy who plays defense, rebounds, works hard, and thinks secondarily about getting his shots."

So then, it's clear that fans appreciate hard work and the underdog like David Wood. It's clear that coaches need role players like David Wood. But what about people whose job it is to talk to the players: the reporters?

One reporter who had never met Wood was pleasantly surprised one preseason game as he waited for the power forward to arrive at a game. As soon as the reporter saw Wood, he stopped the player in the hallway and struck up a conversation. Wood responded like a long lost friend. He had been told by the team P. R. department that the reporter would be there, and he seemed pleased to see him.

Wood invited the writer into the locker room for a postgame

chat, and when they both saw that the interview would take more time, Wood gave the reporter his phone number.

Later, when the two had a bit of trouble hooking up by phone, Wood called the reporter and left a message on his voice-mail, just to make sure they could get together by phone.

Between pro athletes and the reporters who follow them, such a scenario is almost unheard of. That kind of treatment is a breath of fresh air in sports.

"Nobody doesn't like David Wood." It's true of fans, his coach, and reporters. But is it universally true? Not quite. There are times when a few NBA stars might take umbrage with that slogan.

People like James Worthy of the Lakers. Don Chaney recalls the time in Houston when his blue-collar forward made Worthy get a little hot under his.

"He gets in your face and takes guys right out of the game," Chaney remarks.

Another time, during the 1993–94 season, Wood made a lit-tle money for the NBA by getting Rolando Blackman's goat. In a game with the Knicks, Wood shoved Blackman in the back while going for a rebound, which led Blackman to take a swing at the Pistons' forward. He missed, but the NBA didn't. They hit Black-man with a $2,000 fine and an unpaid day off.

"I was surprised," Wood says about the incident. "I talked to him, and he knows I didn't mean anything."

And in still another game, Wood's aggressive style turned Horace Grant into a raging Bull.

Like an innocent kid who didn't know he had set the house afire while playing with matches, Wood pleads not guilty to any dirty work. "I play defense. I think I play really hard on defense and that's what aggravates people. I don't try to aggravate people. I just try to stop them. I just want to win."

Winning was not something the Pistons did much of in 1993–94. So, in an effort to bolster their lineup, they made a trade. Or at least tried to. Not long after they attempted to send Sean Elliott to Houston for Robert Horry only to see the deal fall through when Elliott failed a physical, Detroit wrapped up Olden Polynice and Wood, and shipped them to Sacramento in ex-change for Duane Causwell. Lightning struck the Pistons again as

Causwell failed his physical. After a strange couple of days, Wood arrived back in Detroit, still determined to do what it would take to help the Pistons.

Apparently not much can bother a guy who has made it from Skagit Valley College in Mt. Vernon, Washington, to the Palace of Auburn Hills, the Pistons' homecourt.

Although David Wood loves basketball and plays with the devotion of someone who can't get enough of it, it is not his first love in life. What was important to Wood long before basketball, and what gives him the purpose for which he feels he is in the NBA, is his faith. David Wood has been a Christian far longer than he has been a basketball player.

Ironically, at first he went after the opportunity to be a Christian with a dedication that is not unlike his hoops fervor.

"When I was three years old, I started praying with my mom every night, and I would ask Jesus Christ to come into my heart and forgive me of my sins or my no-nos. I prayed that prayer every night. Then when I hit about eight I realized that you only have to ask Him to save you once. But you do have to confess your sins daily."

As a youngster growing up in Vancouver, Washington, David had a prime example to watch during his formative years. "Our family was really faithful in church. My parents are wonderful, godly people, and I never saw any hypocrisy in them. They did what they said, and said what they did.

"They taught me the principles of God's Word. They went to Bill Gothard's Basic Youth Conflicts and were taught that you should get the Word of God into your kids any way you can.

"I was making 15 cents every two weeks for allowance, so they offered to pay me $5.00 for every chapter of Proverbs that I memorized. So my brother and I did it. I think I memorized the first eleven chapters and he memorized thirteen. This was when we were in junior high. That changed my life. When I was twelve years old, I made a vow to God to read the Word every day for ten minutes. If for some reason I didn't have a Bible, I would just make it up the next day. I've been faithful to that for the last sixteen years."

Today Larry Wood, David's brother, is a minister. And for his part, David says that when his playing days are over, he intends to be an evangelist.

David's playing days began when he was in the fifth grade when he met a man who became his hoops tutor—a man he credits still with helping him make it to the NBA. "We lived six blocks from Marshall Community Center and I would go there every day and help Ted Davis, a friend of mine who was in charge of the community center. I would do chores for him. Set up rooms and sweep the floor, or whatever, and he would teach me the fundamentals of basketball. He was my mentor, and he still is. I've worked out with him since the fifth grade, and I still work out with him when I go home. He's building supervisor at nighttime.

"He had a huge impact on me. I wouldn't be in the NBA if it wasn't for him. He was All-State in Washington in basketball and he was a phenomenal basketball player. An all-around jumpshot. He worked out with me. He taught me my shot and taught me basically all I know about basketball."

Basketball wasn't Wood's only sport, though. "In early elementary school I loved baseball. When you're that young, you can't really shoot a basketball. So I loved baseball. Then I started playing soccer. Then when I was in eighth grade, I dropped everything and started concentrating on basketball. I was 5 feet 7."

Who would have thought David Wood would have an NBA career? Probably no one. Yet Wood didn't lack for confidence as he tried to move up the high school ladder. Fourteen inches and ten years later, he was a pro. But it was unexpected to friends at school.

"I didn't play my sophomore year," he recalls. "I told everyone I was going to play on the varsity, and God really taught me a lot about pride and humility through that. I didn't make the varsity, I didn't make the J. V. I got put on the sophomore team. I was 6 feet 1 and weighed 124 pounds.

"The next year I tried to be humble, but I still was prideful. I told everyone I was going to play on the varsity, and I played on the J. V. team. During my junior year, I was 6 feet 3 and 140 pounds. I learned that God is the one who exalts and lifts somebody up."

One person Wood couldn't lift up when he was in high school was himself. To demonstrate how weak he was, he tells a story on himself. "When I was in ninth grade, we had a really good team. The high school coaches knew I was an athlete even though I wasn't very strong. I signed up for a P.E. class, for badminton. Then we had physical fitness testing, and we had to do pull-ups. I couldn't do any pull-ups. The coaches came and pulled me out of badminton and put me in the weight room for P.E. They said, 'You can get out of the weight room once you do five pull-ups.' So I ended up spending my whole high school career in the weight room. But I can do five pull-ups now."

The strength training must have paid off, for his senior year at Hudson Bay High School was a bit better. Now standing 6 feet 5 and weighing 165, he got a little attention. "I played varsity and made all-league in one newspaper's poll. I just averaged about 11 points and 7 rebounds a game, but we were league champions."

Although he didn't know it at the time, he would eventually grow to be the size of his hero, Larry Bird. And what would have perhaps been more surprising would have been the fact that he would eventually get to play against Bird in the NBA. But for the time being after high school, the NBA couldn't have been much of a hope as he enrolled at Skagit Valley College.

"Physically, I was weak. I couldn't get any scholarship money from four-year schools. It was my goal to play Division I, so I went to Skagit Valley Community College, which was a great move for me. Dave Quall was the coach there, and he was a very good coach. He taught me a lot about defense. I matured and worked super hard and started lifting weights even more."

Wood's second year at Skagit Valley was perhaps the first one in which he showed the promise of post-college basketball. As a late-bloomer who did not reach his full height until after high school, he continued to improve his game as his body continued to grow. In his sophomore year, he shot an amazing 60.9 percent from the floor and averaged 18 points a game. It was not a ticket to the NBA, but it did get him to Division I basketball, as he wished.

He received a full scholarship to the University of Nevada-Reno. Coach Sonny Allen thought about red-shirting the freshman but was so impressed with his improvement that he made Wood the starting center. "I played the five [center spot] and shot three-pointers." It sounds like an odd combination, but it must have pleased Allen, for he let David shoot 113 of them in two years as his man in the middle. He hit 47 treys for 41.6 percent.

The NBA must have been on David's mind by then, for he says that "one of my coaches told me not to worry about the NBA. We have to win tonight. A lot of the guys dream, but you have to dream in order to have the chance. I prayed and felt like if I wanted to go for it and play in the pros, then God would go with me. He would give me the self-discipline."

Wood cites 1 Timothy 1:7: "For God has not given us the power of fear, but of love, power, and self-discipline."

"What I like to tell people is that God never puts the ball in the basket for me, but he definitely gave me the self-discipline to work hard."

Wood was not drafted by any pro team, however, so he decided to take the indirect route to the NBA. First, he went to the

Continental Basketball Association, where he played for two years with the Rockford Lightning, who had drafted him in the second round. "I almost got cut a few times but I kept making the team." Not only did those seasons give him a shot at the NBA, but they also led him to his lifelong partner.

"After I made the team, they had a little article on the front page of the sports page with information about each player. They had a picture of me and my birthdate and everything. This girl named Angie saw that and said, 'I want to meet this guy because we have the same birthday, November 30, 1964.'

"I went to a singles Bible study one night, and she came up to me and told me she had the very same birthday as me. We started talking, and about a month later she asked me out," Wood says, laughing at the apparent turnaround in usual etiquette. Then he explains. "I was in the CBA and poor and didn't have a car, so she asked me out. We started dating and praying and felt it was God's will for us to get married.

"I took all my CBA money, I saved as much of it as I could and bought a ring with it and I proposed to her. We got married the summer after that, which was 1989."

A few months later, Wood got his first exposure to the NBA. The Bulls took a look at him. It wasn't much of a look—two games in which he played two minutes. For many people, that may have been enough. Enough to tell the grandchildren some-day, "I played on the Chicago Bulls with Michael Jordan."

But Wood was dedicated to the task. Ever since fifth grade he had been getting better and better, growing bigger and bigger. Surely he could make a living at this game. He returned to the CBA after being cut by the Bulls, and then he finished the year playing in Italy. The leagues in Europe featured up-and-coming and veteran players who drew applause from the basketball-hun-gry fans and good salaries from the teams. "We had no money until I got a break to go to Italy," David notes. "I made good mon-ey over there."

During this time he also learned a valuable lesson about playing big-time basketball. It's a lesson that NBA players like Ro-lando Blackman and Horace Grant wish he hadn't learned when he sticks to them like a deadbeat relative. "When I made the Chicago Bulls for a while and went back to the CBA, I tried to play cool like the guys who make sure their hair doesn't get mixed up and stuff. I discovered when I was in the CBA the second time that if I don't play hard, I'm not a very good player. If I give it all I've got then I can excel."

With that new drive, Wood crisscrossed the map playing for Athletes In Action and a team in Spain. On the strength of his performance in the Spanish playoffs at the end of the 1990 season, Wood got the attention of Houston.

"I came back from that to a guaranteed contract with the Houston Rockets. They had scouted me, and my agent Kyle Rote, Jr., got me a summer program tryout with them. They were interested in me, and I played exceptionally well, so they signed me."

Although Wood is known for his strong-armed defense, it is offense that really gets his blood flowing. And although it's a rare occurrence for him in the NBA, his favorite feeling is "when you get in rhythm and you get the ball a lot and you catch fire offensively and no one can stop you. I don't get the ball that much, so it doesn't happen a whole lot." But it did once. "When I was with Houston, I scored 27 points against Orlando. I hit some big baskets down the stretch. I had a great year with Houston, but then they didn't want to pay me what I thought I was worth."

So it was back to Spain for the David Wood Traveling Show. There he had what he calls "a good year," and the Rockets agreed with his evaluation, for they signed him to a two-year contract. However, before Wood even suited up for Houston, the team had traded him to San Antonio. He played in sixty-four games. Finally, Coach Chaney brought the workman forward to Detroit, where he worked himself into a starting job for part of the season.

David Wood has worked extremely hard to get a job in the NBA. And for that you have to like him. Day in and day out he contends with a pressure that few people outside of sports know about, and in 1993–94 he endured that pressure with a team that had one of the worst records in basketball.

"One thing people don't realize is that this is a high-pressure job. There is tremendous pressure. I don't think there is any other position that has more pressure than an NBA athlete. The pressure I'm talking about is just trying to maintain a job. If you have a bad game, let's say I shoot 1 for 7, it's in every paper in America. It's not a very pleasurable experience."

But it does have its rewards, of course. For Wood, the biggest reward is that it allows him to have a unique opportunity to talk about his faith. "I want to use this platform that God has given me to be a player who influences kids to walk with Christ. I want to see people saved, and I don't want to just love them and leave them. I want to disciple them and give them a foundation in the Bible and in prayer. I want them to fall in love with Jesus and to obey His commandments."

Young people are especially important to Wood. Asked to provide a training tip for prospective basketball players, Wood offers largely spiritual advice. "The tip that I would have for young people is to just meditate on God's Word. Joshua 1:8 and 9 says, 'Do not let this book of the law depart from your mouth; meditate on it day and night, so that you will be careful to do everything written in it. Then you will be prosperous and successful. Have I not commanded you? Be strong and courageous' [NIV]. We should take God's Word and meditate on it and apply it to whatever we need, whether it is self-discipline or a desire to work hard or have peace before a big game. God's Word is alive and powerful."

Even in his marriage, Wood has discovered that. "When we first got married, I wasn't real disciplined with my time. I would waste time early in the day or late at night watching TV. Then I had my priority list to be the best basketball player I could be, so I would go to the gym at 1 o'clock in the afternoon and lift weights. Then I would go to the gym at night every night to work on basketball skills and that was just eating up all of our time. What I learned to do since was to be more disciplined to not watch late night TV but to go to bed at a good time and get up early. Then I could get done by 6 so we could have the evenings together. You just have to be disciplined to get your priorities right."

How can you not like a guy like this? He's human when so many pro athletes try to pretend they are larger than life. He's humble enough to know how much work it takes to maintain his career. He's loving enough to care for young people and make adjustments for the good of his marriage. He works hard on the court. And he is dedicated off it.

It just may be true. Nobody doesn't like David Wood.

Q & A WITH DAVID WOOD

Q *You mentioned that you would go to the gym for weight training each afternoon and practice every evening. What roles do practice and discipline play in becoming a skill player?*
David: It's so easy to become distracted. If a guy wants to make it in sports and he's not the greatest athlete in the world, he better not be going out on dates five nights a week. He better be in the gym three or four nights a week. It takes a life of discipline to make it in the upper echelons of anything.

Q: *What do you do off the court to relax?*
David: Study the Bible and lift weights. I also like fishing and driving 4-wheel-drive vehicles.

Q: *What is your most memorable moment in the NBA?*
David: I was with Houston and we were playing the L.A. Clippers, and I scored a couple of threes. One was a 40-footer to send the game into overtime, and then I hit a three in the first overtime. I just took over the game for a while. We ended up losing in double overtime, but it was fun for a while. I was the star.

Q: *What ministries do you participate in when you aren't playing ball?*
David: I know God has called me to be an evangelist. My heart is to see souls saved and people discipled. As I'm getting older, I'm learning how to disciple people through my church and an organization called Champions for Christ. Greg Ball is the leader. He is taking me to the next level.

THE NBA ROAD

1987:	Played for the Rockford Lightning (CBA)
September 27, 1988:	Signed as a free agent by Chicago
November 17, 1988:	Waived by Chicago
1988–89:	Played for Rockford Lightning
August 6, 1990:	Signed as a free agent by Houston
October 6, 1992:	Traded from Houston to San Antonio for a second round, 1995 draft pick
October 1, 1993:	Traded from San Antonio to Detroit along with Sean Elliott for Dennis Rodman

THE WOOD FILE

Collegiate Record

Year	School	G	Pts.	Avg.	FGM	FGA	FG%	FT%	Reb.
83/84	Skagit	29	281	9.7	112	205	54.6	70.4	211
84/85	Skagit	26	473	18.1	184	302	60.9	71.9	301
85/86	UN Reno	28	251	9.0	97	190	51.1	66.2	168
86/87	UN Reno	30	363	12.1	127	269	47.2	72.6	281
JC Totals		55	754	13.7	296	507	58.4	71.4	512
NCAA Totals		58	615	10.6	224	459	48.8	70.2	449

CBA Record

Year	Team	G	Pts.	Avg.	FGM	FGA	FG%	FT%	Reb.
87/88	Rockford	42	215	5.1	75	143	52.4	81.4	152
88/89	Rockford	52	491	9.4	157	304	51.6	73.9	315
CBA Totals		94	706	7.5	232	447	51.9	75.7	467

NBA Record (Regular Season)

Year	Team	G	Pts.	Avg.	FGM	FGA	FG%	FT%	Reb.
89/90	Bulls	2	0	0	0	0	0	0	0
90/91	Rockets	82	432	5.3	148	349	42.4	81.2	246
91/92	Played in Europe								
92/93	Spurs	64	155	2.4	52	117	44.4	83.6	97
93/94	Pistons	78	322	4.1	119	259	45.9	75.6	239
NBA Totals		226	909	4.0	319	725	44.0	80.0	582

Pete Maravich
A Special Tribute

VITAL STATISTICS

Born June 22, 1947 in Aliquippa, Pennsylvania
6 feet 5, 200 pounds
College: Louisiana State University
Position: Guard
Retired: 1980

CAREER HIGHLIGHTS

- Named to NBA All-Star team five times
- Led NBA in points and scoring average in 1976–77 (2,273 points, 31.1 points per game)
- Elected to the Naismith Memorial Basketball Hall of Fame (1986)
- Selected to College All-American team three years and named College Player of the Year in 1970
- Led NCAA in scoring average in 1968 (43.8), 1969 (44.2), and 1970 (44.5)
- Holds NCAA Division I career record in five categories: most points, 3,667; highest per-game average, 44.2; most field goals made, 1,387; most field goals attempted, 3,166; most games scoring at least 50 points, 28

PREGAME WARMUP

I gave my life to basketball at seven years of age. Completely. There's no doubt about it. I did some of the craziest things you'd ever think about. We used to live in South Carolina, and I used to dribble my basketball 2½ miles into town. People would stop and say, "Let us give you a ride." I would say, "No, I've got to dribble. I want to dribble." And I'd dribble back home with my left hand. I'd dribble between my legs, around my back. It's a little dangerous to do that today, but I grew up in a small town. I could do it."

PETE MARAVICH

What you know about basketball legend Pete Maravich may depend on how old you are.

If you're over thirty-five, you probably remember the first reports trickling out of Louisiana in 1968. Evening videotape highlights and cable television didn't exist then, but sports columnists and local sports anchors were describing a skinny kid as the greatest thing to happen to basketball since the center jump was eliminated after every basket.

"He's a mop-topped, floppy-socks scoring machine who comes out of the locker room firing," they said, some in awe, some in disgust (calling him a ball hog), and all in envy. The kid had charisma and phenomenal skills. Then you finally watched him play on TV, and you couldn't believe your eyes. You saw impossible passes hit their mark. You saw dribbling exhibitions that you thought were the sole property of the Harlem Globetrotters.

And you saw shooting exhibitions that were nothing short of miraculous. Bank shots, jump shots, off-balance shots, reverse layups, occasional corkscrews. Because of his quick release and a ready willingness to fire, they called the kid The Pistol.

Some commentators began to compare the kid to the spectacular playmaker, dribbler, and shooter from the Boston Celtics,

Hall of Fame guard Bob Cousy. But Pete Maravich made Cousy look like a beginner. Pete the Prestidigitator became the greatest magician in college basketball since Oscar Robertson.

If you're under thirty-five, you may know Pete Maravich through an ongoing media blitz. His video series *Homework Basketball* is an instructional mini-lesson for Pistol Pete wanna-bes. Maybe you've viewed *The Pistol: Birth of a Legend,* the movie of his hoops debutant year as an eighth grader. Or maybe you've seen an occasional fleeting glimpse of his magical moves on one of the cable network's trips into the past.

No matter your age, if you're a basketball fan you have grown to appreciate the showmanship and the unbelievable talent of the man they called Pistol Pete.

Only a few players in the history of basketball have changed the game—and are remembered as pioneers. Those players not only performed well and helped their teams, as all great players do, but they also left a mark on the game. They altered the way it would be appreciated from then on.

George Mikan, the first mobile big man in the sport, did that. Cousy, who changed the way guards were viewed and even set the stage for Maravich, made his mark. Julius Erving taught players how to fly as his drives to the hoop often climaxed in monster dunks. Earvin "Magic" Johnson, who benefited from the Maravich mystique, carried the game to new heights.

These and other engineers of change left the game better than when they started, yet they were different from Maravich in an important way. From the earliest days of his life, Pete seemed to have it in mind to change the game. His contribution was by no means an accident. It was the result of the leadership of a challenging father, who successfully instilled in his son the desire to change the game.

As you watch the game today, you can see the effects Maravich had on the game with his showman-like skills. He opened the way for players to go beyond the basics in ballhandling. When you see no-look passes, routine between-the-legs dribbling, and fake behind-the-back passes, you are seeing improvements that The Pistol popularized.

Part of the excitement of the tricks Maravich did with the ball is that they were things he taught himself through hundreds of hours of practice. They are not skills that take an incredible vertical leap or a Michael Jordan-like acrobatic ability. They can be done by regular guys with talent. They are not above-the-rim antics reserved for skywalkers like Dr. J, Michael, and David Thompson.

Pete Maravich was bestowed a dream by his father—a dream to become the best basketball player in the world. And Pete took that dream seriously. Perhaps more than any athlete, Pete gave himself to his sport in total commitment.

It was a commitment that led him to play varsity basketball as an eighth grader, to become the greatest scorer in NCAA history, and to earn a place in the Basketball Hall of Fame. Then at age forty, eight years after he retired, Pete Maravich died of a massive heart attack.

But his story is more than incredible basketball and sudden death. In this special tribute to Pistol Pete Maravich, we will let Pete himself tell the story, for he learned to do it so well. As he told the following details from his heart to young people wherever he went, they could feel his intense desire. He wanted them to discover that Jesus satisfies far more than basketball—and he wanted them to turn their lives over to the Savior he loved so much.

Here, then, in Pete's words, is his story of an enduring love for basketball and an even greater love for His Savior, Jesus Christ.

The only thing I've ever known in my life was basketball—from four years of age. In fact, my dad said he took a picture of me when I was born, and he would show it to people and say, "That boy is born to play basketball."

At four years old, I was already playing. At five I was playing competitively on a league team. When I was seven, my dad came to me and said, "Pete, you're not dedicated enough. Let me tell you something. I make $2,900 a year as a head basketball coach, and I can't send you to college. But if you listen to me and let me teach you, and let me develop you, let me tell you what you can have."

"What's that, Dad?"

"Number 1, you get a scholarship," he said. "I can't pay your way to school, there's no possible way. Now, when you get there, it'll be $20,000, $25,000, $30,0000. I just don't have it. But you can get a scholarship, and if you get a scholarship, Pete, just maybe you'll make it to the pros. If you get to the pros, Pete, maybe you will be on a team that will win the world championship. And they'll give you a big diamond ring, and you'll have your name on it. It'll have 'World Champions' written on it. You'll be the best player in the world on that particular day, you and eleven other players. You can go and show everybody. You wear your ring, and you can tell everybody that you're world champions. Not only that, they'll pay you to play. They'll pay you to play basketball."

Well, to a seven-year-old, that opened my eyes. I decided right then and there: That was it—no other sports. I'll dedicate my life to basketball. Committed completely. In fact, my dad used to tell me when I went to bed at night, "You think, you pray, you sleep, you dream, you walk, you run basketball. That's all I want you to do." And that's all I did.

I gave my life to basketball at seven years of age. Completely. . . . I did some of the craziest things you'd ever think about. We used to live in South Carolina, and I used to dribble my basketball 2½ miles into town. People would stop and say, "Let us give you a ride." I would say, "No, I've got to dribble. I want to dribble." And I'd dribble back home with my left hand. I'd dribble between my legs, around my back. It's a little dangerous to do that today, but I grew up in a small town. I could do it.

When I finally got a bicycle, I learned to dribble to town riding my bicycle. I got quite a few stares, riding a bicycle down the highway, dribbling a basketball. But I did it. I taught myself how to do it. I got so crazy.

My dad came to me one day and said, "Pete, bring your basketball."

I said, "Why?"

"We're going somewhere, get in the car." And I got in the car. He drove out on the highway. He looked around and there were no cars coming. He said, "Now put yourself out of the passenger side of the car. I'm going to drive at various speeds, and I want to see if you can control the basketball.

"Dad, are you nuts? What's happened to you?"

"No, I'm not nuts. You do as I say."

"OK."

And he drove at 5, 10, and 15 MPH. We'd stop. I'd get the ball, and so on and so on. I never understood why he would want that. I never understood, but I understand now. Whatever he could put into me, where he could encourage me and see I was the only one doing something, he knew I would be more confident.

I used to go to bed at night with a basketball. I slept with a basketball until I was thirteen years old. I would say three things, and I would shoot the ball up in the air as I tried to go to sleep because I couldn't get back up and play basketball. I'd say, "Fingertip control, back spin, follow-through. Fingertip control, back spin, follow-through." I would finally fall asleep and the ball would fall to the floor.

Some nights there were thunderstorms. I would sneak out the window. I'd go out there in the thunderstorm in the rain in my pajamas and tennis shoes, and I'd dribble in the mud. There was this hard spot with mud and everything splashing in my face. But I figured if I could dribble there—if I could play there—I could easily do it on the court.

I used to go to movie theaters when it was over 100 degrees at 3 in the afternoon. Nobody was in the theater, just me. Everybody else was out playing, being at the lake, swimming and everything. I'd go in the front row. I'd sit on the right aisle. Through the first half of the movie I would dribble the basketball, and I'd sit the second half on the left side and would dribble the basketball on the carpet by the aisle.

I had an early church life. My mother and father were church people. I remember when I lived in Aliquippa, Pennsylvania, they were members of a church. But they didn't have a relationship with Jesus Christ. There were churchtians, not Christians. But my mother and dad were very good people. They met all the needs of their family. They loved us. Because Dad was a coach, we had some sorry nights, and we had some happy nights. But that was part of it.

I used to go to church, but I'd sit there with a little piece of paper and a pencil, and I'd take it and go "1, 2, 3." I'd count a minute and mark it off. I felt if I was in church, if I was in Sunday school, somebody in L.A. or New York was playing basketball, and when it came time to get that scholarship, I just wouldn't get it. That's how committed I was.

Oh, I believed in God. Who doesn't believe in God? But the God I believed in was impersonal, and the God I believed in was just there when I needed something or was there when I got hurt.

I walked my own way. I had my own dreams, my goals were set. They were set in concrete and nobody was going to change me. I walked that way for 14½ years.

Finally, right before I was fifteen, my best friend came to me and said, "Pete, why don't you drink a beer?"

I said no, but he kept on and on. Finally I said, "OK, OK, I'll try one." So I said the best place to drink it is on the steps of the Methodist church at 8:00. And that's what we did. He went and got it, and he sat on the steps and I took that first drink.

I remember taking that first step, that first beer in my life. And I'm here to tell you that that beer, that first sip almost destroyed my life. It's only by the mercies of God that I'm even standing here. But it almost destroyed my life. Ninety-eight percent of everybody in jail today started with that first drink. Over 500,000 in correctional institutions today, over 500,000 committed their crime while under the influence of the mind-altering substance. I've been in prisons and I've talked to prisoners, and they said, "Pete, I don't remember committing my crime. I was so drugged out. I was so spaced out. I was gone." But they're there, they made the choice to do that. I made the choice to live the life I live today.

But at eighteen years old, my dedication, my discipline, my obedience to basketball started to dwindle. You see, God had given me so much talent, I played so long, that I could go months without playing, and just go out and do it.

At eighteen, I entered LSU as a scholarship player. That summer I was to go out to a Campus Crusade for Christ camp. I was asked to come out there to put a showtime on. And I said I would be very happy to go out there.

I took a friend with me, and we had a good time going out, a good worldly time. We stopped at every bar, we took four, five days to get there. I drove out there, I chased as many ladies as I could find. And I drank.

You see, that was me. As I grew up, I saw all those hypocrites in church. And instead of understanding that my life was my concern, and I'm a unique individual in God's creation, I let other people determine my destiny.

We got on this campus, and I saw these people, and they were all sitting around playing music. And they were singing songs under trees, and they were holding hands in prayer. And I was completely embarrassed.

"I've got to get out of here," I said.

"Yes, let's get the clinic going, and then let's get out of here," my friend says.

So I checked in, and I asked, "When do I put on the clinic?"

"Pete, we've got a thousand people here," the director said. "If you will just hold on, you'll be with this group."

"Well, OK." I stayed there three days. I never put a clinic on. But for three days, I heard who Jesus Christ was. There was no running from it. And on the third night Bill Bright, the founder of Campus Crusade, gave a message and an invitation. My friend finally stood with tears in his eyes and said, "Pete, I'm going forward. I've accepted Christ."

"You're nuts! What's wrong with you? Why don't you just sit down here, you're kind of embarrassing me." But he went forward. I reached out and grabbed him by the arm, and he pulled away. I tried to steal away his salvation. There's many ways to steal your salvation. It usually comes in the form of peer pressure. But I tried to steal his. I wanted him to be like me. I couldn't understand what was going on in his life, and didn't care either.

I flatly rejected Christ when I was eighteen years old. I said, "God, I don't want you. I don't need you. I've got my plan right here. I'm going to play pro basketball. I've already got my scholarship. I'm going to get a world championship and make a million dollars. And then I'll look into this." And that's what happened in my life up to that point.

I went to LSU and I set some fifty, sixty basketball records. I don't know how many I set. But I set a lot. I got more trophies and awards and plaques and honorary mayorships, keys to cities, telegrams from presidents and governors and senators in my attic than you can imagine.

I've got a trophy 6-feet-5 inches tall, the same height as me, still in the box from 1972, collecting dust. I've finally realized that that's what happens to trophies—they end up collecting dust in attics. Because with that and about 50 cents you can buy a cup of coffee. They're meaningless because you've got nobody to share it with. Even though God gave it all to me, I never glorified Him, I just glorified me.

I had everything. I had popularity. I had fame in college. I averaged over 44 points a game for three years, the all-time leading scorer in the history of college basketball.

And then in 1970 I signed the largest contract in the history of sports. Greater than anyone in any sport at that time. It made the *Guinness Book of World Records.* It was there for thirty days and then somebody beat me out.

But it was there, and I remember sitting in the press conference, thinking, *Boy, Dad, aren't you proud of me? I got a scholarship. I got the NBA. I got a chance for the world championship now, and I'm signed for over a million dollars.*

This is great, and now if I get my ring, I can just stop and play tennis, and go off and just live happily ever after. But it just didn't happen that way, because the person I was on the court was not the person off the court.

You see, at 14½, alcohol came into my life. It came as a toehold. It just came as a toehold, but it grew into a foothold. And then a stronghold. And then a possession. Alcohol did that to me. Alcohol possessed my life. Alcohol possessed members of my family. And I was just one of the pack.

During the seventies, I searched. All of a sudden I said, "I want to know what life's about." And I searched. Believe me, I was a commitment person. I got into karate for 4½ years. I thought that would take a lot of pressure off me, because I was getting beat up a lot. I wanted to learn how to take care of myself, so I went with an instructor who taught me how.

But that led me into transcendental meditation. I thought I needed more; I was too stressed out. And that took me into yoga. Put me into a different religion: Hinduism. I read everything I could on it. I believed in reincarnation at one time. But then all of a sudden it left me. I would try something else. So I started reading books about philosophy.

You see, I don't have a degree. I didn't graduate from LSU. I said, "Well, if I'm going to have anything, I'm going to learn. I have to be able to say the right things at parties. I'm at all these parties while the cocaine is being sniffed up and the beer being drunk. I've got to be able to talk. I've got to be able to converse."

So I was into philosophy. And I got into hypnosis. I got into visualization techniques, and I got very much into UFOs and ufologies. I truly believed in UFOs. In fact, I believed I was going to be the first person taken by a UFO. That's how much I believed in it. . . . I went from there and kept searching.

The person who was on the court was a person who could express his freedom. The court was my refuge, because when I left the court, I was back in reality. And I was back to alcohol and back to the things I hated but couldn't get rid of.

I found out that I wanted to rebel, and I did. I got heavily into nutrition and was a vegetarian for 3½ years. In fact, one year I fasted for twenty-five days. I got life-extending drugs from eastern Europe because I knew pharmacologists. I was going to be 150 years old. I thought that would make a difference. I thought it would make a difference if I was healthy and felt good and impressed people, but it didn't.

In 1980 I quit basketball. I quit bitterly. I quit from immaturity. I quit because we had a first son and I wanted to be a role model to him, and I knew I wasn't a role model to anybody if I couldn't be a role model to my son.

So for two years I became a recluse; I was in turmoil and despondency and depression. I put on a front to everybody, but when I got home, I was nearly tearing my guts out. Because you see, I couldn't find the answer.

I would take my one-year-old son and sit down and I would do seven- or eight-year-old puzzles. For an hour or two a day I would put his hand on them. I said, "Jason, you're going to have what I didn't have. You're going to be smart. And your daddy is a dummy."

Many things filled my life, but they didn't work. You see, I've driven every car you could ever drive. I drove Rolls Royces, BMWs, Mercedes, Porsches, Cadillacs. I used to carry $5,000 in cash around at all times. I did that because I just never knew when I wanted to hop over to the Orient or something. I've lived the life. I've been in the fast lane. And I'm here to tell you that the fast lane is a dead lane. It's totally dead.

One night, late in 1982, I went to bed. It was like any other night. I was at my home on the lake. I had everything. Friends who loved me. Family who loved me. My guts were tearing out. Why wasn't I happy? Why didn't I have the success I was supposed to have had when I thought back to when I was seven? Where was the happiness? Where's the enjoyment? It wasn't there.

At night when I went to bed, things started coming up in my mind. Perverted things—perverted things I did in my life. Things that I was so sick over. It just broke me down. They kept coming. They wouldn't leave. I was being tortured in my mind, and I didn't understand why.

I didn't know where to go. I didn't know who to call out to. But I called out to God.

"God, I don't know that I could even be saved, because I know what a sinner I am. I don't know that You can forgive me, because I don't understand. But if You don't save me, I won't be around at all." And right at that point, I reflected back to when I was eighteen. When I rejected Him. It all came clear to me. I saw the love of Christ right at that moment in my life. As I was getting off my bed, early in the morning, while it was still dark, I invited Christ into my life.

The Lord spoke to me. He said, "Be strong and lift thine own heart." It resonated through my room. I was so shocked and so stunned, I reached over. I grabbed my wife. I woke her up. She thought somebody had broken into the house. I said, "Jackie, Jackie, did you hear what God said? Did you hear what God said? He said, 'Be strong and lift up thine own heart.' He assured me. I know I'm going to be saved, Jackie."

Well, Jackie didn't understand that, and Jackie didn't understand me, for she had been through a lot. I don't even know why she was with me. Anybody else would have left a long time ago.

But I got off that bed, and I very crudely asked for forgiveness for my sins. And I asked Christ into my life.

It wasn't just some prayer. It was from my heart. I cried out to God because I had nowhere else to go. The riches didn't do it. And if I had been poor, that wouldn't have done it. God saved me that night.

Pete Maravich retired from pro basketball at age thirty-two, having thrilled fans across the country with his magical performances and finally concluding his career in Boston Gardens, home of the legendary Bob Cousy. And Pete Maravich himself became a legend, playing in the NBA All-Star game five times and leading the league one year with a 31.1 scoring average.

He devoted most of his time after his conversion to the two things he enjoyed the most in life: playing basketball and telling people about his love for Jesus and their need for a Savior. He spent the last six years of his life traveling the country, telling how he found happiness in Jesus Christ after a lifetime of searching for joy in fame, money, and the many other interests he developed.

On January 5, 1988, Peter Maravich played a pickup basketball game in a church gym in Southern California. He was in town to record a radio interview on Focus on the Family, and the host of the program, James Dobson, invited Pete to join him and friends for their morning workout. Along with Dobson, former UCLA center Ralph Drollinger, and others, Pete was enjoying the morning scrimmage. He went over to a chair to sit down, commenting as he did that he was really having a good time. The next thing his friends knew, Pete was on the floor. He was not breathing.

Before medical help could arrive, Pistol Pete Maravich was dead. An autopsy revealed a congenital heart condition that no one knew he had. It was a problem that usually took the lives of young people before they turned twenty.

Yet God had let Pete live. He had let him reject the simple plan of salvation at age eighteen and had allowed him to enjoy one of the most amazing basketball careers ever. He had let Pete

change the game and almost destroy himself. Then God had rescued him, turned him into a dedicated spokesman for the gospel,
and let him create a legacy of basketball greatness that will never
be matched.

And when Pete Maravich died at age forty, he died a success.
Not because of those trophies that are still collecting dust, but
because of his unwavering faith in Jesus Christ. It is a story of
faith that still lives today and is still influencing young people
who need to know that no matter what they gain in life, if they
don't have Jesus as Savior, it is all as worthless as an old pair of
floppy basketball socks.

THE NBA ROAD

1970:	Selected by the Atlanta Hawks in the first round (third pick)
May 3, 1974:	Traded to the New Orleans Jazz for Dean Meminger, Bob Kaufman, and draft choices
1979:	New Orleans Jazz became Utah Jazz
January 17, 1980:	Waived by Utah Jazz
January 22, 1980:	Signed by Boston Celtics

THE MARAVICH FILE

Collegiate Record

Year	School	G	Pts.	Avg.	FGM	FGA	FG%	FT%	Asst.
67/68	LSU	26	1138	43.8	432	1022	42.3	81.1	105
68/69	LSU	26	1148	44.2	433	976	44.4	74.6	128
69/70	LSU	31	1381	44.5	522	1168	44.7	77.3	192
NCAA Totals		**83**	**3667**	**44.2**	**1387**	**3166**	**43.8**	**77.5**	**425**

NBA Record (Regular Season)

Year	Team	G	Pts.	Avg.	FGM	FGA	FG%	FT%	Asst.
70/71	Hawks	81	1880	23.2	738	1613	45.8	80.0	355
71/72	Hawks	66	1275	19.3	460	1077	42.7	81.1	393
72/73	Hawks	79	2063	26.1	789	1789	44.1	80.0	546
73/74	Hawks	76	2107	27.7	819	1791	45.7	82.6	396
74/75	Jazz	79	1700	21.5	655	1562	41.9	81.1	488
75/76	Jazz	62	1604	25.9	604	1316	45.9	83.5	332
76/77	Jazz	73	2273	31.1	886	2047	43.3	87.0	392
77/78	Jazz	50	1352	27.0	556	1253	44.4	87.0	335
78/79	Jazz	49	1105	22.6	436	1035	42.1	84.1	243
79/80	Celtics	43	589	13.7	244	543	44.9	86.7	83
NBA Totals		**658**	**15948**	**24.2**	**6187**	**14026**	**44.1**	**82.0**	**3563**